A New History of Tanzania

Isaria N. Kimambo
Gregory H. Maddox
Salvatory S. Nyanto

MKUKI NA NYOTA
DAR−ES−SALAAM

PUBLISHED BY
Mkuki na Nyota Publishers Ltd
P. O. Box 4246
Dar es Salaam, Tanzania
www.mkukinanyota.com

© Isaria N. Kimambo, Gregory H. Maddox, Salvatory S. Nyanto, 2017

ISBN 978-9987-75-399-4

All rights reserved. No part of this publication may be reproduced, stored in a retrieval system or transmitted in any form or by any means, electronic, mechanical, photocopying, recording, or otherwise, without the prior written permission of Mkuki na Nyota Publishers Ltd.

Visit www.mkukinanyota.com to read more about and to purchase any of Mkuki na Nyota books. You will also find featured authors, interviews and news about other publisher/author events. Sign up for our e-newsletters for updates on new releases and other announcements.

Distributed world wide outside Africa by African Books Collective.
www.africanbookscollective.com

Contents

Foreword... ix
Preface.. xi
Acknowledgements.. xiii
Abbreviations.. xv
Introduction... 1

PART ONE.. 7

Chapter One
Sources and Environment in The History of Tanzania 11

Chapter Two
The Making of Human Communities in Tanzania.......................... 25

Chapter Three
Early Community Formations to 11Th Century: The Coastal Belt 37

Chapter Four
Early Community Formations: The Interior to 11Th Century.................. 46

PART TWO 55

Chapter Five
From Simple to Complex Communities:
Development of Socio-Political Organisations in Tanzania 56

Chapter Six
Commodity Production and Exchange to 1800 74

Chapter Seven
The Development of Swahili Civilisation.................................80

PART THREE 85

Chapter Eight
The Integration of the Tanzanian Interior
in the Capitalist System 87

Chapter Nine
The Ngoni Invasion and Its Impact...95

Chapter Ten
The Expansion of European Influence to 1890 101

PART FOUR...106

Chapter Eleven
Imperialism and Colonialism:
The Scramble and Partition of Africa..................................... 114

Chapter Twelve
Colonial Conquest and African Resistance............................... 121

Chapter Thirteen
The Colonial Economy 131

Chapter Fourteen
Colonial Administration
in Tanzania From the Germans to the British............................ 142

Chapter Fifteen
The Political Economy of Zanzibar....................................... 147

Chapter Sixteen
Nationalism in Tanzania... 153

PART FIVE..167

Chapter Seventeen
The Early Years of Independence up to 1967............................ 171

Chapter Eighteen
The Arusha Declaration and Sectoral Development 177

Chapter Nineteen
Economic Liberalisation and Multiparty Politics......................... 189

Chapter Twenty
From Neo-Colonialism to Globalisation 193
Postscript: A Note on Sources and Methods............................. 197

Maps and Figures

Map 1: The making of human communities in Tanzania
from the Seventh to the Ninth Centuries, A.D 35

Figure 1: Peoples of East Africa: Linguistic Classification 36

Foreword

We are pleased to see *A New History of Tanzania* available to students, academicians, visitors, and ordinary men and women in Tanzania and elsewhere. We have been aware for a number of years of the difficulties of getting relevant and appropriate texts for teaching History and other subjects. For this reason, we encourage our academic staff to collaborate with colleagues at our own university and elsewhere to produce up to date quality reading materials such as this book, for even if the one published in 1969 were still available it would have been seriously out of date.

We are satisfied that the new book covers all important topics in the history of Tanzania and uses the most recent sources. We hope other staff members will learn from experience and produce teaching materials for their courses. We are grateful to Professor Gregory Maddox from Texas Southern University in the USA, Texas who has had interest in cooperating with us for the benefit of our two institutions, and Salvatory Stephen Nyanto, a Tanzanian, Lecturer at the University of Dar es Salaam, and a Ph.D. candidate at the University of Iowa in the USA. His supervisor, Prof. James Giblin is also interested in collaborating with TUDARCO.

Prof. Uswege Minga
Provost,
Tumaini University, Dar es Salaam College
January, 2017.

Preface

A New History of Tanzania takes its name from lecture series introduced for the first time in the University of Dar es Salaam by Professor Isaria Kimambo in 2002. Before this time, History of Tanzania was taught as part of the History of East Africa. Introduction of this new course made it possible to study Tanzanian history in depth without affecting the teaching of the History of East Africa. It has been necessary to use the name *A New History of Tanzania* because there was *A History of Tanzania* published in 1969 by East African Publishing House in Nairobi for the Historical Association of Tanzania and, after East African Publishing House (EAPH) died out, it was reprinted in EAPH 1997 for the Historical Association of Tanzania by Kapsel Educational Publications. Unfortunately, the book has been out of print and Kapsel has also failed to continue as a publisher.

The new publication has come into being because Tumaini University Dar es Salaam College (TUDARCO) leadership has seen how difficult it has been for its history students to get reading material. When Professor Isaria N. Kimambo volunteered to use his inaugural lecture notes for the History of Tanzania at UDSM, the possibility for *A New History of Tanzania* appeared. Working together with two other colleagues, Prof. Gregory H. Maddox and Salvatory S. Nyanto, the new history has been completed. It is an outline history of Tanzania, quite different from its predecessor.

Prof. Isaria N. Kimambo
Tumaini University, Dar es Salaam College
January, 2017

Acknowledgements

This book owes its present shape because of years of painstaking research and writings from which it draws most of its supporting evidence. Although historians spend most of their time in the archives, libraries and offices, collecting pieces of surviving evidence, writing a book of this nature is always a collective responsibility. We gratefully acknowledge the contribution of numerous institutions and individuals towards the publication of the book. We are indebted to the Managing Director of Mkuki na Nyota Publishers, Walter Bgoya, and the administration of Tumaini University, Dar es Salaam College, for supporting this project. Their criticisms and suggestions made us, on several occasions, revisit parts of the manuscript.

We are also grateful to the coordinator of the African Archaeological Network (AAN), of the University of Dar es Salaam, Prof. Felix A. Chami, for his constructive comments about Bantu migration, Swahili pottery cultural seriation, and farming communities along the coast of Tanzania. We gained a lot from his works and through the many discussions we had with him. His suggestions and criticisms have been instrumental in shaping various arguments presented in the book. Prof. Betram B. Mapunda of the University of Dar es Salaam deserves a note too. His archaeological interventions on the Maji Maji uprising enlightened our understanding of the war beyond written and oral sources. Nonetheless, these individuals should not be held accountable for the shortcomings of this book. The shortcomings of this book remain our responsibility.

Finally, we owe a vast debt to the Director General of the National Museum of Tanzania and House of Culture, Prof. Audax ZP Mabulla, and the Tanzania Information Services for letting us use the photos of the independence of Tanganyika, the union of Tanganyika and Zanzibar, and the Arusha Declaration. We hope that this book will appeal to history students of secondary schools, colleges, and universities. It will also be useful to academicians, visitors and ordinary men and women who have long wished to see a book of this kind.

Salvatory Stephen Nyanto,
Department of History
University of Dar es Salaam
January, 2017.

Abbreviations

AA	African Association
ASP	Afro Shirazi Party
ASU	Afro Shirazi Union
AD	After Christ
ANC	African National Congress
ANU	African National Union
BC	Before Christ
BCE	Before Christian Era
CMS	Church Missionary Society
CCM	Chama cha Mapinduzi
CUF	Civic United Front
CRDB	Commercial Rural Development Bank
CE	Common Era
DC	District Commissioner
DNA	Deoxyribonucleic Acid
EIW	Early Iron Working
EEC	European Economic Community
EIA	Early Iron Age
ESR	Education for Self-Reliance
GATT	General Agreement on Tariffs and Trade
GDP	Gross Domestic Product
IMF	International Monetary Fund

KNPA	Kilimanjaro Native Planters Association
KNCU	Kilimanjaro Native Cooperative Union
LMS	London Missionary Society
NPSS	National Party for the Subjects of Sultan
NBC	National Bank of Commerce
NEC	National Executive Council
NGOs	Non-Governmental Organisations
NAP	National Agricultural Development Project
NUTA	National Union of Tanganyika Workers
NPSS	National Party for the Subjects of Sultan
OECD	Organisation for Economic Cooperation
OAU	Organisation of African Unity
PW	Plain Ware
PIW	Pre-Iron Working
SW	Swahili Ware
SCOPO	The Standing Committee on Parastatal Organisations
SIDO	Small Industrial Development Organisation
TANU	Tanganyika African Union
TAA	Tanganyika African Association
TFL	Tanganyika Federation of Labour
TPH	Tanzania Publishing House
TIW	Triangular Incised Ware
TUDARCO	Tumaini University Dar es Salaam College
UMCA	Universities' Mission to Central Africa
UN	United Nations
URT	United Republic of Tanzania
UDSM	University of Dar es Salaam
UTP	United Tanganyika Party
UPE	Universal Primary Education
WWI	First World War
WWII	Second World War
WB	World Bank
WTO	World Trade Organisation

YAU	Young African Union
ZNP	Zanzibar Nationalist Party
ZPPP	Zanzibar and Pemba Peoples Party

Introduction

Tanzania remains a relatively new nation, having come into existence in its recent form just over five decades ago. While the land and the people who have lived there have the subject of a great deal of historical research, there remains no readily accessible and concise history of the country. The aim of this volume is to fill that void.

This volume will tell the stories of communities that have lived in the territory that has become Tanzania. In no part of the world have humans lived longer than in Tanzania as it is part of cradle of humanity in eastern Africa where humans first evolved around 200,000 years ago. While historians cannot reach that far back in the discovery of information about the human past, this volume will explore the deep history of human societies in the area. Such stories begin with the relationship between human societies and the environments in which they live. Rather than seeing such a relationship as a duality, it must be understood that environments create human societies and human societies shape their environments. Within this environmental context human society adapt to and adapt the conditions under which they live. Over the course of time they create diverse communities adapted to different environments with different cultures and languages. Numerous communities have called Tanzania home, many speaking widely varying languages.

Given the variety of environments, communities developed many different ways of ensuring enough food to support their populations. Agriculture and cattle keeping spread into the area as long as 5000 years ago. The earliest farmers grew grains such as sorghum and millet. Cattle keepers had to develop complex methods of keeping cattle safe from disease as well as ensuring adequate water and fodder. Technologies developed including metal working and irrigation to enhance production. In Tanzania as elsewhere, these societies did not live in isolation from each other. They developed trade relations based on the different products that could be produced in different environments. They shared technologies and ideas. Spouses moved between communities. When conditions became severe enough, communities in whole or part, sought to relocate. These types of movements often led to conflict, but sometimes to accommodation.

These communities began to develop elaborate cultural and political structures in order to regulate relations among community members, and protect the community from others. Political structures took many forms across the landscape of Tanzania over time. Some societies developed centralised states ruled by hereditary rulers. Others worked more as federations of kin-groups, clans. Still others used age groups that linked communities across large areas. Conflict over resources including people commonly occurred.

The communities that came to exist within Tanzania developed not just with each other but with societies outside the borders of the current country and even across the Indian Ocean from a very early stage. Goods, ideas, and people moved from the interior to coast to the lands beyond. These contacts brought East African communities into conversation with others across the globe. Many came to share a religion, Islam, with communities around the Indian Ocean. Such contacts also brought conflict and sometimes slave trading.

The contact of Islam brought by Muslims from Arabia and Persia with the African communities of the East African Coast led to the expansion of the already existing Swahili language–that eventually became one of the defining features of Tanzania. Swahili civilisation developed and spread along the East African coast from what is now Somalia to Mozambique and to islands in the Indian Ocean from about the beginning of the current era. The language developed as part of the great expansion of Bantu languages into eastern Africa. A common material culture indicates the spread of a society along the coast based on exploitation of maritime resources and trade. Its settlements grew into sizeable towns with stone architecture showing influences from Arabia and Persia. These towns became city states, linked in trade but each with its own ruler often claiming descent from Arabia or Persia. The towns in turn maintained trade links with communities in the interior with Islam and the Swahili language spreading gradually along the trade networks.

Contact with the outside world intensified after the sixteenth century of the current era. European expansion began with Portuguese expeditions along the coast of Africa. The city of Kilwa, at the time the richest of the Swahili cities because of the gold from what is now Zimbabwe, became the first attacked by the Portuguese and the first to have European installation placed on it. While the Portuguese presence in East Africa was relatively fleeting, it marked the beginning of the period when the capitalist world system centred in Europe expanded to every corner of the globe. In East Africa, eventually an alliance of local forces and Arab merchants and sultans from Omani drove the Portuguese out.

In the eighteenth and nineteenth centuries, trade increased driven by the growth of commerce with Europe. East Africa became a source of commodities and labour in the form of slaves used to produce commodities that fed trade in the Indian Ocean. Societies in the interior of East Africa were all changed by this increase in intensity. Warfare expanded and states grew in part in response to the demand for slaves on the coast. Elephants were hunted almost to extinction to feed demand in Europe and Asia. On the coast, the Omani sultans from their seat of power in Zanzibar oversaw the development of an empire comprising of the coastal cities and dominating the much more numerous caravan routes to the interior. Plantations developed on the coast that produced spices, grain, and sugar for trade in the Indian Ocean.

In the late nineteenth century, European powers began their final expansion of their colonial empires, and the theme of conquest and resistance become the next major focus of this book. Rivalry for control over resources and markets drove what became known as the Scramble for Africa. Racism and paternalism provided its justification. Explorers and missionaries came first, seeking to spread Christianity and commerce. In Europe agreements divided the continent. The mainland became German sphere of influence while Zanzibar became a British Protectorate. African societies though had other ideas about recognising their new overlords. Many came to admire the material and technological advances brought by Europeans and some found solace in the coming of the Gospel. Even those, though, joined in resisting the loss of sovereignty that colonial conquest entailed. While the sultan in Zanzibar reluctantly signed the agreement for the creation of a protectorate, his subjects staged a revolt that led the British to bombard Stone Town. On the mainland, resistance took many forms. African leaders often made calculations about when and who to fight. But fighting was almost constant during the first two decades of German rule. As late as 1905 peoples in the southern mainland rose up in revolt in the Maji Maji rising that shook the colonial state to its core.

Like peoples across Africa, the peoples of Zanzibar and the mainland experienced colonial domination across the first decades of the twentieth century. During the era of colonial rule communication increased across the breadth of the colonies that became known as Tanganyika and Zanzibar. The Germans and British promoted economic integration with their imperial economies. Once the allies defeated the Germans in World War I, in a campaign fought in East Africa using mostly colonial troops, both Tanganyika and Zanzibar became part of British East Africa along with Kenya and Uganda. The next theme taken up is the reconstructing of African societies politically, economically, and culturally under colonial rule.

The colonial era brought the permanent linkage of Tanzania's communities into the global world order economically and politically. It turned Africans into producers of commodities destined primarily for global markets. It made them subjects of an imperial political order rather than just members of their own communities. It brought them into closer contact with each other and gave them a language in which to communicate. More Tanzanians became members of the great religious traditions of Islam and Christianity. It united them in a struggle for freedom from an imperial domination.

By the 1950s, Britain and the other imperial powers began to realise that economically and politically they could not hold on to their African empires indefinitely. This change occurred partly because of the decline in global power of the of imperial states after World War II and the rise of the cold war rivalry between the United States of America and the Soviet Union. But it also occurred because across Africa, people mobilised to demand independence. In Tanganyika, the anti-colonial movement gained support rather late compared to other African colonies, but its leaders remained more unified in the support of independence. In Zanzibar, the independence movement became divided between those who supported independence under the rule of the Sultan of Zanzibar and the maintenance of paternalistic social relations between Arabs and Africans and those who sought to only independence but the creation of a new political order that gave the African majority the power to rule. Under the leadership of TANU and Julius Kambarage Nyerere, Tanganyika moved towards independence relatively smoothly and achieved it in 1961. In Zanzibar, political conflict put off independence until 1963. Within a month, an uprising led by the Afro-Shirazi Party overthrew the Sultan in a violent revolt and declared Zanzibar a revolutionary state.

Nyerere became the first Premier and then President of the Republic of Tanganyika. In the early years after independence, the new country faced many major challenges. Tanganyikans demanded an end to the influence of foreigners in the government and economy. The government tried to chart a neutral course in foreign affairs in an age when the Cold War demanded countries to choose a side. The country became a foremost support of African liberation for the rest of the continent, especially in white-ruled southern Africa. An army revolt and the revolution in Zanzibar presented particular dangers to the government. The government responded by proposing a union with Zanzibar in 1964 that created the United Republic of Tanzania with a Union government and an autonomous government for Zanzibar.

African nationalist thought had always been partial to a socialist analysis that equated colonial domination with capitalist exploitation. In the years immediately after independence and then union, Nyerere and leaders in Tanzania struggled with unfulfilled expectations that independence would radically transform people's lives in the new country. In the mid-1960s, Nyerere began to extend his own thoughts about the situation of Tanzania and other African countries into what became known as Ujamaa—"familyhood" best translated as African Socialism. In 1967, Nyerere issued the Arusha declaration that committed Tanzania to African socialism and one-party rule.

Ujamaa na Kujitegemea—Socialism and Self-Reliance—led to the nationalisation of most of the large – scale economic enterprises in the country. It promoted the movement of rural peoples into Ujamaa villages so that they could receive access to services and education. It encouraged them to work together in communal farms. It tried to make primary education and health care available to all. It promoted the use of Kiswahili as a national language. From 1967 to 1986 it remained the guiding ideology of the new nation.

It succeeded in many respects in building a sense of nationhood on the mainland and fostering a society that sought to solve its problems through consensus. Tanzania remained a stalwart support of liberation in southern Africa, hosting liberation movements from Mozambique, Zimbabwe, and South Africa. Its military fought against intrusions from Portuguese colonial forces before the liberation of that country in 1980. In 1979, Uganda under Iddi Amin invaded the northwest Tanzania, and the Tanzanian military mobilised to drive Ugandan forces out and overthrow Amin.

But after 1979, the Tanzanian economy collapsed. The decline was partly caused by the dramatic rise in oil prices on the world market and decline in other commodity prices that made up Tanzania's exports. But many blamed the decline on Tanzania's socialist policies that stifled production. Led by the IMF, many developing countries were forced to accept "structural adjustment" programmes that reduced government spending on social programmes and denationalised industry. Tanzania resisted, but continuing economic decline led Nyerere to retire in 1985, and his successor Ali Hassan Mwinyi to reach a deal with the IMF in 1986. While exports and inflows of investments increased, many Tanzanians saw their living standards decline dramatically because of the changes. Access to health care and education declined. Employment declined as previously nationalised firms reduced workforces under new private owners. In 1992, the country even moved away from one-party rule, allowing opposition parties and liberalising the press.

Political competition and global openness have occurred in a context where continued economic growth has brought some benefits to many in the country. Public services to citizens expanded in the 1990s and 2000s so that many more children attend school, even to the university level. Access to health has increased such that infant mortality declined dramatically and life expectancy increased. Yet growing disparities between rich and poor left many Tanzanians feeling left out of the changes. While the ruling party has maintained its hold on power, opposition leaders have merged as powerful voices of protest. This volume will weave through the human story of the history of Tanzania. It relies on the growing scholarship of historians and others on that narrative both inside and outside the country. Each chapter will end with a brief reference list as a guide to the most important of the literature available on subjects covered. It will present the evidence and enable readers to reach their own judgements on the history of Tanzania.

PART ONE

Environment and Community
Formations in Tanzania

The first section of this book constitutes four chapters about sources and the environment, the making of human communities in Tanzania, and early community formations in Tanzania. It provides important clues to the understanding of the history of Tanzania from the Stone Age to the eleventh century of the Christian era. The first chapter provides an account of the sources, and relationship between environment and history. Apart from exposing our readers to a wide range of sources, the chapter also adopts the emphasis given by James Giblin and Gregory Maddox that proper understanding of the interaction between people and their environment is necessary at all historical periods. It addresses twofold aspects: environment as the determinant of human activities, and the ways human change/remake the landscape. It also provides a brief account of location and evolution of boundaries that form Tanzania, and important physical features that have over time shaped different historical processes.

Tanzanian societies are diverse in linguistic and cultural compositions. This diversity is demonstrated in the second chapter that delves into the making of human communities in Tanzania. It departs from the claim that assumes that the Stone Age people did not exist in a region assumed to be the cradle of mankind. In fact we are discussing a process of population movements that led to intermingling of people of different historical, ethnic and linguistic backgrounds that settled in this country at different times. The chapter sheds light on physical and linguistic classifications to show how peoples of Tanzania have been classified by colonial and post-colonial scholars. Relying on linguistic classification, the chapter surveys migrations and socio-economic activities of the Khoisan, Bantu, Nilotes, and Cushitic speaking communities that inhabited modern Tanzania at different times and places. This chapter is important as it shows the fact that the making of human communities in Tanzania has been an interplay of different ommunities with different linguistic and cultural backgrounds.

In the third chapter, community formations are studied in detail. The first section surveys community formations on the coast belt from the first century A.D to the seventh century A.D. It relies on Graeco-Roman, Arabic, Chinese, and Portuguese documents to indicate the possibility of getting a picture of coastal communities formed by the first century A.D. The second period explores communities along the coast from the seventh to the eleventh centuries A.D with greater availability of documentary and archaeological sources including writings of Arab travelers. As demonstrated in the chapter, until the ninth century of the

Christian era, most of the communities had probably developed what one might call "proto-Swahili" language whose further refinement and expansion by words from other languages belong to a later period. The mixture of indigenous people and immigrants resulted in an ethnically mixed and economically specialised society.

This section ends up with the fourth chapter that relies on Christopher Ehret's analysis to provide an account of the transformations of the East African interior from the seventh to the eleventh centuries. Such transformations corresponded with new ethnic expansions that posed new challenges to be addressed by settled communities. The chapter concentrates on Stone Age hunters and gatherers, mixed farmers, and Bantu communities in the interior. Stone Age hunters and gatherers are early inhabitants who lived by hunting and foraging. They lived in caves or forests and painted on rocks. This kind of existence did not require any tools more sophisticated than stone knives and digging sticks. Mixed farmers included both agriculturalists and pastoralists. Following the advent of iron, communities increased agricultural productivity and expanded into new areas for agriculture which had hitherto been untouched by hunters and gatherers. By the eleventh century of the Christian era, most of the Bantu communities had expanded quickly after their revolutionary transition in the savanna region south of the rain forest. Since they were iron using communities they had advantage over other Stone Age communities for they quickly occupied the more favourable areas of the coast including islands, northeastern and Great Lakes region.

Chapter One

Sources and Environment in The History of Tanzania

Introduction

The intentions of this chapter are twofold. The first intention is to present the sources that historians use in reconstructing the past processes and events. Such sources include archaeology, historical linguistics, oral traditions, and anthropology. The second objective adopts the emphasis of Giblin and Maddox in the introduction to the *Custodians of the Land* (Giblin and Maddox, 1996, p. 2-9) that proper understanding of the interaction between people and their environment is necessary at all historical periods. The debate among historians took two different positions on the relationship between human societies and environment: Primitive Africa and Merrie Africa. Primitive Africa approach saw pre-colonial Tanzanians having inhabited hostile environment constantly facing famine, epidemics and demographic reversals before achieving somewhat greater security in the colonial period. The Merrie Africa approach saw stable pre-colonial communities living in harmony with nature before suffering depopulation, ecological disasters and economic exploitation under colonial rule. This became an attractive debate but none of these interpretations reveal the reality which should be "Communities have continually used their economic, political, cultural and moral resources to prosper in the ever-changing ecological circumstances" (ibid, p.3).

Sources of History

Archaeology

Archaeology is the study of past cultures through material remains. Archaeology and history are related because the two are concerned about the human past. Archaeology operates on a deeper time scale than history. Archaeology goes into the origins of culture and humanity as far back as two million years ago where written records and oral traditions--the evidence used by historians—cannot reach. History and archaeology complement each other in the later period to produce a better understanding of the past (Mapunda, 2010, p. 221). Although archaeology uses material remains it nonetheless relies on history to tell the past processes and events from those material cultures. This synthesis has resulted in a new discipline called historical archaeology which is a sub-discipline of archaeology that shares the time scope and methods with history and uses archival and oral sources. Peter Schmidt has incorporated archaeology and history in studying social and technological transformations of northwestern Tanzania for the past three thousand years (ibid, p. 222). Likewise, Betram Mapunda has studied the social and technological transformations of societies in southwestern Tanzania (Mapunda 1995, 2010). Thomas Biginagwa also ventured into the field of historical archaeology by studying the archaeology of the nineteenth-century caravan route of northeastern Tanzania (Biginagwa, 2012).

Archaeology, like history, faces challenges in reconstructing the past. It is always a challenging task to link the present in which artifacts are perceived and experienced and the past in which they were made and used. However, both history and archaeology use interpretive linking principles to establish the validity of their data as authentic records of the past (McIntosh, 2005, p. 52). History has set of rules and procedures for interrogating and criticizing sources. Archaeology has also developed its own procedures for interrogating and evaluating the material remains—artifacts, structures, and features—as records of the past (ibid, p. 58). Archaeologists, like historians, use chronology and analogy to reconstruct the past. As McIntosh assets, archaeological reconstructions of past processes are based on claims that "certain sets of archaeological entities were produced contemporaneously as part of a cultural system" (ibid, p. 58-59). Archaeologists also build a picture of the past by constructing networks of chronological arguments about material patterns that could have been produced by human action and interaction. Thus, when archaeologists produce a narrative of the past that explains change over time, they usually recognise the changes in the patterns of ordered material remains (ibid). To mediate between the past and the present, archaeologists also use analogy on the existing features and structures. Analogy becomes effective when some forms of cultural relationships and continuity between the past and present groups can be established (ibid, p. 60).

In recent years, biologists have contributed another source of evidence for understanding deep human history in East Africa. In decoding the human genome, the genetic map for each human being, biologists have also begun to make estimates for when changes in that genetic map occurred and the relationship between existing populations based on when common ancestors lived. The species ancestral to humans lived in eastern Africa as much as 2 million years ago. At about that time, they began to make and use stone tools, with some of the earliest examples coming from Oldupai Gorge in northern Tanzania. They gradually spread out of Africa. While earlier theories argued that these examples of the genus Homo continued to interbreed across the globe and gradually evolved into modern humans, DNA evidence from different parts of the world has established that about 200,000 years ago, modern humans emerged in eastern and southern Africa. The older view also contradicts with what scholars know about the patterns of evolution of other mammals that have become more diversified into numerous species over a span of time (Ehret, 2002, p. 20). It is also an indisputable fact that Africa is the cradle of humanity. Archaeological evidence from various sites of Africa have indicated that the species of Homo sapiens had come fully into being more than 200,000 years ago. Skulls found in various sites dating from 130,000 to 100,000 years ago show that the oldest genus Homo existed in Africa before moving to Asia and Europe. This view is supported by DNA evidence that, relying on both genetics passed from mother to daughter and evidence of Y-chromosome from males, demonstrates the fact that the greatest genetic diversity of Homo sapiens is found in Africa (Ehret, 2002, p.21).

Anthropology

Anthropology generally studies societies and their cultures. There are two branches of anthropology: physical and social anthropology. Physical anthropology is commonly called human or biological anthropology. It studies the biological aspects of human species. Among the fields of the physical anthropology include paleoanthropology that essentially looks at aspects of hominid evolution (Keita, 2005, p. 112). Driven by the influence of Social Darwinism, anthropology was used to describe and classify the evolution of humankind. Such categories of "race", though no longer being used in scholarship, have left their marks on the studies of Africa. Biological and racial categories gave rise to the so called "Hamitic myth" that was used to describe and classify some African biological, linguistic, and cultural aspects. In the same vein, peoples of African continent were divided into "races" and "social units" as markers of establishing differences among groups. These biological and social constructs remained dominant in the fields of biological anthropology and African history throughout the colonial period (ibid, p. 113).

Anthropology, as an academic discipline, was introduced in Africa as a colonial package in the late nineteenth century. Colonial anthropologists preoccupied with two issues. One was to identify the universal characteristics of humankind though acknowledging diversity in cultures. The other was to trace the evolution of human societies through different stages of evolution in order to establish evidence of cultural variation among societies (Moore, 1994, p. 8). A few scholars of the late nineteenth century travelled writing about societies in Africa that they visited. On the whole, the majority anthropologists of the time relied on writings of travellers, explorers, and missionaries. Relying on the writings of scanty evidence—with disagreements about centres of civilisation, independent invention, and diffusion—some argued that all human beings had certain ideas and characteristics in common. They also used the same sources to establish a typology of different stages of social development. The lowest stage was considered savagery, followed by barbarism, and the highest form of social development was civilisation (ibid). The drive for European colonisation in Africa provided an impetus for anthropology in Africa. Colonisation increased the demand for ethnographic knowledge about societies that Europeans were going to govern. Prompted by the works of anthropologists, colonial authorities regarded the people and societies they governed as socially, culturally, economically, technically and morally "backward". Such social and biological constructs and the "civilising mission" of colonial states paralleled each other throughout the colonial period (ibid, p. 9).

Historical Linguistics

Lyle Campbell, views historical linguistics as primarily being concerned about studying language change. It is also, among other things, used to solve historical problems of concern to society which extend far beyond linguistics (Campbell, 2006, p. 1). Historical linguistics is different from history and archaeology in terms of method. Whereas historians and archaeologists directly deal with evidence of the past—in terms of material evidence or written records—historical linguists deal with languages that evolve over time. Since earlier forms of languages rarely exist with exception of written languages, linguists always start with the present forms of languages to enable them establish hypotheses about their earlier stages and about communities that spoke those languages (Nurse & Spear, 1985, p. 8). Again, unlike historical and archaeological data, linguistic data are secondary and are derived from historical languages that historians intend to study. The more languages evolve the more they absorb new materials, develop new patterns, and preserve the inherited materials that are transmitted from one generation to another. As Derek Nurse and Thomas Spear assert, the most common linguistic form is the word. Words and languages in general change when speakers come into contact with other people who speak another language and begin to use some of their words. This leads to the emergence of dialects due to internal differentiation (age, sex, or occupation for example) and due to geographical distance with speakers of the same language. Notwithstanding the lexical exchange arising from the encounter of two languages, all the daughter languages retain some vocabularies that their speakers recognise as being similar though they might have undergone slight changes (ibid, p. 9).

For decades, historians of Africa, including Christopher Ehret, have employed linguistic evidence to reconstruct the African past. Ehret argues that languages contain potential information on the history of the people who have spoken it in the past (Ehret, 2006, p. 86). As he notes, "every language is an archive of many thousands of individual artifacts of the past. Such artifacts are the words of the language, hard evidence that can be rigorously placed into linguistic stratigraphy" (ibid). From this excerpt, it is clear that vocabularies of a particular language are tools from which historians can draw past experiences, knowledge, and cultural practices of members of different societies. Because people's ideas, behaviours, and practices changed in the history of past societies, the vocabularies that described people's ideas, behaviours, and practices underwent changes in two ways. People both changed the meaning of existing words and adopted, invented, or discarded words to fit new circumstances. Histories of change and development in the past, as Ehret contends, leave "imprint on histories of thousands of individual words with which members of the society express all the various aspects of their lives" (ibid). Unlike other disciplines, historical linguistics cannot identify individual characters in history, it nevertheless offers a set of tools for examining the general long term processes and developments within a particular community or society over many years in the past. Again, historical linguistics does not provide exact dating, not even as close as the broad ranges that archaeology can, but its data relate directly to the whole range of cultural elements that consists of longer-term processes and human developments in particular communities or societies (ibid, p. 87).

One of the branches of historical linguistics is linguistic prehistory which is of interest for historians. It uses historical linguistic findings for cultural and historical interpretations. Linguistic prehistory compares information from historical linguistics with information from archaeology, ethno history, history, ethnographic analogy, human biology, and other sources of information on people's past in order to obtain a clear picture of the past (Campbell, 2006, p. 378). The field deals—among other things—with linguistic homeland and migration theory, cultural inventories from reconstructed vocabularies of proto-languages, loanwords, place names, classification of languages, internal reconstruction, dialect distributions to mention just a few in order to provide pertinent information about the past (ibid). In Chritopher Ehret's *An African Classical Age*, he uses language as key evidence to examine the history of peoples and their livelihoods in Eastern and Southern Africa. He, in particular, examines how societies changed and evolved over 1,400 years, a period that underwent crucial economic and technological transformations across the continent (Ehret, 2002, xvii).

Oral Histories/Oral Tradition

Oral histories refer to lived experiences, hearsay or eyewitness accounts about events and situations that occurred during the lifetime of the informants (Vansina, 1985, p. 12). Jan Vansina provides a typology of oral histories as oral testimonies and eyewitness accounts of groups and individuals who saw, experienced and participated in the events (Vansina, 1965, p. 4-5). Oral traditions on the other hand, refer to stories and people's experiences that are passed from one generation to another. Oral tradition, as Vansina puts it, encompasses both a process and its products. The products are oral messages that have at least a generation old. The process refers to the transmission of various oral messages by word of mouth over time until such messages disappear (ibid, p. 3). William Moss views oral traditions as spontaneous expressions of the identity, functions, customs, purposes and generational continuity that are not immediate personal experience of those who hold them in memory. Rather, experiences of previous generations that are retold in the present as understood by the present generation (Moss, 1988, p. 9).

Oral history was given prominence in the historiography of African history in the 1960s. A number of conferences were organised and research centers were established among African universities for documentation and research. Among the centres established to promote the use of oral histories in scholarship were at the universities of Legon in Ghana, Ibadan in Nigeria, Makerere in Uganda, and Khartoum in Sudan (Alagoa, 1990, p. 3). In Tanzania, like other African countries, historians of the 1960s embarked on oral histories, supplemented by available written sources, as a method of reconstructing past processes and events. For instance, Isaria Kimambo became the first Tanzanian historian to use oral traditions or oral histories in his reconstruction of the political history of the Pare of Northeastern Tanzania in 1967. He adopted the traditional method of using generations each consisting of thirty years following the first known date in Pare history recorded by von Decken in 1861 (Kimambo, 1967, p. viii, 1969, p.xii). Likewise, Steven Feierman collected oral traditions of the Shambaa making it possible to reconstruct a history of the Shambaa (1974, 1992). Israel Katoke was among the first generation of historians who used oral traditions to reconstruct a history of the Karagwe kingdom (Katoke, 1973). Oral tradition as a methodology has since the 1960s continued to be an important historical methodology in Africa. While oral traditions have their limitations, most notably in that they exist only for still extant social formations at the time of their collection and hence carry little information on states or societies that had ceased to exist, they remain an important pathway into the African past.

The Boundaries of Tanzania

European invaders created the boundaries of what today we know as Tanzania in the 1880s. The Germans occupied what came to be known as German East Africa and settled boundaries internationally with the British who had occupied neighbouring territories: Kenya, Uganda and the Islands of Zanzibar and Pemba. Today Tanzania extends from latitude 1° to 11° south and from longitude 29° east. On the eastern side it borders the Indian Ocean; on the south it borders Mozambique, Malawi and Zambia; on the west it borders the Democratic Republic of Congo (formerly Zaïre), Rwanda and Burundi; on the north it borders Uganda and Kenya. Tanzania has a land area of 886223 square kilometres. By the year 2015, the country had a population of over 40 million. The Anglo-German Agreement of 1886 fixed a boundary from the Indian Ocean by a line extending from the Umba river and to the eastern shore of the Lake Victoria in the northeast to the Ruvuma River in the south. The British zone (today Kenya) extended from the German border to the Juba River in the north. Germany's recognition of the Congo Free State (later the Belgian Congo) set Lake Tanganyika as the western border. The Anglo-German Agreement of 1890 fixed latitude one-degree south as boundary with Uganda in the north. The German colony of German East Africa included Rwanda and Burundi. German rule in Tanganyika ended when the First World War of 1914-1918 ended. Mainland Tanzania was separated from Rwanda and Burundi when it was given to Britain as a colony (mandated territory) under the League of Nations. Rwanda and Burundi were given to the Belgians under similar agreements.

Since the Germans had named Tanzania Mainland Deutsch Ostafrika it was necessary for the British to find another name after taking over the territory in 1920. British officials proposed several names including "Smutsland", "Ebumea", "New Maryland", "Windsorland" and "Victoria". The British Government however rejected all these names and directed that local names be proposed instead. Following this directive, the names "Kilimanjaro" and "Tabora" were proposed but the Government rejected them as well. A little later in the same year, "Tanganyika protectorate" was proposed by an assistant to the Minister of Colonies and was accepted by the Government. Before the advent of the German colonial rule, the big lake in the western part of the country was known in Kiswahili as Lake Tanganyika – the land beyond Tanga. The British Imperial Government eventually substituted the word "Protectorate" with "Territory", and henceforth the official name of the country became "Tanganyika Territory" (URT, p. 14). The country known as Tanzania today came into being on 26th April 1964 when the two former British colonies of Tanganyika and Zanzibar united to form the United Republic of Tanzania (Itandala, 1992: 20). The name came from combining the first three letters of each of the two countries and adding "ia" at the end. The ceremony of forming the union under the new name included mixing soil from the two countries on 26th April 1964.

Geography and Climate

The boundaries of modern Tanzania contain a varied geography with many different types of climates. Tanzania includes the islands of

Zanzibar – Unguja and Pemba – as well as Mafia. The mainland has a narrow coastal plain with many potential harbours along its shoreline. Altitude rises gradually until it reaches a chain of mountain ranges stretching from the border with Kenya to the border with Mozambique. Beyond the mountain ranges lies the Central Plateau which occupies the territory until it reaches the western branch of the Great Rift Valley. The Rift Valley extends from Ethiopia to South Africa. In Tanzania it forms two branches, the western one running through Tabora, Singida, and Iringa Regions and the eastern branch which includes the Great Lakes of Tanganayika and Nyassa. Tanzania's climates are determined by two principle factors – the annual variation in the monsoon winds blowing off the Indian Ocean and altitude. The monsoon winds blow from the northeast from October to December – a season called Kaskazi in Kiswahili – bringing the "short rains" to the islands and much of mainland Tanzania. The winds begin to shift and by March blow from the southwest during the season called Kusi. From March on the winds push moisture back over the mainland bringing the long rains to most of Tanzania. From June to September little rain falls as the winds blow from land towards the sea. This season pattern of winds would allow sailors to sail up and down the East African coast and brought the rains that nurtured plants and animals. Altitude affected these patterns as the highland regions west of the coast received more rain on their east faces and blocked moisture from reaching the Central Plateau. In the far west, the Great Lakes of Victoria, Tanganyika, and Nyassa provided another source of moisture that brought rain to the surrounding lands.

The islands and the coast share a similar climate because of the monsoons. Unguja island is the largest and receives less rainfall. It covers 1658 kilometer square and lies 39 kilometers from the mainland. Water flows towards the west over most of the island with the south and east much drier. Pemba to the north has a high central ridge and greater rainfall. It has supported more intensive agriculture in the past. It covers 984 kilometers square and lies 56 kilometers from Tanga on the mainland and 48 kilometres north northeast of Unguja. Mafia is smaller and flatter and has a much smaller population. It occupies 435 kilometer square and lies south of Unguja. It is governed as part of mainland Tanzania.

The coast plain is narrow and dotted with many inlets that have served as harbours from the Kenyan border to Mozambique. The coastline stretches 804 kilometers along the Indian Ocean. For a distance from shore varying from 16 to 64 kilometers, a low plain, no more than 300 meters above sea level, has a tropical environment. In the past mangroves and other types of tropical trees covered much of the land, but today human action has reduced the natural tree cover dramatically. The city of Dar es Salaam and other towns such as Tanga, Pangani, Bagamoyo, Lindi, and Mtwara lie on the plain.

West of the coastal plain lies a plateau with an elevation of up to 1000 meters. This area includes much of Pare, Korogwe, Muheza, Handeni and Bagamoyo districts and most of Morogoro, Lindi, Ruvuma and Mtwara regions. The region receives less rainfall than the coast and in some areas is actually arid. It has wide plains with hill regions interspersed. It is covered by savanna grasses with some tree cover in better watered areas.

The Eastern Arc mountains stretch from Kenya through northeast Tanzania down to the Southern Highlands of southern Tanzania. From the volcanic highlands around Mt. Meru to Mt. Kilimanjaro – Africa's tallest mountain and the world's largest free standing mountain – to the Pares, the Usambaras, the Ngulu, the Ulugurus, the Livingstone range, and the Southern Highlands the altitude rises from 1000 meters to 4000 meters. The eastern faces of these ranges receive regular and large quantities rainfall along with having in many cases fertile soils. The western faces receive less rainfall. At the lower levels vegetation is similar to the surrounding savannas while in the past woodlands covered the upper slopes. On the very tallest climate turns alpine – meaning that temperatures are too cold for most species of trees – and glaciers cover the peak of the tallest. The highest mountains include Kilimanjaro at 5890 metres, Meru 4566 meters, Loolmalasin 3648 meters, and Hanang 3418 meters. In the southwest the Mbeya Range reaches 2834 meters, and in the Uporoto mountains Mount Rungwe (2960 meters). All the main rivers of Tanzania rise in these mountains. These include the Ruvuma, the Rufiji, the Ruaha, the Wami, and the Pangani.

West of Kilimanjaro, the volcanic highlands border the Serengeti Plain. The Serengeti National Park, which neighbours the Ngorongoro Crater, is renowned for hosting in large numbers, the big five animals, namely: elephants, giraffes, rhinoceros, lions and buffalos. Every year millions of wildebeests migrate from the Serengeti to the Maasai Mara National park in Kenya and back. This migration is recognized as one of the eight new wonders of the world (URT, p. 4). Ngorongoro Crater is one of the most impressive features, an extinct volcano, it now forms "a big circular pit" like a depression of land several metres deep which today serves as a spectacular natural zoo. It is situated in the greatest animal sanctuary in the world known as Serengeti National Park.

The Rift Valley runs through western and central Tanzania from north to south. A wide depression of land with the valley has two branches east and west. The eastern branch stretches from Ethiopia and passes through western Kenya and northwestern and central Tanzania before reaching Lake Nyasa and the Zambezi River. The western branch starts from Lake Albert and forms Lakes Edward, Kivu, Tanganyika, and Rukwa before merging with the eastern branch between the Uporoto mountains and Mbeya Range, not far from Lake Nyasa. Lakes Natron, Manyara and Eyasi are situated in the eastern branch of the Rift Valley. Both branches of the Rift Valley are a result of faulting or breaking of the earth's surface thousands of years ago. The Fifty Years' Report of Tanzania mainland comments about the three big lakes which border the country. "Lake Victoria which is located in the north of the country is the largest in Africa and the third largest fresh water in the world. Lake Tanganyika which is located on the western side of the country, is the world's longest and the second deepest, Lake Nyasa located to the south west of the country, is also among the deepest lakes in the world." (URT, p. 4).

The Central Plateau occupies most of central part of Tanzania, bounded by the highlands of the east and south, by Lake Tanganyika and highlands extending from Rwanda and Burundi in the west and Lake Victoria in the north. It is a bowl like plateau with 1000-2000 meters above sea level. Soils are generally poor and rainfall less than 750 milimeters except in the Lake Victoria basin where it is higher. Most of the rain falls in a single wet season between October and May. Very little rain falls during dry season. It is less hot and humid than coastal belt but it is warmer and more humid than the highlands. Most of it is made up of open grasslands with a thin cover of trees cover most the area. The semi-arid regions of Dodoma, Singida, Shinyanga and Tabora regions are covered mainly by the shrubs and thin thickets of thorn-bush. These constitute about two-thirds of the central plateau and are either uninhabited or thinly populated. Miombo and mitundu woodlands cover the better watered parts.

Environment and Human Activities

Natural environment and climate are often thought of as setting limits to human efforts in the use of natural resources to satisfy human needs. Areas with fertile soils and reliable rainfall of more than 750 milimeters a year (such as northeastern highlands and Lake Victoria basin) have always attracted larger number of people than the arid areas in the lowlands and central plateau. Systems of agriculture and livestock keeping and fishing have been the range of activities highlighting historical development of communities in these areas. Parts with poor soils and marginal rainfall such as parts of Dodoma, Singida, Shinyanga and Tabora regions could support hunting and gathering, pastoralism and precarious agriculture. Yet climate and environment themselves change over time, and human activity, in particular the development of technology, expand those constraints. Modern climate systems generally came into place about 13,000 years ago – the beginning of Holocene Era – and before that the earth had gone through long periods of warming and cooling lasting tens of thousands of years that created remarkably different landscapes than those that have existed in the historic era. Even within the Holocene, cycles of warmer or cooler climate associated with wetter or drier conditions respectively, occur regularly such as the global cooler period in the three centuries preceding the twentieth century. The development of technologies like metal working greatly increased the efficiency of agriculture, and in the last two centuries the industrial revolution has even further changed humanity's relationship with the environment. Over the last century, the burning of fossil fuels has increased the amount of carbon in the atmosphere which has led to global warming. This warming trend has already altered the earth's climate leading to greater instability in weather patterns as well as the decline in ice cover at the poles as well as in glaciers such those on Mt. Kilimanjaro.

One of the geographical features that has continuously affected human activities in the history of Tanzania are rivers and Lakes. Archaeological evidence suggests that they facilitated cultural developments and communication networks among the ancient peoples of the Great Lakes and the Rift Valley. Besides rivers and lakes, the coast, characterised by wetter climatic conditions and seasonal monsoon winds, facilitated the growth of trade networks between the Indian Ocean and the outside world (the Red Sea, the Persian Gulf and Southeast Asia). It also led to the development of towns as commercial centres along the East African coast--dating back to the Neolithic period--whose inhabitants constantly engaged in agriculture, fishing and trade (Chami, 1994; 2006:13-17). The coast—favoured by its climatic conditions, has up to now continued to influence cultural and commercial contacts between the people of the coast, mainlanders, and those from the outside world.

Apart from trade and communication, varied environments supported different agricultural activities and skilled crafts. In the woodland savanna, by the nineteenth-century agriculture involved cutting, burning bushes, sowing grains for a few seasons, and planting root crops that did not need much soil fertility. However, continuous slash and burn activities led to the clearance of forests that had adverse impact on both the land and the entire farming system. Among the Turu of Singida, millet and sorghum became the main staple crops to communities in semi-arid regions because they could withstand aridity and could support sparse population. Conversely, banana remained a staple crop in high-rainfall areas such as Usambara and Uhaya as it could support dense populations and required less labour too (Iliffe, 1979:14-15). Division of labour between sexes dominated the two agricultural systems. In many areas, women did all the agricultural works while men engaged in herding, hunting, and homestead management. Notwithstanding women's dominance in agriculture, Nyakyusa and Nyamwezi men were skilled cultivators too (ibid, p. 16).

Although environments are generally regarded as influencing human activities, the landscape can also be remade by human activities. Iron smelting in Buhaya offers an example of environmental changes that are affected by human activities. Archaeological evidence indicates that the evolution of iron technology and permanent agriculture has had caused environmental changes over the past 2,000 to 3,000 years (Schmidt, 1997:401). The increasing scale of iron production between 300 and 500 CE led to the clearance of forests in costal valleys and hill tops and forced iron smelters to clear forests in distant areas to obtain charcoal for smelting and forging. By the beginning of the first millennium kinship groups in villages started penetrating further in western Buhaya in order to exploit new opportunities and resources for both agriculture and iron production (ibid, p. 405-411). The magnitude of forest depletion increased between 12,000 and 15,000 CE due to banana cultivation and increasing cattle herding that in consequence increased deforestation in Buhaya. Following the formation of centralised states in the late seventeenth century, deforestation was intensified due to taxation and regulations imposed on iron production to meet the needs of kings and indigenous rain makers (ibid, p. 417-418).

References

Chami, Felix A. *The Tanzanian Coast in the First Millennium AD: An Archaeology of the Iron Working, Farming Communities*. Uppsala: Societas Archaeological Uppsaliensis, 1994.

_____. *The Unity of African Ancient History 3000 BC to AD 500*. Dar es Salaam: E &D Limited.

Iliffe, John. *A Modern History of Tanganyika*. Cambridge, Cambrigde University Press, 1979.

Itandala, Buluda A. *History of Tanzania to 1890*. Dar es Salaam, Open University of Tanzania, 1997.

Koponen, Juhani. *People and Production in the late Pre-colonial Tanzania*. Uppsala, 1988.

Maddox, Gregory, Giblin, James, & Kimambo, Isaria N., eds., *Custodian of the Land: Ecology and Culture in the History of Tanzania*. Dar es Salaam, Mkuki na Nyota, 1996.

Schmidt, Peter R. "Archaeological Views on a History of Landscape Change in East Africa". *Journal of African History*. Vol. 38, No.3, 1997.

United Republic of Tanzania, *Report on the Fifty years of Independence, 2011*. Dar es Salaam, 2011.

Chapter Two

The Making of Human Communities in Tanzania

Introduction

The history of the human communities in the lands that came to make up Tanzania is much longer than the history of the country formed by colonial rule in the 1890s. Tanzania is part of the cradle of humanity that stretches from Ethiopia to South Africa. The ancestors of modern humans evolved in this broad swatch of eastern Africa at least 2 million years ago. Some of the earliest evidence for tool making by human ancestors comes from Olduvai [Oldupai] Gorge in northern Tanzania. Modern humans, homo sapiens sapiens, evolved in the same area about 200,000 years ago and began to spread out of Africa about 70,000 years ago. During this long time span, as John E.G Sutton notes, similar active beings making stone tools and living by hunting, foraging, and scavenging existed in many parts of the world. By modern standards the progress was slow but, during the late Stone Age, "commencing about ten thousand years ago man started in some parts of the world to assert himself over nature by providing his own food – that is by cultivation of plants and the taming of animals" (Sutton, 1968, p. 7). As the human population of Africa grew slowly groups began to develop different technologies to exploit different resources. They developed different languages as separation increased. They continued to evolve genetically in very subtle ways as communities adapted to differing environments and through random mutation of genes. For these earliest times we use three different types of evidence to try to understand the movements and interactions of human communities: archaeology, historical linguistics, and more recently genetic data. Archaeologically, several sites in addition to Olduvai [Oldupai] provide evidence of the slow differentiation in stone tool technology among the earliest human communities of Tanzania, particularly at Isimila in Iringa region.

The Language Families of Tanzania

Until the 1960s, colonial social scientists often had used racial classifications to explain the existing populations of Tanzania. Conflating language and physical appearance, they fit Tanzanians and Africans generally into schemas that generally sought to prove that Europeans were superior by nature. Such explanations failed, especially in light of the constant intermixing of linguistic and cultural groups. From the 1960s, African historians came to see the racial classification and migration explanations to be quite unsatisfactory. They were racist and irrational. They confused language, culture, and biology. The peoples of Africa had constantly intermingled and shared elements of culture and language meaning that no group was "pure." These explanations also confused socio-economic groups, such as hunters and gatherers with "races" such as the "Bushmen."

Because of these problems, scholars began to concentrate on what they could actually know rather than on supposition based on false evidence. Through careful study of existing languages, relationships between languages can be established and hypotheses about geographic origins of related languages and timescales of their spread developed. The making of human communities in Tanzania can be explained in terms of migration of these languages from certain centres of origin. As populations speaking the same language move farther away from each other and cease to interact with each other regularly, their languages will gradually become more different. As they interact with other populations speaking other languages, they will borrow terms from each other. Over a period of time, the two groups will speak different languages, not mutually understandable, but retaining certain characteristics in vocabulary and grammar. Linguists by carefully studying existing languages can arrange them in families indicating how closely related to each other (or how recently they divided from each other). Africa is home to four major language families – Afroasiatic, Nilo-Saharan, Niger-Congo, and Khoisan – and examples of each are spoken in Tanzania. While people certainly moved and brought their languages with them, the movement of languages also included people already living in an area adopting the language of the newcomers. Such language change could occur because of conquest or perhaps more likely because the newcomers brought a new, more successful set of technologies. Likewise, migrants could adopt the language of their hosts, perhaps adding new vocabulary to the host language. Genetic analysis of African populations shows such admixtures are more the norm than otherwise. Combining linguistic history with careful use of archaeological data and increasingly genetic information we can begin to draw the broad outline of the history of human populations from up to 20,000 years ago (Ehret, 2002, 26-35).

The Khoisan Languages

Post-colonial archaeologists, historians and linguists like John Sutton, Christopher Ehret, Thomas Spear and Derek Nurse have theorised that the first human community they can identify as Stone Age hunters and gatherers of Tanzania and the rest of East Africa spoke Khoisan languages. They base this conclusion on the existence of a common archaeological tradition, a set of similar artifacts, found at sites dated to between 20,000 and to very recent times. This East African Microlithic culture spread from southern Ethiopia gradually across all of East Africa and into southern Africa as far as what is now Namibia. The tool kit indicates that these communities survived on hunting and foraging. Rock paintings in cave shelters are often associated with these sites, including in Kondoa District. Today, groups speaking Khoisan languages in southern Africa historically have lived by hunting and foraging. Khoisan languages are distinctive for the clicks they use. The Sandawe of central Tanzania speak a language in the Khoisan family, and until recently lived by hunting and gathering. Other surviving hunters and food gatherers in north- central Tanzania who might have spoken Khoisan before being heavily influenced or linguistically absorbed by incoming groups include Hadzabe, Qwaza, Asa and Aramanik. The clicks in their languages, especially the Hadza in Tanzania and Dahalo in Kenya show that their ancestors were once Khoisan speakers (Ehret, 2002, 51-55).

The Cushitic Languages

Chushitic languages are a branch of the Afroasiatic language family, a group of languages spoken in eastern and northern Africa and in southwest Asia. The Afroasiatic family includes the Berber languages of

North Africa, the various languages of Ethiopia, and Semitic languages such as Arabic and Hebrew in southwest Asia. In East Africa, languages in this family come from the Cushitic branch. There are two Cushitic branches — eastern and southern, which spread from Ethiopia. Groups speaking these languages seem to have first brought cattle keeping and agriculture to East Africa. Most of those which spread to Tanzania were of the southern branch. Cushitic speaking people of the southern branch expanded into the highlands bordering the Rift valley in western Kenya and north eastern Tanzania from Ethiopia during the second millennium BC bringing with them cattle and finger millet.

Historians have five bodies of evidence for this explanation. The first piece of evidence is the presence of burial sites and cairns (or stone mounds) in the Rift Valley area of Kenya and Tanzania which do not exist elsewhere in East Africa, except Ethiopia. Secondly, skeleton evidence from a number of burial sites show affinities with similar burials in what is now Ethiopia. Thirdly, the presence of circumcision as initiation rite, a taboo against fish eating and other cultural traits which were wide spread among modern populations in Kenya and northeastern Tanzania would indicate earlier Cushitic influences. Fourth, radio-carbon dates from the burial sites indicate settlement by 1000 BC. Finally, archaeological evidence uncovered by Leakey and others show that the first millennium BC Cushites probably practiced agriculture and herded animal. Most members of this language group have been absorbed by their Bantu and Nilotic neighbours. Their remnant in Tanzania today are Iraqw or Mbulu (Wambulu), Gorowa, Alawa (Alagwa), Burungi, Ngomvia and Qwaza of Mbulu, Babati, Kondoa and Dodoma districts; the Asa and Aramanik of Maasailand, and the Mbugu or Vama'a who live in the Shambaa mountains (Ehret, 1998, 8-10).

The first Southern Cushites had settled in Southern Kenya during the 3rd Millennium B.C and some of their linguistic descendants spread still further South as central Southern Tanzania by the late Second Millennium. People speaking the early Southern Cushitic languages can be identified as makers of various archaeological cultures which belong to the Savana Pastoral Neolithic tradition of East Africa (Ehret, 1988, p. 617). The Southern Cushites from their first settlement kept cattle and small livestock as well as apparently donkeys. What is not clearly seen in the archaeological record but clearly seen in the linguistic evidence is that Southern Cushites were grain cultivators. Some of them from fairly early times used both irrigation and animal manure. The Southern Cushites of early first Millennium A.D varied a lot. Along Tana River and parts of coastal interior lived Dahaloans. At least one hunter-gatherer community in modern Witu area had taken up the Dahalo language as its own giving up its former Khoisan language but bringing in a number of Khoisan words with click sounds into the new language.

In the deeper interior, were the Rift Southern Cushites. One such society known in oral tradition as Mbisha lived in the Taita Hills. Around Mount Kilimanjaro and southward in Masai steppe, the old Asa-speaking communities lived, while in parts of central Tanzania they closely related to the old Kw'aza. At the time the three societies probably spoke dialects of a related language. Both Old Asa and Old Kw'aza societies apparently co-existed. West of the Rift valley in Tanzania lay the West Rift people, at one time probably extending through all the areas south of Mau forest of Kenya as far west as South-western Lake Victoria but by +600 probably centred on the Serengeti and Ngorongoro region. Most of the Western Rift Cushites of the 7th century may have been pre-eminently pastoral as were those of Kilimanjaro and the Taita Hills. The Southern Cushitic communities of the era spoke Mbuguan languages. Such languages were of two sets: one Kirinyaga Cushites preceeded Bantu settlers on Mount Kenya. They are probably the people remembered as the Gamba in modern day traditions. The second Mbuguan group, the Old Ma'a were probably centred by this time in north-eastern Tanzania probably to the east of the Old Asa and south of the Pangani River in parts of Upper Wami watershed where the ecological conditions allowed existence of cattle-raising (Ehret, 1988, p. 619).

The Central Sudanic Speakers (Moru-Madi)

Far to the west, in the Great Lakes region Central Sudanic-speaking communities seem to have held the same kind of historical position as the Southern Cushites had in Central and East Africa. They came to East Africa as herders of cattle and small livestock and cultivators of sorghum and finger millet. The Central Sudanic languages first rose to prominence in the areas near the Nile River in Southern Sudan and far Northern Uganda, probably in the third millennium before Christian era. Sometime later, a new front of central Sudanic settlement opened up to the mouth of Lake Victoria basin. Evidence of pollen studies reveal changes in vegetation attributed to agricultural activities in the basin about 3,000 years ago just north of Lake Victoria. In archaeology the probable reflection of this cultural and economic expansion of central Sudanic is Kansyore pottery. Like their contemporaries, the Southern Cushites to the east of the Great Lakes region, the Central Sudanic farmers and herders of the last three millennia before the Christian era entered into close relations with neighbouring food collecting communities. Another reflection can be seen in the wide adoption of Kansyore pottery by hunter-gatherers along the west and to the south of Lake Victoria. May have assimilated the hunter-gatherers more rapidly and thoroughly than did the Southern Cushites.

The Nilotic Speaking Peoples

The Nilotic language group is a sub-sub-group of the family known as Chari Nile, divided into central Sudanic and Eastern Sudanic. The Nilotic sub-branch comes from the Eastern Sudanic which developed in Southeastern Sudan and Southeastern Ethiopia. From there different branches of the language groups moved into Northern part of East Africa and from there to Tanzania at different times: Highland or Southern Nilotes, Plains or Eastern Nilotes and River–Lake or Western Nilotes. They acquired iron technology before expanding into East Africa. Highland or Southern Nilotes gradually expanded southeastwards into the highlands bordering the Rift Valley in the first millennium A.D. In this, there are two sub-language groups: Kalenjin (Western Kenya) and Tatoga who moved southwards into northeastern Tanzania. They include the Barbaig of Hanang (until recently known by nick name as Wamang'ati), the Gisamajeng (Mbulu), the Bajud, Buradig and Lake Eyasi and Kitangiri; the Ghumbieg, Mangadg, Reimojig, Daragwajeg and Bianjid in the Wambere River in Iramba, Igunga and Singida districts and the Iseimajeg and Rudageig of Ruvana valley in Serengeti district (Itandala, 1992, p. 34). Plains or Eastern Nilotes have three branches: the Bari in the Nile Valley, the Karamajong in northeastern Uganda and northwestern Kenya; the Maa or Maasai who expanded into the Rift valley in Kenya by the 9th and by the 16th centuries had moved to the Rift valley in Tanzania up to the central region. In Tanzania, River-Lake Nilotes or Western Nilotes include the Luo people who expanded southwards from Kenya into Tarime District of north Mara and interacted with Bantu speaking groups. As Christopher Ehret contends, the Moru-Madi group a branch of Central Sudanic Speakers was widespread in small groups in East and Central Africa. In most of East Africa they were completely absorbed by Bantu, Nilotic and Cushitic groups. Some of them still live in south western Uganda, southern Sudan and northwestern Congo (Zaire).

On the eastern part of Lake Victoria, the initial challenge to the predominant position of the first farmers came from the Southern Nilotes who began to move southwards out of Uganda-Sudan bordering regions sometimes around the middle of the first millennium before the Christian era and are to be identified as makers of the Elmenteira archaeological tradition. The Southern Nilotes took up residence in the higher areas along and to the west of the Central Rift Valley in Kenya, incorporating a considerable body of Southern Cushites into their society and apparently entering into close economic relations with hunter-gatherers' communities of the forested fringes of the Rift Valley and with the more purely pastoral Southern Cushitic people who continued to occupy the valley floor. From the hunters they would have obtained products such as honey, bees wax and skins, while with herders of the Rift Valley they would probably exchange grain for livestock. By the seventh century A.D, two distinct descendant societies of the early Southern Nilotes had emerged: the pre-Kalenjin, and the Tato from whom modern Datoga derive. The Tato were centred at first, it would seem, in the Loita highlands, and spread at some later period, but before 1100 southward from there into the Old Asa country of the Maasai steppe.

The Bantu Speaking People

Bantu languages make up the largest language group in Tanzania and East Africa in terms of number of speakers, yet the languages spread into East Africa after languages of the other three great African language families. Bantu is a sub-sub group of the Niger-Congo family; languages of that family are spoken all over West Africa, across Central Africa, and down eastern Africa all the way to South Africa. Bantu emerged in the savanna region of eastern Nigeria and Cameroon in the pre-Christian era (second millennium BC). The Bantu spread south and east into equatorial forest zone and from there into the savanna areas of east and central Africa during the first millennium B.C. Once communities speaking these languages reached the savannas they became grain cultivators, iron working people and livestock keepers adopting many techniques from their new Nilo-Saharan and Cushitic neighbours. There are many debates about Bantu expansion. It is important to bear in mind that the expansion in Tanzania was in small groups at a time from the east to the Great Lakes and from north east into the coastal area. Community formation involved also much interaction with other peoples, especially the Cushitic speaking people. By the first millennium A.D Bantu speaking communities had become the biggest occupiers of most of the coastal and interior of Tanzania. We shall elaborate on this process of social formation in the next chapter.

The more serious challenge to the earlier ways of agricultural life was posed by the Early Iron Age Bantu expansion into East Africa. It was a challenge not always immediately evident. For the Bantu immigrants were initially rather selective in their areas of settlement. The far west of the Great Lakes region speaking a number of different dialects of a language known to the modern scholars as proto-Bantu—in parts of the western, central and southern Lakes region earlier than the middle of the last millennium B.C. By this point in time two major kinds of economic change were under way in the northwestern part of East Africa. One was the spread of iron working with its attendant effects on the technology of tool-making: the age of stone-tools was thus beginning to draw to an end rather earlier there than elsewhere in Eastern Africa.

The second probably greater long-range development was the emergence of a more complex agriculture, principally among the communities speaking proto-Eastern Bantu language. Coming with the livelihood based in yam cultivation, they had begun to adopt in addition the crops of the farming societies who had preceded them in the eastern side of the continent, gaining a new potential flexibility in adapting to the great variety of East African environments (Ehret, 1988, p. 622). By the close of the era, a few Eastern Bantu communities under the influence of Central Sudanic neighbours and, to the south of Lake Victoria, of Southern Cushites, as well, had also begun to take an increasing interest in cattle-raising. Moreover, the population of people speaking Eastern Bantu dialects apparently grew considerably during the last several centuries before the Christian era by absorbing many of the east while Sudanese and probably by natural increases as well, at the turn of the era, the Eastern Bantu of the Great Lakes region and the adjoining parts of eastern Zaïre had grown into a sufficiently large population to support vast new scattering of Bantu immigrants into new and distant regions of settlement all across eastern and southern Africa.

In East Africa some of the new settlers went far to the east, to the coastal areas of Southern Kenya and to parts of mountainous areas of northeastern Tanzania, in particular to the Pare and Ngulu ranges. These were the makers of Kwale pottery. A slightly later offshoot of this settlement had arrived Mount Kenya by the 5th century A.D. That latter group of settlers probably brought the dialect of Eastern Bantu which was ancestral to Thagicu languages spoken across the eastern highlands of Kenya today. Archaeological continuity between Kwale ware, and Gatung'ang'a pottery of the 12th century on Mount Kilimanjaro, and more recent wares, though not fully demonstrated, seems a plausible hypothesis. The people of Pare mountains settlement can be suggested to have spoken the closely related dialect from which the later Chaga, Dawida, and Soghala languages derive. A second movement of early

Eastern Bantu into coastal East Africa was that of the north-east-coastal people, probably by or before the middle of the first millennium A.D.

Among historians who have propagated the idea of "Bantu expansions" include Christopher Ehret. In his article about Bantu expansions, Ehret argues not for one great "Bantu Expansion". Rather, he suggests a variety of regional and local expansions with different cross-cultural encounters, and socio-political and cultural change that make the vast distribution of modern Bantu communities (Ehret 2001, p. 5). As speakers of Bantu languages spread across the vast area, they adopted different ideas and practices of non-Bantu speaking communities in the different regions where they moved. Such a process, in consequence, made them more diverse than other Bantu-speaking communities (ibid, p. 7). He further gives credit to the Bantu-speaking communities for introducing the domestication of cattle and agriculture from southern Tanzania. This was engineered, in East Africa, by the arrival of the new population that he calls "Mashariki Bantu" in 1000B.C. They are said, in the view of Ehret, to be the first instigators of early agricultural innovation in Eastern Africa. Such a planting tradition originated among the people who spoke languages of Niger-Congo language family, and the initial stages in the development of agriculture was before the fifth century before the Christian era with yams being the key indigenous crop (Ehret, 1998, p. 13). Ehret argues as well that iron working in East Africa could have come from a separate origin than that of the Middle East and Europe, being independently invented in the Central African Sudan about the beginning of the last millennium before the current era (ibid, pp. 15-16).

Felix Chami has most famously questioned the relevance of the idea of Bantu expansion for East African history. Chami argues that archaeological research does not show evidence of a massive movement of people into eastern Africa bringing new technology with them. Rather sites show a gradual development of new ways of producing subsistence and new styles of material culture. He suggests that theories of the development of agriculture put too much emphasis on Bantu speakers both adopting grain cultivation from earlier communities and then bringing it for the first time to coastal and southern regions in what is now Tanzania. The differences between the views of linguistic historians and archaeologists lie perhaps in the nature of the evidence they use. The artifacts used by archaeologists to develop their theories of change cannot tell the language spoken by the people who created them. Likewise, the evidence of language change cannot be as precise in its dating as archaeology can in the dating of the creation of artifacts and sites. Perhaps more importantly, even if the evidence for the timing of language change proves accurate the continuity of material culture indicates that the changes were gradual and not abrupt and probably involved communities gradually adopting new languages more than large movements of population.

Map 1: The Making of Human Communities in Tanzania from the Seventh to the Nineth Centuries, A.D

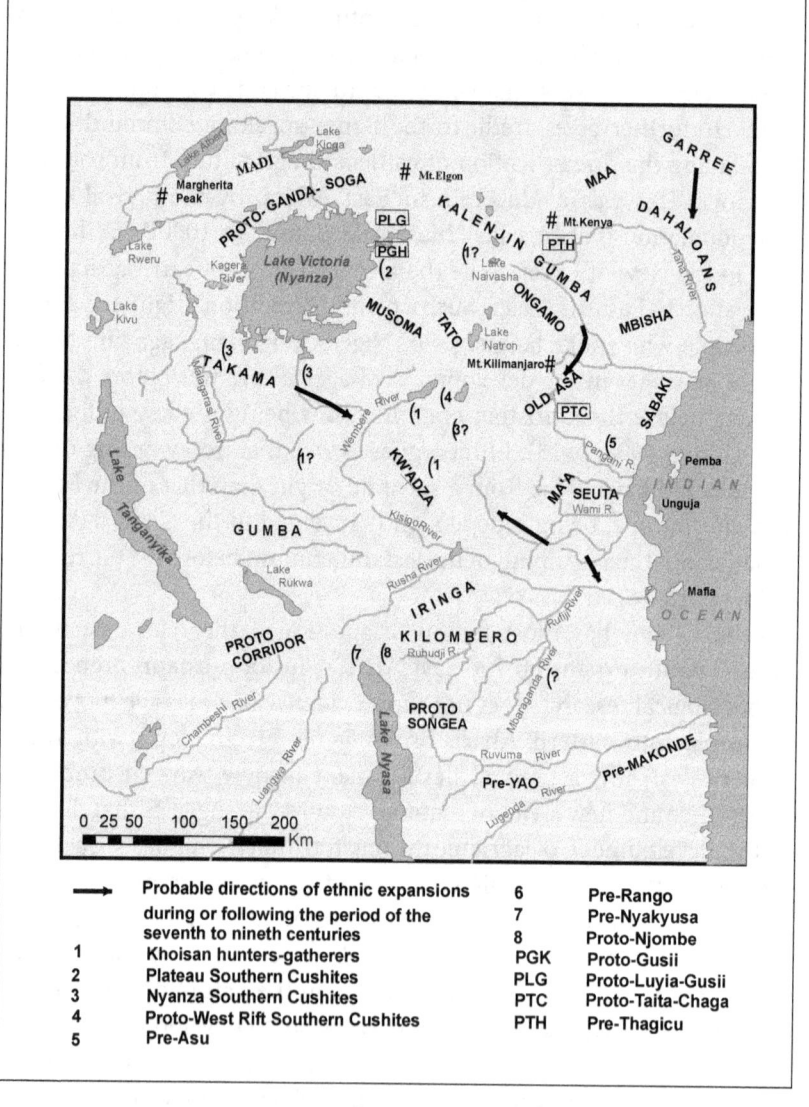

Source: Modified from Christopher Ehret, 1988.

Figure 1: Peoples of East Africa: Linguistic Classification

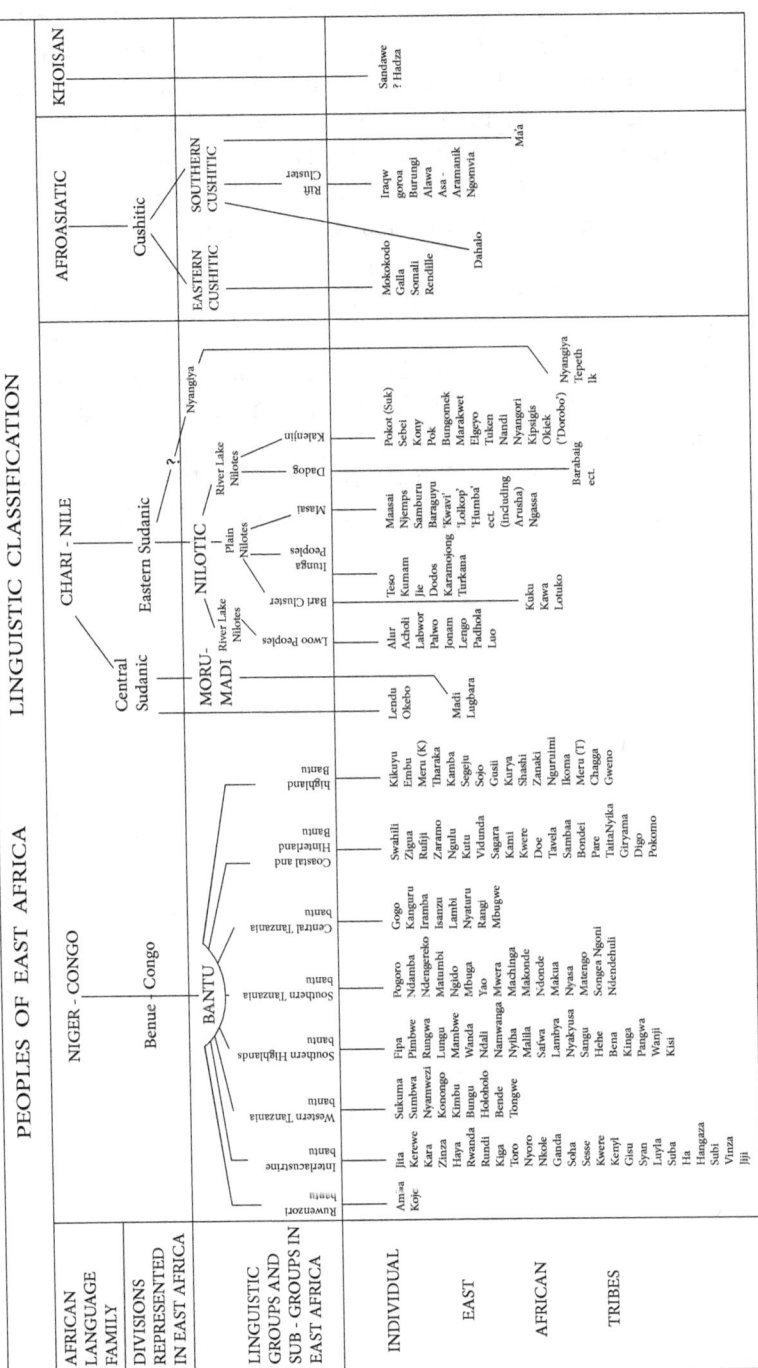

References

Chami, Felix. "A Response to Christopher Ehret's "Bantu Expansions", *International Journal of African Historica Studies*. Vol. 34, No.3, 2001.

Ehret, Christopher, "The East African Interior" in M. Elfasi and I. Hrbek, eds., *General History of Africa: Africa from the Seventh to the Eleventh Century*. California, Heinemann. UNESCO, 1988.

_____. *An African Classical Age: Eastern and Southern Africa in World History*. 1000 B.C to A.D. 400, Charlottesville: University Press of Virginia, Oxford: James Currey, 1998.

Itandala, A.B., *History of Tanzania to 1890*. Dar es Salaam: Open University of Tanzania, 1997.

Sutton, John E.G. "The Peopling of Tanzania" in Kimambo, I.N and Temu, A.J. eds., *A History of Tanzania*. Nairobi, East Africa Publishing House, 1969.

_____. "The Settlement of East Africa" in Ogot, B.A. *Zamani: A survey of East African History*. Nairobi: East African Publishing House, 1974.

Chapter Three

Early Community Formations to 11th Century: The Coastal Belt

Introduction

"One of the outstanding characteristics of the East African coast has been its relative accessibility, not only from the interior but also from the sea" (Sheriff, 1981, p. 551).

The East African coast served as a large gateway to the rest of the world for East Africans. Archaeological finds from the Benadir Coast in present day Somalia down to Sofala in Mozambique show evidence of trade goods from outside of Africa including glass beads and metal goods dating back to the beginning of the current era. Felix Chami and colleagues had documented Roman beads and others of Middle Eastern origin dating to about the third century of the current era at sites in the Rufiji Delta (Chami, 1999) and Neville Chittick documented Roman coins from several sites along the East African coast. Yet, dearth of historical sources makes it impossible to reconstruct the history with confidence especially in the period before the 7th century. From the available sources, we can divide the history of the broader East African as well as the Tanzanian coast before the 12th century into two sections. The first period surveys community formations on the coast belt from the first century A.D to the seventh century A.D with limited indications from Graeco-Roman, Arabic, and Chinese documentary sources. The second period explores communities along the coast from the seventh to the fifteenth centuries A.D with greater availability of documentary and archaeological sources including writings of Arab travelers.

The Tanzanian Coast 1st – 7th Century A.D

Graeco-Roman documents provide evidence for a picture of coastal communities formed by the first century A.D. Two documents are important. The first is *The Periplus of the Earythrean Sea* written by anonymous Greek commercial agent perhaps in the 1st century AD. It provides an eye witness account of commercial contact between the East African Coast, the Middle East and the Mediterranean regions. It also provides a thorough description of routes, ports, and goods involved in the contact between the coast and the outside world. The second document is Claudius Ptolemy's *Geography*, perhaps first written in the 2nd century but re-written with additions perhaps in the 4th century. Some 6th century materials, like Cosmas Indicopleustes' *Christian Topography* brings the picture close to the 7th century. Three important factors can be seen from these documents. First, the writers describe the existence of settled communities on the Coast populated by the people of "very great" stature. Oliver suggests that this may be reference to the Cushitic communities who had settled in many parts of East Africa by the early period of Christian era. Many other writers have not accepted this, because we know that Bantu speaking people had reached the coast by this time. The *Periplus* gives a clear indication about the economic activities of these people in agriculture, fishing, use of dug-out canoes and small sewed boats but no deep sea dhows. The socio-political picture is also mentioned; they had chiefs at each of the market towns. International trade certainly played an important role in local economies.

Apart from settled communities, there is also the existence of international contact. In this period commercial interests in the Middle East developed contacts with East Africa, with India, and with the Mediterranean world. The existence of monsoon winds allowed ships and merchants to travel between East African coast and the Middle East in a round trip lasting one year as seen in the first chapter. By the beginning of the Christian era Indian Ocean sailors already used these winds to sail north and south on the East African Coast. Trade was stimulated by intense rivalry among Greek successor states after the death of Alexander. The Seleucids in Persia controlled overland routes to India and even China and the Ptolemy's of Egypt used the Red Sea route. South-west Arabia (Aden) occupied a crucial middleman's position and appropriated its share of the profits developing trade with

East African area from about early 2nd century B.C. The rise of the Roman Empire created peaceful conditions for trade and the demand of oriental commodities in the Mediterranean. Finally, the East African coast became assimilated into the Roman economic system. The Romans called the East African coast Azania–perhaps a general name referring to a series of market towns, each independent with its own chief. The Periplus mentions a number of places in what is now Somalia. The only market town along the coast south of Ras Hafun mentioned was Rhapta. Ptolemy says it was located on a river "not far from the sea." The identification of the location of this big trading town has been a problem. Some have claimed that Msasani, a small town three miles north of Dar es Salaam, traded with Egypt and was the port that the *Periplus* and Ptolemy called Rhapta (Freeman-Grenville, 1962: 22). Sheriff eventually came to conclusion that Rhapta could have been on the Pangani River. Ptolemy called it a "metropolis" which implied the capital of a state.

Recent archaeological work by Felix Chami seems to point to the Rufiji region. Thus by the middle of the 2nd century A.D, Tanzania had been drawn into international system of trade. As the Roman Empire entered its period of decline in the 3rd century the market for luxuries contracted considerably. Direct trade with East African may have ceased altogether. The trading settlements along the East African coast seem to have remained fairly small. The most important exports consisted of tropical goods, especially ivory, rhinoceros horn, and tortoise shell. Imports included beads and coins, both used as currencies in exchange, fine pottery, cloth, including silk, and perhaps some metal goods. As East African communities already worked iron to make agricultural implements and weapons, the imports would have been specialised and high value. The trade centres, such as those at Pangani and the Rufiji delta would have become centres for not just trade but also possibly political influence.

The Tanzanian Coast 7th – 15th Century AD

Arabic and Chinese documents provide clues for the understanding of the East African Coast between the seventh and eleventh centuries A.D. These medieval documents were written by either traders who visited the Coast or by city dwellers in the Middle East who probably depended on travellers' tales. Prominent among the documents from the ninth to the twelfth centuries include those of Tuan Cheng-shih (863A.D), Al-Masudi (9th Century), Buzurg Ibn Sahriyar (10th century), and Ibn

Hawqual (10th century). Among the most detailed documents about the East African Coast is that of Al-Masudi. In his account, he states that the coast was inhabited by black people with autonomous rulers (*falme*). He identified Sofala and Kumbalu Island as two important areas along the East African Coast (which he called the land of the Zanj) that developed trade contacts between Siraf (present Oman) and the Coast. He noted that the town of Sofala produced gold, ivory, tortoise shell and amber as items for trade. Besides precious minerals, its inhabitants also engaged in the cultivation of bananas and coconuts (Chami, 1994:26, Freeman-Grenville, 1962b, pp. 1-17).

Later documents from Asia between the 10th and 15th centuries A.D. give a clearer picture of conditions along the coast. These documents include those of Al-Idirs (1100-1066), Chao Ju Kua (1226), Abu Al-Fida (1273-1331), Marco Polo (1295), Ibn Battuta (1331), and Abu Al-Mahasin (1441). Both Al-Idirs and Ibn Battuta provide a detailed account of the today's coastal cities at Unguja, Zanzibar, Mogadishu, Malindi, Mombasa, Sofala, and Kilwa. The two travellers describe the inhabitants of these places as efficient cultivators of fruits, sorghum, sugar-cane, bananas, rice, and camphor trees. Both Al-Idris and Ibn Battuta mention iron mining and smelting centres at Malindi, Mombasa, and Sofala. Apart from trade and farming, the inhabitants of the coastal towns engaged in pearl-collecting, hunted for skins and ivory. Because of constant contact with the Middle East and the Mediterranean world, the inhabitants of the coast, as Ibn Battuta asserts, had by the 14th century been integrated into the Islamic world (Chami 1994: 27).

Portuguese documents are the last documents that report about the East African coast in the medieval period. Vasco Da Gama's voyage to find an alternative route to India for Portugal led the way. He arrived on the East African coast in 1498 on his way to India. He was followed by several expeditions that generated a great deal of information about the East African Coast. Prominent among the written works include that of Joao de Barros' *Decadas da Asia*. The work demonstrates the coast's long development of trade contacts with the outside world especially the Arab world. The work singles out Kilwa, Mombasa, and Mogadishu as towns that emerged competing against each other for trade monopoly. He notes that Kilwa for centuries controlled the southern coast up to Sofala and the routes to the gold producing region of Mwanamutapa in present-day Zimbabwe. Besides trade, de Barros mentions fishing as among the main occupations of the people of Kilwa. Men in Kilwa and other small villages also practiced crafts and arts that they inherited from their families. He noted that cloth and gold were the main items exchanged between Kilwa and the kingdom of Mwanamutapa (Chami, 1994:27, G.S.P. Freeman-Grenville, 1962a: 197). Furthermore, in his *Decade I, Book VIII*, de Barros identifies Mogadishu, and Barawa as having been founded about seventy years before the formation of Kilwa in about 887 A.D (Fereman-Grenvile, 1962a, p. 22-23).

The flourishing of the Swahili city-states coincides with the beginning of the Islamic era. Much of the colonial era scholarship assumed that coastal communities were created by or through influence of immigrant groups arising from Islamised Arab and Persian settlers. The colonial scholars were greatly influenced by a bias similar to the "Hamitic myth" which interpreted change on the coast (and elsewhere) in terms of diffusion from some superior cultural centres rather than as result of peoples' adaptation to their changing environment. The false interpretations were built in two stages. Prior to Neville Chittick's work in the 1960s the prevailing interpretation was that after the rise of Islam in the 7th century, there was expansion of people, to begin with, from the Persian Gulf into the East African coast. By the 10th century AD immigrants from Shiraz in Persia built a big empire with its centre in Kilwa. Chittick's research changed the picture to show that such a development did not take place until the 12th century and that the people came not directly from the Persian Gulf, but from Shiraz dominated settlements on the Benadir coast. Thus Chittick killed the concept of "Zenj Empire" but reinforced the picture of outside influence in the explanation of formation of coastal communities by stressing the Indian Ocean outlook of their developments. Recent research even though still limited, has shown that there was more community continuity starting long before the Islamic period.

Masao and Mutoro have documented a number of archaeological sites which have demonstrated the existence in the region, not only of human activities but also human settlements going back beyond the frequently quoted ninth century of the Christian era (Masao and Mutoro, 1988, p. 593). Thus archaeological evidence in all cases indicates that there were local inhabitants with their own civilisation before the coming of the Muslim Arabs and Persians. The available evidence also supports the contention that at least for the central and southern parts of the East Coast the inhabitants were Bantu speaking. Many more sources written by Arab authors have come to light. Some were known before but were not fully utilised. For example, al-Masudi who visited the coast in 916-917 A.D stresses the non-Muslim character of the Zandj states. The impression from the Arab writers of this period is that political power in all coastal settlements had been in the hands of indigenous Africans. At the same time the Arabic sources show constantly expanding trade between East African coast and the lands surrounding the Indian Ocean. This is a continuation of the picture of the Graeco-Roman period. Although the earlier big urban centres of the time disappeared, other settlements took their place as centres of trade.

Social Organisation on the Coast

Coastal settlements seem to have always governed themselves and maintained their independence. Their links with each other followed patterns of alliance and hostility. Villages built of mud and wattle lay scattered along the coast. The layout of the large centres of the Graeco-Roman period is still not known. By the 9th century, most of the communities probably spoke what one might call the "proto-Swahili" language whose further refinement and expansion by words from other languages belong to a later period. The mixture of indigenous people and immigrants resulted in an ethnically mixed and economically specialised society. This led to the characteristic pattern of socio-economic differentiation and social stratification.

The role of Muslims and their numbers has been exaggerated. Although Islam had reached the Benadir coast by the 8th century and southern part of the East African Coast by the 11th century, it was not until the 14th century that a distinctive Islamic coast civilisation differentiated itself. Besides Islam, architecture dominated Swahili coastal settlements. Before the 9th century, the majority of the buildings in many of the settlements were mud and wattle with roofs of thatch. Gradually, stone houses came in as stratification and economic differentiation appeared. Many scholars have attributed the stone architecture to Persian and Arabic influences. Masao and Mutoro argue that, "this diffusionist view is eschewed here in favour of more acceptable explanation. It has already been pointed out that in no one region in the Near East are there sufficiently numerous or detailed parallels to enable clear conclusions on Persian or Arabic to be made" (Cf. Masao and Mutoro, 1988). They point to the increase in stone buildings as a process of continuous development based on local conditions and increasing trade.

Economic Activities

In economic terms, coastal society was "an urban-rural continuum" with many earning their living from agriculture. In Benadir in the north pastoralism also existed. The practice of townsmen going into the country for 3 or 4 months every year to cultivate was probably a common practice. The chief crops included sorghum, yams, bananas, coconuts and sugar cane. Honey is mentioned by some sources but it is not clear whether bees were kept or collected from the forest. A Chinese source says yams replaced grains in Zanzibar. In Kilwa, evidence shows that the only grain grown was sorghum. Arab writers insist that Zandj people were fish eaters. Fishing was a general activity all over the coast, but in some places it was the main occupation. Arab writers do not comment much on boat building. Buzurg bin Shahriyar mentions numerous boats that surrounded Arab ships near the coast of Sofala. He also says some Zandj served as the ship captains on the Indian Ocean an indication that East Africans were acquainted with not only coastal navigation but also with that of the high seas (see Masao and Mutoro, 1988, pp. 609-610).

The picture we get north of Juba River and southwards is not yet clear. Al-Masudi reports that cattle were employed by the Zandj as riding oxen (with saddles and reins) in war. Al-Idrisi on the other hand, categorically insists on the absence of any beasts of burden or cattle along the East African coast. Other Arab authors are totally silent. In modern times, cattle could not be kept in areas near the coast due to tsetse fly, but in the past areas may have existed cleared of enough bush to be free of the fly. Other economic activities included hunting and mining. Hunting must have been part of the basic economy. Arab authors were fascinated chiefly by elephant hunting but they also mention other animals including hunting techniques. East Africans hunted leopards, lions, dogs and monkeys. Hunting focused both on producing skins or ivory for export and meat for consumption. Gold drew a great deal of attention from Arab authors especially at Sofala and Kilwa. Local people seem to have valued iron and copper more. Al-Idrisi mentions iron exports but his accounts poses problems because evidence of large-scale smelting has been found only in the vicinity of Mombasa and Malindi. Since Bantu speaking peoples arrived in this area with knowledge of iron, this lack of direct evidence does not mean that smelting activities did not exist near the coast. Smelting could have taken place both localized and small in scale. Since iron working was occurring in the hinterland, iron goods also could have moved from interior to the coast.

Commercial Activities

From the time of the Graeco-Roman period, settlements on the coast had become big and urban centres and grew and declined because of trade. From the 7th century an expanding market in Islamic countries offered new possibilities. Trade grew both in volume and in variety. Major items attractive to Arabs, Persians, Indians and Indonesians included ivory, tortoise shell, ambergris, incense, spices, slaves, gold and iron. Some of the items attracted even ninth century Chinese visitors. According to al-Idrisi, the Arabs of Oman kidnapped children to take into slavery. The slave trade poses a problem of interpretation. For the period between 7th and 12th centuries there is no direct evidence on slave trading. Foreign traders procured slaves by capturing or abducting local people rather than purchasing them from local sources. In the long run this method was hardly effective and could produce only a restricted number of slaves. Trade relations could not be maintained by this method. On the other hand, the mass employment of the so called Zandj slaves in irrigation works in lower Iraq leading to ninth century famous slave revolt, would indicate that there was a continuous flow of enslaved peoples from East Africa, perhaps mostly from the northern part of the coast, to the Islamic world.

Large towns tended to be oriented more towards international trade than small ones which depended more on agriculture and fishing. But frequent interaction between the settlements regardless their sizes existed. Some of the imported items could circulate even to those who were not directly trading with the foreigners. Excavations at Kilwa before the dynastic period (about 12th century) indicated imported items including Islamic pottery and glass beads, cornelian beads from India, and porcelain from China. Excavations at Manda in the north and Kilwa in the south show that in levels dated to ninth century there were no glass beads which would indicate that these centres did not have much trade during this period.

References

Chami, Felix A. *The Tanzanian Coast in the First Millennium A.D: An Archaeology of the Iron-Working, Farming Communities.* Uppsala: Soceietas Archaeologica Upsaliensis, 1994.

_____ *The Unity of African Ancient History, 3000 BC –AD 500.* Dar es Salaam: E & D Limited, 2006.

Chittick, Neville H. "The Coast before the Arrival of the Portuguese" in Ogot, ed., *Zamani: A Survey of East African History*. Nairobi: East African Publishing House, 1973.

Freeman-Grenville, G.S.P. *The Medieval History of the Coast of Tanganyika*. London, New York, and Toronto: Oxford University Press, 1962a.

_____. *The East African Coast: Select Documents from the first to the earlier nineteenth century*. Oxford: Clarendon Press, 1962b.

Masao, Fidelis T. and H.W. Mutoro, "The East African Coast and the Comoro Islands" *General History of Africa*, Vol III, 1988.

Sheriff, A.M. H. "The East African Coast and Its Role in Maritime Trade." in G. Mokhtar, Ancient civilisations of Africa. Paris, UNESCO. *General History of Africa*, Vol II, UNESCO, 1981.

Chapter Four

Early Community Formations: The Interior to 11th Century

Introduction

"The seventh to eleventh centuries of the Christian era appear on the whole to have been a period of consolidation of previous trends in the East African interior. The notable ethnic and economic transformations of the earliest Iron Age lay several centuries in the past, at the turn of the eras and during the two or three centuries thereafter when Bantu communities spread into widely scattered areas and iron technology began widely to be practiced. The next era of equivalent transformation would not be for centuries still to come. That is not all to say that the period of the seventh to eleventh centuries was without interest. New ethnic expansions took place changing the linguistic map and creating new challenges to be dealt with by established communities. And sometimes the accumulation of small changes grew into something new and significantly different from just the sum of its parts". (Ehret 1988, p. 616).

Christopher Ehret's observations shed light on transformations in the East African interior from the seventh to the eleventh centuries. Such transformations corresponded with new ethnic formations that posed new challenges to be addressed by settled communities. Building on Ehret's observation, this chapter attempts to reconstruct the way or ways of life as far as the combined archaeological, anthropological and linguistic evidences will allow. The linguistic picture has already been set in the second chapter but this chapter looks at community life. At this stage linguistic differentiation was still taking place. But by the 11th century many proto-languages had been formed and settlement in major favourable ecological zones had been accomplished.

The Stone Age Hunters and Gatherers

In Tanzania we have a more complete archaeological record of the Stone-Age period from time culturally modern human beings appeared about 70,000 years ago to the more recent period. From the emergence of the culturally modern humans until the rise of agriculture and domesticated livestock beginning about 5000 years ago in East Africa all people lived by some form of hunting and gathering. People lived mostly in small mobile bands that moved regularly to take advantage of different types of food across the seasons. They made tools out of stone including spear and arrow heads, axes, knives, digging sticks, and hammers. The types of resources they exploited depended on the environment in which they lived. Those that lived near large bodies of water such as lakes and rivers fished and collected fruits and grains that grew permanently along the waterways. In the savannas groups followed and hunted game such as antelope and wildebeest. In almost all cases, vegetation such as fruits, nuts, berries, and wild grain made up most of the diet. These tended to be collected mostly by women while men focused more on hunting.

Before about 5000 years ago, most of these communities that lived in Tanzania probably spoke Khoisan languages. As agriculture and livestock spread, foraging communities in most cases assimilated into the new agricultural societies. In some, though, small groups of foragers came to live in symbiosis with agricultural communities as happened with the Twa in the Great Lakes Region who came to speak a Bantu language like their neighbours. The Dhahalo of eastern Kenya came to speak a Cushitic language. In Tanzania, only small groups remained foragers by about 1000 years ago. The Sandawe of Kondoa speak a Khoisan language. Other groups speak Cushitic languages – Hadzabe, Asa, Aramanik, and Qwaza; Bantu – Sonjo; and Nilotic – Ogiek or Ndorobo. Over the colonial and independent eras, most of these groups have been forced to abandon a pure foraging lifeway and take up agriculture.

The First Agriculturalists and Pastoralists

The earliest farmers and herders probably spoke Cushitic languages and filtered south interspersed with hunting and gathering populations. The coming of iron in East Africa increased agricultural productivity and boosted the expansion of new areas for agriculture which had hitherto been untouched by hunters and gatherers. More importantly, iron tools helped farmers to cope with high rainfall regions and thick forests where the banana has become the main crop (Sutton, 1973, p. 76). We have already seen that the first food producers were Cushitic speaking peoples. We saw that they expanded into the Rift Valley as early as second millennium BC. We noted explanations for their existence. Ehret's linguistic evidence shows that Cushitic communities with variety of settled agricultural life existed in most of Tanzania, not only in the Rift Valley but stretching to highland areas of northeast to Lake Victoria Basin and up to the coast. Their reliance on stone tools limited their ability to clear land for agricultural expansion. When iron working technology arrived (associated with Bantu and Nilotic speakers), many of the Cushitic communities were absorbed. Ehret also mentions another widespread group from the central Sudanic language group (Moru Madi) which in our area completely disappeared, although they were cultivators and livestock keepers.

Communities combined the cultivation of food crops and livestock keeping. This could also be in addition to hunting, honey collecting and fishing. They include members from all main linguistic groups: Bantu, Cushites and Nilotes. Most Cushitic groups (Iraqw, Gorowa and Burungi) have had this combination since the Stone Age period. Bantu speakers seem to have adopted herding and grain cultivation after arrival in the Great Lakes region and their interaction with both Cushitic and Nilotic groups. People like the Wasukuma, Wanyamwezi, Wagogo, Wanyaturu, Wakuria and others are modern examples. The best example of Nilotes are the Waarusha and the Parakuyo.

Bantu Communities

From the first to the eleventh century, Bantu speaking communities had expanded quickly after their revolutionary transition in the savanna region south of the rain forest. As iron using communities they had advantage over other Stone Age communities, and they quickly occupied the more favourable areas of the coast including islands, the northeastern highlands, and the Great Lakes areas. Ehret argues that by the 11th century, most Bantu speaking peoples had settled in their main territories, had formed the proto-languages of their main branches, but further ethnic differentiation occurred later as they continued to expand in occupying areas within their main environments. The Bantu speaking communities had the advantage of growing grains sorghum and millet already introduced by Cushitic and Central Sudanic farmers. They probably also adopted livestock including sheep, cattle, donkeys, and chickens from Cushitic, Nilotic and Central Sudanic groups. Evidence for early Bantu expansion comes from both linguistic and archaeological studies. The dating of the spread of iron and agriculture using radiocarbon techniques correlates closely with the estimated spread of Bantu languages in eastern, central and southern Tanzania. Archaeologists have used the presence of "dimple based" and "channelled-based" types of pottery as evidence of Bantu speakers.

In most instances, Bantu speaking communities settled in various types of environments and cultivated crops most suited to the ecology. They adopted bananas in the highlands of Unyakyusa, Kilimanjaro, Meru and Bukoba at a very early date. They grew grains such as sorghum and millet in grasslands like those of Mwanza, Shinyanga, Kigoma, Dodoma and Singida regions. Where possible they kept cattle. Although agriculture became the main subsistence activity they hunted and fished. Unlike hunters and gatherers, and pastoralists, who were nomadic, cultivators were forced to live sedentary life by the nature of their economy. Secondly agricultural production made storage or accumulation, management and distribution of the harvest necessary across the year. These tasks called for cooperation and managerial leadership. Kinship relations, clans and lineages played an important part in this kind of leadership. Because of this cohesion and solidarity, the family became the unit of production of the means of subsistence. Elders emerged as the leaders of the community.

The expansion of Early Iron Age Bantu posed a challenge to early agricultural life in East Africa. Around the middle of the last millennium before the Christian era, two kinds of economic changes occurred in the north-western part of East Africa. The first was the spread of iron-working that gradually replaced Stone Age tools. The second was the emergence of complex agriculture among the communities of proto-Eastern Bantu language (Ehret, 1988, p. 621). The emergence of both iron-working and complex agricultural communities led to the spread of Eastern Bantu farming communities in different areas of the interior especially in central and southern Great Lakes region, the immediate hinterland of central and southern Tanzania, the Pare Mountains, along the western sides of Lake Victoria, in central southern Tanzania, and in north-central Tanzania (ibid, p.623).

The primary factor for the distribution of Bantu farming communities was the relationship between Bantu settlements and favourable climatic areas with sufficient rainfall. By the seventh century, many areas in the Tanzanian interior remained unoccupied by food producing communities. Among the regions include many areas of central, western, and south-western Tanzania. Cultural change seems to have occurred though. The expansion of Bantu settlements into the interior of East Africa corresponded with the movement of the Lelesu-pottery ware in the dry areas of central Tanzania. It remains unknown whether this Lelesu community adapted to the new environment by changing from grain cultivation to hunting. It is also unknown whether these foraging communities continued to speak Khoisan languages or used the languages of their agricultural neighbours (ibid, p. 624).

The period from the seventh to the eleventh centuries of the Christian era marked various significant changes. First, the majority of Bantu-speaking communities remained largely within relatively restricted ecological boundaries of their Early Iron Age settlement areas and only gradually expanded within and outside their boundaries to meet the needs of the growing populations. Secondly, as linguistic evidence attests, there was a continuing process of assimilation of non-Bantu-speaking communities in many areas of the Tanzanian interior. For instance, in north-eastern Tanzania a considerable number of Old Ma'a speakers were incorporated into proto-Seuta society when the territories of Seuta expanded in the Ngulu Mountains and Uzigula. This demonstrates the extent to which Ma'a speakers exploited diverse potentialities of new areas that hitherto had not been colonised before their incorporation into the proto-Seuta society.

The third factor stems from climatic variations and interactions with other communities that eventually increased differences and distinctions among Bantu communities in the interior. At the beginning of the first millennium, nearly all Bantu of East Africa spoke dialects of a single Eastern Bantu language. By the seventh century such commonalities were coming to an end and by the eleventh century separate languages could be noticed among the Eastern Bantu societies. They included the North-east-Coastal language consisting of Seuta, Sabaki, Ruvu, and Asu dialects, Lacustrine languages of the Great Lakes region consisting of dialects spoken by communities in southern Lake Victoria, the proto-Gusii-Kuria on the south-eastern Lake Victoria, proto Luiya-Gisu of north-eastern side of Lake Victoria, Thagicu spoken by makers of Gatang'ang'a were of Mount Kilimanjaro, proto-Chaga spoken by the makers of Maore pottery ware in North Pare and the Taita Hills. The proto-Chaga language had three dialects of which two of them were spoken in the Taita area, while other languages were spoken as far as Southern Tanzania (Ehret, p. 627).

Besides differences and distinctions of the Eastern Bantu languages, by the second half of the first millennium of the Christian era, considerable movements of Bantu-speaking communities took place in the Great Lakes region that increased expansion of territories inhabited by the original Lacustrine societies. The original Lacustrine societies among the early Iron Age Bantu communities settled in the heavily forested areas of western and south-western shores of Lake Victoria. Such societies were associated with Urewe pottery ware from Bukoba that are associated with early iron-working sites. Constant outward movement of Lacustrine communities in the first millennium of the Christian era gave rise to the emergence of Lacustrine dialects. Among the evolved dialects included the Rwanda-Ha and Konjo languages of the Western Rift Valley. What prompted the outward movements of Lacustrine societies included environmental exhaustion caused by population growth, increasing agricultural demands, and forest clearing to make charcoal for iron-smelting (Ehret, p. 628, Schmidt, 1997).

In what is now southern Tanzania, Bantu languages expanded slowly after the beginning of the current era. A major centre of the adaptation of grain cultivation occurred in the Njombe highlands during the first millennium of the current era. Bantu communities continued expanding further south into the modern countries of Malawi, Zambia, Zimbabwe, and South Africa. A second stream expanded down the coast and its hinterlands into what is now Mozambique.

Economically, Bantu-speaking communities practiced different types of farming and grew various types of crops including sorghum, finger millet, and kept cattle as well. By the end of the first millennium of the Christian era, indigenous varieties of yam were still dominant foods of some of the Bantu speakers of the East African interior. Besides indigenous yams, South-east Asian crops including Asian yams, taro, and bananas were grown by Bantu-speaking communities. The reason for growing these crops was due to favourable climatic conditions and early Bantu speaker's acquaintance with planting agriculture. What accounts for the growth of South Asian crops into the interior of Tanzania stems from the fact that crops and seeds could move from one region to another by way of trade, contact with neibhouring societies, and expanding agriculture in societies. The merging of both indigenous and foreign crops had a significant contribution to the success of the Bantu economy and agricultural production as well. In the Tanzanian interior, the period between 600 to 1100, Bantu-speaking communities relied more on grain crops than on yams. The West Ruvu community engaged in cattle-raising and grew grain crops as well as the Kimbu, Nyamwezi-Sukuma, Rimi (Nyaturu), and Nyiramba (Ehret, 1988, p. 632, Sutton, 1973, p. 71).

The other notable crop was the cultivation of banana crops in highland areas of the Tanzanian interior paving the way for the evolution of highland planting agriculture. The knowledge of banana cultivation diffused in the interior in the second half of the first millennium of the Christian era via the Pare region and Kenya. The systematic use of irrigation made highland banana agriculture in northeastern Tanzania very productive. Apart from the northern Tanzania coast and Kenya, the knowledge of banana cultivation spread in the interior from the south and west. Linguistic evidence points to the spread of bananas into the Great Lakes region from the south (Malawi and the Zambezi basin), through Congo Basin, and across West Africa. By 1100 the introduction of banana from the south had spread the knowledge of the crop into many areas of the Great Lakes region including the Bukoba area. The introduction of banana in Bukoba and other parts of the Great Lakes region was largely prompted by the need to expand food production in the face of a series of environmental pressures (Ehret, 1988, p. 634). It can therefore be argued that food production in East Africa never originated from the same source. Rather, different crops with different methods of domesticating animals originated from multiple sources at different times. This, in consequence, led to the evolution of complex agriculture in the interior of Tanzania and East Africa in general (Sutton, 1973, p. 73).

As far as social organisation is concerned, the most common residential unit in all interior Bantu-speaking communities was the pattern of a neighbourhood of scattered homesteads otherwise known as the village. At the turn of the first millennium of the Christian era, village life had become common among the Bantu although such a pattern had earlier dominated Nilotic and Cushitic modes of life. As Bantu absorbed Cushitic or and Nilotic communities, the older Nilotic or Cushitic pattern of residence was preserved in some parts of Kenya highlands and in northern Tanzania. In the southern interior, a village mode of life tended to dominate Bantu-speaking communities. Like Southern Cushitic speakers, early Bantu societies consisted of several clans each under the leadership of a clan head. However, the role of a Bantu chiefship was largely political while that of the Cushites was mainly for the allocation of land. More importantly, the chiefly roles of Bantu communities in the interior became modified by cultural assimilation with non-Bantu communities. Social organisation went hand in hand with peoples' religious systems. Throughout the interior and the Great Lakes region, Bantu-speakers at the beginning of the Iron Age developed a set of beliefs in the existence of a high God, but directed prayers to meet their needs to ancestors. Evil was often attributable to human relations and gave rise to belief in witches and sorcerers. In north Pare and Kilimanjaro, the God-sun metaphor dominated Chaga religious thought at the beginning of the second millennium of the Christian era (Ehret, 1988, pp. 636, 640).

Nilotes and Mixed Farmers

The expansion of Nilotic languages into East Africa and the Rift Valley region of Kenya and Tanzania have already been discussed. The span of expansion from periods similar to Bantu expansion (for Highland Nilotes) in the first millennium A.D to most recent periods of the 19th century (for Luo speaking people) is the widest of any of the great language families in Tanzania. Another point to note is that although most of Nilotic groups had a tendency towards mixed economy (agriculture and pastoralism), some communities, especially the Maasai speakers have tended to become mainly pastoralists. Pastoralist communities include Tatoga and Maasai groups living in Arusha, Serengeti, Dodoma, Singida, Shinyanga and Mara Regions. Many of them still depend on cattle for their livelihood. They tend to move around following pastures for their herds across the seasons. Residential groups are not stable either in size, composition or location. But families tended to be stable because of owning property in cattle. Unlike gatherers who had no permanent leadership, the Tatoga and Maasai pastoralists had permanent leadership by male elders but leaderships tended not to be centralised. They also had strong age-grades and age-sets that promoted cooperation across large areas and among many kin groups.

Both Nilotic and Cushitic-speaking communities continued throughout the seventh and eleventh centuries to dominate the grasslands and high plains of the central interior of East Africa. But, as Ehret asserts, the territories of Southern Nilotes were increasing while those of the Cushites were relatively declining. Examples of Nilotic-speaking communities include Dadoga and Maasai. According to Ehret, the Dadoga evolved throughout the period as a society dominated by pastoral economy from the west side of the Rift Valley in southern Kenya to the northern and central Maasai plains in Tanzania. As they expanded their settlements from Kenya to the Maasai plains, the Nilotes co-existed with the Asa who were specialised in hunter-gathering activities. Despite the co-existence, the Asa maintained their East Rift language which is different from the Asu Bantu language as it is often confused (Ehret, 1988, p. 629). Economically, the Nilotes raised cattle and cultivated grains. Driven by such an economy, the Nilotes were in conflict for land with the pastoral Southern Cushitic-speaking communities. In due course, Southern Nilotes incorporated the dominant Cushitic communities. For instance, the Maa-Ongmo, in their course of spreading, were incorporated into Southern Nilotes (ibid, p. 632).

References

Ehret, Christopher. "The East African Interior", Elfasi, M, Elfasi, ed, in *General History of Africa: Africa from Seventh to Eleventh Century* Vol. III. UNESCO, 1988.

Itandala, Buluda A. "History of Tanzania to 1890", The Open University of Tanzania, 1997.

Sutton, John E.G. "East Africa before Seventh Century" in Mokhtar, G (ED.) *General History of Africa: Ancient Civilisations of Africa*, Vol II, UNESCO, 1981.

PART TWO

From Simple to Complex Communities

Chapter Five

From Simple to Complex Communities: Northwestern Tanzania

Section I: Development of Socio-Political Organisations in Tanzania

Introduction

In the previous chapter we discussed the development of different types of means of subsistence, based on both the continuing expansion of new technologies such as agriculture, animal husbandry, and metal working. Communities specialised in foraging, keeping domestic livestock, and agriculture primarily based on the particular environments in which they lived. This chapter explores the development of socio-political orgnisations in Tanzania. The first section provides a general account of different types of socio-political organisations while the second section provides details, for different parts of the country, of specific socio-political organisations that developed in the pre-colonial period. We argue that the development of socio-political organisations in Tanzania was not homogenous. Rather, it was complex and involved an interplay of variegated forces across the country.

Kinship Organisation

In precolonial Tanzania, internal relations in many societies, as Juhani Koponen argues, were dominated by kinship. It was the kind of social organisation that was characterised by kinship groups based on kinship relations. Heads of families or kinship groups acted as leaders and led other members in performing several functions. Kinship organisation provided a basis for social and political organisation in many precolonial societies across Africa. Clans or kinship groups traced membership either patrilineally (inheritance on the father's side) or matrilineally (inheritance on the mother's side) depending on societies. In many societies kinship organisation ran from the lineage (the descendants of a single ancestor) to a clan (the descendants of an ancestor in the distant past such that all members of the clan could exactly trace their relationship to each other). Organisation in descent groups laid the foundation of kinship organisation forming complex societies. For instance, along the East African coast, the natives in the Swahili towns identified themselves with patrilineal descent groups called *kabila* or *taifa* to differentiate themselves from the newcomers (Koponen, 1988, pp. 209-211). Other sophisticated communities that developed social organisation on the basis of descent groups included those of west Usambara, and the Chagga of Kilimanjaro to mention just a few (Feierman, 1974, Kimambo, 1969, Koponen, 1988, p. 211). In Unyamwezi, the lowest unit of social organisation was the family under one man. Each family claimed land (*itongo, matongo*) for cultivation. Several families formed clans (*kaya*) that were led by *bazengakaya*. The *bazengakaya* were in principle, founders of the clan or members of the founding family. And several clans formed villages (*gunguli*) that were under *watemi* (territorial chiefs) and assistants called *banangwa*. Families and clans were free to break off to form other *gungulis* in search of fertile land (Abrahams, 1967b, pp. 55-56).

Politically, as John Iliffe contends, many Tanzanian societies were stateless that nevertheless adapted to different environmental circumstances. This stems from the fact that relations between human beings and nature were stronger than those of human beings themselves. Areas with abundant high rainfall developed a well-defined political system. However, that was not the case for all communities. For instance, though the Iraqw lived in an environmentally favoured climate, practicing intensive agriculture, and often in conflict with neibhouring communities, they never developed political institutions above the clan. Kinship organisation was in most instances dominant in the less populated and tsetse free areas of south eastern Tanzania. The Makonde of south-eastern Tanzania, as Iliffe asserts, developed both matrilineal kinship and territorial kinship (*chilambo*) grouping as units of kinship organization. The former consisted of several kinship groups while the latter was led by a leader (*mkulungwa*) who descended from the pioneer colonisers[1] of the land (Iliffe, 1979, p. 21).

Age-Grades/Age-Set Organisation

Age-Set organisation refers to a social organisation where division of labour is based on age. Age-set organisation is commonly referred to as age set, age grades or age classes. Age-set is more elaborate among the Maasai, the Parakuyo, and Arusha. The Chagga, Sonjo, and the Gogo also adopted an age grades system based on that of the neigbouring Maa-speakers (Maasai) (Koponen, 1988, p. 288). Juhani Koponen provided a thorough description of the age-set system among the Maasai of northern Tanzania whose intervals between one age-set and the other does not exceed fifteen years with elaborate economic and social functions. Men and women passed through the age grades simultaneously but separately. The youth from zero to eight years were exempted from manual work. Those between 15 and 30 years were the *il mourauk* (warriors, and initiates of the society). They performed military function in defending the society against invasion and herded cattle which ranged long distances in search of pasture and water. Those between 30 and 45 years were known as *il piron*. These junior elders could marry and managed herds. And elders between 45 and 60 years were *il dasat*. These senior elders performed both religious (ritual) and political functions of the society. Nonetheless in nearly all societies certain tasks such as scaring birds and monkeys in the farms, milking and grazing cattle were boys' duties while girls, along with their mothers, performed domestic duties (ibid, p. 289).

Environmental Control and Political Authority

In all types of precolonial societies survival depended on environmental conditions. Drought could kill crops and cause animals to die threatening starvation for whole communities. Communities developed different ways of countering these risks including planting fields in different microenvironments, moving livestock long distances in search of water and pasture, and maintaining relationships with neigbouring communities that allowed for trade in times of need. They also developed ritual means of seeking to control the environment, and control of these rituals was

---

1 The idea of "colonisation" is John Iliffe's concept to mean the first conqueror of the land or immigrants into the land that was hitherto inhabited. For a detailed account of the idea of "colonisation" see Iliffe, *Africans: The History of a Continent* (Cambridge: Cambridge University Press, 1995) pp.62-126.

often the expression of political authority. A few members of the society emerged to form specialised classes of rainmakers and ritual leaders. Among the Zigua of Handeni in northeastern Tanzania, as James Giblin reiterates, this type of political authority formed the basis of precolonial environmental control. Although Handeni never developed centralised states, relations between patrons and clients led to the growth of stable farming communities that played a central role in the management of vegetation, wildlife, and controlled disease-bearing insects (Giblin, 1996, p. 128). Steven Feierman provides a similar argument about the politics of environmental control in his study among the Shambaa of northeastern Tanzania. He argues that the people of Shambaai believed that political conflict harmed the land while proper political authorities restored or healed the land. An action that damaged the land was described as "power against power" or "force against force". This was seen in the conflict between Kilindi chiefs or between important rain makers. The politics of "power against power" as harming the land were at the heart of Kilindi political structure to the extent that the notion of restoring the land was used to describe actions for increasing fertility. In due course, chiefs struggled to cover the land to establish themselves as dominant rainmakers for each local chief worked to dominate competitors within his territory (Feierman, 1992, pp. 78-85).

In a similar vein, western Tanzania developed certain kinds of political authorities that played a leading role in environmental control and conservation. Drawing examples from Buha in the present-day Kigoma region, Michelle Wagner and Joseph Mbwiliza show the role of *bateko* in environmental control. *Bateko* performed several functions in Buha: they were duty bound to allocate land for settlement and cultivation, they blessed farmers' seeds at the beginning of the planting season, provided advice and medicine to the villagers, and acted as a medium of land spirits (*ibisigo*) in rivers and in sacred groves (*amaholezo*) (Mbwiliza, 1979, p. 11). The relationship between nature spirits and human beings was reciprocal. While the *muteko* served the spirits by performing rituals and direct communities in matters of the environment, the spirits in turn ensured environmental security to all human beings. Consequently, *bateko* assumed both social and spiritual authorities over boundary conflicts and resources (Wagner, 1996, p. 182).

In many areas, rainmakers assumed authority in pre-colonial Tanzania. Because of their functions, rain makers rivaled kings and chiefs. However, rain making did not by itself convey political authority.

Rather, individuals sought political legitimacy through a number of factors including control over the use of force and trade. These leaders sometimes appropriated claims to control the environment that increased their control over society through political organisation (Koponen, 1988, p. 194).

State Organisation

In many cases high rainfall, permanent agriculture, and dense population seems closely related to the development of territorial states. States had a permanent administrative structure, often headed by a hereditary ruler, and a defined territory and groups of subjects or citizens. While states could be small, usually they covered more territory and had more subjects than chiefdoms that covered only a few villages or settlements. Despite the association of states with dense populations, as Iliffe cautions us, not all such areas developed elaborate state structures. He cites the Iraqw who never developed centralised political institutions despite the fact that they lived in an environmentally favoured climate. Iliffe explains the development of centralised political systems through what he calls the "dynamics of colonisation" that enabled pioneering men to break away from existing political control to form new political institutions. In certain cases then new states formed due to the interaction of peoples of varied social and cultural backgrounds who required strong authorities to facilitate their course of interaction and bury their differences (Iliffe, 1979, p. 21). Other states notably those of Ugweno in north Pare and Usambara, came into existence due to the evolution of small chiefdoms dominated by certain lineages who performed more ritualistic duties than administrative and gradually enlarged the scope of their authority while assuming more administrative tasks (Kimambo, 1969a, 1969 b, pp. 15-16). The formation of complex communities in centralised states in Tanzania was not homogenous. It was complex and involved an interplay of different forces.

Section II: Development of Complex Communities in Tanzania

Northeastern Tanzania

The northeastern highland areas of Usambara, Pare, Kilimanjaro, Meru and the Maasai steppe or plains bordering the eastern arm of the Rift valley form the northeastern region. We have already seen how parts of this region were inhabited by iron-using Bantu agriculturalists, Nilotic pastoralists and Cushitic mixed farmers since the beginning of the first millennium A.D. The region continued to attract immigrants long after 1000 A.D. In fact many people appear to have settled there between 10th and 18th centuries. Most of these later immigrants mainly settled on highlands of Usambara, Pare and Kilimanjaro where climatic and environmental conditions were more favourable. The development of banana cultivation increased populations in the best watered highland regions. State societies appeared after 1000 A.D. Stahl (1964), Isaria Kimambo (1969) and Steven Feierman (1974) have shown that the Chagga, Pare and Shambaa states arose between 15th and 18th centuries. They were not a product of military conquest or diffusion of political ideas from elsewhere as claimed earlier by colonial scholars. According to existing oral traditions in the region, iron working clans were the groups of people responsible for establishing several of these states. In Upare, for example, the Shana iron making clan is said to have established the Gweno state just before the 16th century. This state was later taken over by the Suya clan.

The beginning of the Shambaa kingdom was initiated by the Wakina Tui iron producers in the Vugha-Bumbuli area of southern Usambara. But the centralisation and expansion of the kingdom was carried on by Mbegha and his successors in the 18th and 19th centuries. The Chagga on the slopes of Mount Kilimanjaro formed states that controlled territory stretching from the highest habitable lands towards the peak of the mountain to large areas in the lowlands that surround the mountain. Each state was divided from its neighbours by natural boundaries such as valleys and streams, and together they divided the entire mountain like a pie cut into slices. Each had a ruling clan that claimed to have founded the state and held the allegiance of the other clans that lived in its territory.

In semi-arid areas bordering the northeastern highlands such as the Maasai plains, Handeni, Kondoa, the Tatoga area and Unyaturu, arid environmental conditions limited the number of people which these areas could support. As a result, people living in this area (the Maasai, Zigua, Datoga and Nyaturu) did not establish states as their neighbours in the highlands. Their social organisation was based on age-grades and age-sets that linked people from across large areas into common age grades that ritual leaders could mobilise for defence or warfare.

Northwestern Tanzania

From about 11th century, communities started experiencing changes in agricultural and mixed farming communities than in pastoral communities. These changes were social, economic and political in nature. This was due to three causes. First, increase in contact or coming together of people of different languages, cultures and origin. Movements of people were still taking place. Secondly, possession of iron technology by Bantu, Nilotic and other Tanzanian peoples during the first millennium A.D promoted agricultural and animal production activities. This led not only to production of more food and increased population but also evolution of more complex communities: greater social and economic differentiation. Centralised political leadership and institutions appeared. Thirdly, differentiated communities which the original order of equality and equal access to resources has been destroyed by division of people according to wealth and privileges. The differentiated communities with centralised social and political institutions are generally known as Kingdoms or States. A state is a political unit which has centralised government with powers to collect tribute or taxes, to draft people for public works or for war and to make laws and enforce them in its territory.

Northwestern Tanzania includes what now is the Kagera and Kigoma administrative regions. They form part of what is known today as the Great Lakes Region of East Africa (or previously the interlacustrine region). Because of its fertile soil and high rainfall this area was one of the earliest parts to be settled by iron-using Bantu speaking cultivators and pastoralists. The area has two climate zones: the lake shore zone which lies within 24 kilometers from Lake Victoria where rainfall is more abundant and reliable. And the grassland belt which extends from Kagera to highland areas of Kigoma. Agriculture and cattle keeping are possible in both zones. But the Lake Victoria zone was more suitable for banana growing as well as production of other crops than cattle keeping while the grassland zone is more suitable for cattle keeping than for the growing of banana and other crops.

Before the formation of Kingdoms, the area was thinly populated by small groups of cultivators organised on kinship basis. They lived side-by-side with similarly organised groups of cattle keepers. As population increased through migration from the neighbouring areas (such as southwestern Uganda, Rwanda and Burundi) and by natural increase, the kinship organisation started breaking up because it failed to cope with the problems caused by a growing mixed population. The kinship organisation was also undermined by social differentiation which had already started within clans by 1000 A.D. This differentiation led to specialised groups of iron workers, pot-makers, craftsmen, rain makers, medicine men and clan leaders. Some of the clans and the specialised groups within them became richer and more powerful than others. In Karagwe, for example the Basita clan is said to have became fairly big and influencial by 1000 A.D. Similarly, clans such as the Batundu, Bahunga, Bayano and Baheta became big and influencial socially, economically and politically after 1000 A.D in Kyamutwara, Ihangiro and Buzinza. Gradually, these clans placed several other clans under their control.

It was this rise of some clans to dominate which probably led to the formation of kingdoms of Karagwe, Kyamutwara, Ihangiro and Buzinza. Then by about 16th century, these kingdoms are said to have been taken over by a Hima pastoral group known as *Bahinda*. Oral tradition in this area claim that the Bahinda were descendants of the Bachwezi rulers of the empire of Bunyoro-Kitara in western Uganda, who invaded the area, conquered it and founded the kingdoms. They are said to have done so when the Bachwezi were replaced as rulers in Bunyoro by a Luo group from southern Sudan known as Babito. Colonial scholars claimed that the Bachwezi were Hamitic invaders and conquerors of western Uganda from Ethiopia. This means that the Bahinda and their Bachwezi forefathers were supposed to be Hamites from Ethiopia. But there is no convincing evidence for this claim. This is regarded as one of the manifestation of the Hamitic myth we mentioned earlier.

Further to the south, in Buha, leaders of the dominant founder clans known as *Bateko* "became wealthy and powerful as time went on" (Itandala, 1997, p. 49). They were the people responsible for allocating land to families in their village communities. In this way, eventually they became landlords demanding goods and labour services from individuals to whom land was allocated. So differentiation had taken place before kingdoms were formed. Then by about 16th century or probably later, a north Buha kingdom was established north and east of the Malagarasi River by a Tutsi dyanasty known as *Bahumbi*. This north Buha kingdom later became divided into several smaller kingdoms known as Buyogoma, Buyungu and Muhambwe. A south Buha kingdom was also established south of the Malagarasi River by another Tutsi ruling family known as *Bakimbiri*. This kingdom became divided into several small kingdoms later in the 19th century. By the nineteenth century, the whole region of Buha comprised of six centralised kingdoms in both pre-colonial and the colonial periods. These kingdoms were Nkalinzi,

Heru, Bushingo, Nkanda-Luguru, Buyungu and Muhambwe (Scherer, 1959: 844). It was believed that the Batusi belonged to the larger movement of Nilotic pastoralists who migrated into East Africa during the second half of the second millennium of the Christian era. However, oral and written accounts associate Batusi to the Nilotic speaking Luo. Despite being pastoral, these Batusi are said to have adopted clan organisation which was typical Bantu. It is mostly likely that pastoral Batusi adopted the clan organisation when they encountered Bantu speaking communities (Mbwiliza, 2001, p. 73)

It was also claimed by colonial anthropologists and historians that the Tutsi rulers of Rwanda, Burundi and the Ha kingdoms were Hamitic conquerors from the Ethiopia highlands. However, there is no evidence to support this claim from the oral traditions of the people. Both the Bahima and Batutsi are Bantu speaking with no indication that they might have been assimilated Cushitic minorities. The physical appearance between them and the agricultural people can probably be explained in terms of differences in diet and selective breeding over a long time. The Hima and Tutsi living on meat, milk, blood and marrying exclusively within their own socio-economic group. One can therefore reasonably conclude that the Hima or Tutsi pastoralists in the Great Lakes region were not conquerors but local people who rose to power from within.

Social and Political Features of the Kingdoms

The most notable feature was the patron-clientage relationship. This is sometimes referred to as patronage or clientage. This can be defined as the giving of favours and privileges by rulers to their subordinate officials in exchange for services and loyalty. The giver of favours is known as patron or master, while the receiver of favours from a patron is known as client. In the Lake Victoria zone of this area, where cattle were less numerous and less important, this relationship was based on land. The Bahinda rulers, though a minority, eventually managed to establish firm control over the subject clans. As it was in the kingdom of Buganda to the north, the *Omukama* (king) in each Haya kingdom first strove to reduce the power of the clan leader in the districts of his territory. He did so by replacing them as district heads with his own appointees known as *abakungu*. Originally only members of the royal family (*abalangira*) were appointed; later even commoners were appointed to these positions.

Because of their monopoly of political power, the *abakama* (kings) in the Haya kingdoms eventually seized control of most of the productive land and divided it up into large estates known as *nyarubanja*. The nyarubanja were then given by the abakama to their abakungu appointees, relatives and friends as rewards in return for their services and loyalty. Once land had been allocated, the people living in it automatically became tenants and clients of the new landlord. These landlords became known as *abatwazi* while the tenant cultivators became known as *abatwarwa*. In this relationship, the *omutwazi* or patron provided protection and the use of a plot of land for the production of food and other goods to the *omutwarwa* or client in return for the provision of goods such as bananas, beer, backcloth, coffee beans and labour services.

The introduction of the *nyarubanja* system of land tenure led to the establishment of new social relations which replaced the old communal clan relations. It established, not only the patron-client relationship between the cultivators and the *Bahima* ruling group, but also a hierarchical administrative system in which the cultivators were replaced in a political system made up of a series of regional administrators rising to the *omukama* at the top. In the grassland areas of Karagwe and Kigoma region, the basis of patron-client relationship was cattle. This relationship was known as *ubugabire* (clientship) in the Ha kingdoms. At first, it was based on land when the *Bateko* or clan leaders acquired clients by giving plot of land to individuals in exchange for goods and labour services. After the rise of the Batutsi pastoralists to power, cattle became the basis of patronage. Under this system, the *umwami* (king) in each Ha kingdom gave cattle to his senior regional administrative officials known as *abatware* in order to make them serve him well and loyally. The ascendancy of Batusi into power shows how a few pastoralists were able to exert dominion over the majority in Buha. This temps to argue in favour of the now discarded Hamitic myth. However, what accounts for the Tutsi dominance is the fact that they used cattle to subdue indigenous populations of Buha who had no cattle. It was through a special form of cattle contract that made Batusi pastoralists acquire political rights over the indigenous population making ubugabire central in the state formation of Buha (Mbwiliza, 2001, p. 76).

The *mwami* (king) could create a title and appoint one to hold the office. Very often, these were *Batware* who remained in the villages. They could not be transferred unless there was serious problem that would make them at logger heads with the mwami. The office of Batware was hereditary making it possible to appoint people who were influential and familiar with the problems of the specific area. Having been given political positions and cattle, the *abatware* were not only expected to serve the *umwami* well but also to show their faithfulness or loyalty to him by annually visiting him and giving him presents. They could also receive personal gifts from individuals who sought their favour (Mbwiliza, 2001, pp. 83-84). Similarly, his officials at different levels gave cattle to their juniors as rewards for their services and support. They also loaned cattle to poor people, both Batutsi and Bahutu in exchange for goods, services and respect. An ordinary client obtained protection and custody of cattle from his patron in exchange for goods, services and respect. An ordinary client obtained protection and the custody of cattle from his patron in exchange for goods such as beer, iron tools, pots, crafts and labour services such as building houses or compound fences, collecting firewood and cultivation of patron's fields. However, it was not only the ruling group had its clients in Karagwe and Ha kingdoms. Ordinary Bahima and Batutsi cattle owner got clients also by loaning and giving cattle to poor people in exchange for goods, services and recognition of their superiority. This implies that the patron-client system was used by *Bahima or Batutsi* cattle owners to exploit non-cattle owners especially the *Bairu or Bahutu* agriculturalists. It is clear that by 1800 the people of northwestern Tanzania had established many small kingdoms. These kingdoms especially in the cattle zone had a rigid class system which was like caste system. The economic system had also become complex by mixing pastoralism with agriculture. It was the clientage system which was the special mark of these communities.

Western and Central Tanzania (Ntemi Region)

Across much of what would become Tanzania, the period after 1000 saw the development of political structures that would still exist in some form as late as the nineteenth century. These political structures varied in size and population, often conforming to ecological constraints that put limits on communication and trade They generally built on village level communities and sought to integrate groups of settlements into larger communities. Their rulers relied on concepts of heredity to justify their positions, but they also answered to concepts of working for the communal good that meant that they could be replaced if they failed to "heal" or "cool" the land – in other words to ensure peace and security and good harvests. Ideas circulated widely, as did people, across much of what would become Tanzania so that people spoke of political authority its ritual and spiritual undergirdings in much the same way from Lake Victoria to the Usambaras and from Mt. Kilimanjaro to the Ruvuma River.

Ntemi – Cooling the land

The use of the concept of *Utemi* to justify political authority is one of the most striking examples of the commonality of dialogue and exchange of ideas in pre-colonial East Africa. Across almost the whole of western and central Tanzania the ruler of each political unit was known as *mtemi* or *mutemi*. Communities in Usukuma, Unyamwezi, Iramba, Ugogo and Ukimbu all use this term in some form to name their political and ritual leaders. The concept seems to have spread from the west to east. As it spread, of course, it changed as local communities adapted it their own situations. In some cases, the concept became the basis for rather sizable states with the mtemi or mutemi in effect claiming rights and powers of a king with authority over tens of thousands of people. In others, such as especially Ugogo, many *watemi* ruled each claiming jurisdiction over his own *yisi* (country) and people that might number in the low few thousands.

Claims to hold ritual authority in the broader area usually began as claims to lead the first (or first agricultural) settlers. The leaders of these communities became known as *batemi* or *watemi* (derived from kutema, meaning cutting down trees or cleaning the bush in a given area) because they were the people who directed the bush-clearing operations in their areas of settlements. Thus, batemi appeared as communities adopted sedentary way of life and increased agricultural activity. But these early batemi were no more than village or neighbourhood heads. However, their position as the descendants of first settlers gave them ritual authority to cool the land, especially by calling the rains. Their authority was limited to small communities mainly of their own lineages or clans. As the population of the region increased due to immigration or natural increase, contact between different clan communities also increased. This, in turn, created new problems which could not be solved by the existing organisation. There was increased struggle for resources and dominance between leaders of different neighbouring communities. In this struggle, clans such as Babinza, Bakwimba, Basega, Basiya, Bakamba and Basagali emerged victorious and became ruling groups in Usukuma and Unyamwezi.

Formation of Larger Units (Butemi)

The formation of larger political units in Ntemiship societies was due to the amalgamation of several villages, a process that began in the 16th century. In Unymwezi, for instance, the lowest unit of social organisation was the family under one man. Each family claimed land (*itongo, matongo*) for cultivation. Several families formed clans (*kaya*) that were led by *bazengakaya*. The *bazengakaya* were in principle, founders of the clan or members of the founding family. And several clans formed villages (*gunguli*) that were under *watemi*'s assistants called *banangwa*. Families and clans (*kayas*) were free to break off to form other *gungulis* in search of fertile land. The largest form of social and political organisation was the chiefdom that was made up of several villages (*gungulis*). Each chiefdom (*butemi, ichalo*) was under a paramount chief (*mtemi*) assisted by *banyikulu* or *bagohogoho* "men of chief's court" (royal bodyguards of the chief's regalia), village headmen (*banagwa*) and *ngabe* (ritual officers of the chiefdom) (Abrahams, 1967b, pp. 55-56). Different ntemi states were founded at different times. Their formation elevated the butemi (kingship) from its simple beginnings to more elaborate political institution. The ntemi became the title the ruler of a fairly big plural society or community instead of being a leader of a small lineage or clan community as before.

Ntemi states were, in general, fairly numerous and much smaller than those of northwestern Tanzania. In Usambara alone for example there were about 30 small states just before introduction of colonial rule (Itandala, 1997, p. 57). Unyamwezi had by the nineteenth and twentieth centuries many chiefdoms. In the present Tabora, Urambo, Sikonge and Uyui districts, there were eleven chiefdoms: Kiwere, Ngulu, Ugunda, Karunde, Uyui, Ibili, Busagali, Bukumbi, Ulyankulu, Uyowa, and Unyanyembe. An in the present Nzega, and Igunga districts, there were eight chiefdoms: Puge, Ndala, Unyambiyu, Nyawa, Karitu, Mwakarunde; Mwangoye, and Busongo. In all these chiefdoms, Unyanyembe was the largest and most populous chiefdom in Unyamwezi throughout the nineteenth century except in the 1860s and 1870s when it was challenged by *mtemi* Mirambo. (Abrahams, 1967a, p. 55-56, 1967b, pp. 28-36). There were also numerous chiefdoms in Ugogo, numbering by some counts over 80 in the late nineteenth century. There were three reasons for the emergence of Ntemi states. First, they were formed by different ruling clans in different places of the region and at different times. Second, availability of plenty of land in areas near the original states, encouraged people to move, making imperative the shifting cultivation of grain crops. Thirdly, limited surplus. It was difficult in the ntemi region to produce a big surplus food which could support large ruling classes because the region had less fertile soils and little irregular rainfall annually. For these reasons, what emerged in this region were many small states all with small ruling classes. These states were even more numerous and much smaller in Ugogo where climatic and environmental conditions were favourable.

Throughout the region, people mixed agriculture, animal husbandry, and the exploitation of natural resources through hunting, fishing and gathering. Besides cultivating grain crops and raising livestock, they fished, hunted, collected honey and engaged in commodity exchange or trading. By 1800, the Wasukuma and Wanyamwezi had developed caravan trading among themselves and between them and distant areas such as northwestern Tanzania, northern Zambia, the Shaba or Katanga region of Congo and the Mrima coast. This access to trade goods in return for ivory, captives and transport services in the form of porters increased the wealth differential in these communities. Just as the basis of authority for butemi lay in their perceived ability to ensure social peace and fertility so too they had to redistribute some of their new wealth throughout their communities. Especially during times when harvests failed due to drought, they had to ensure the survival of their community or risk losing their claim to cool the land (Itandala, 1997, pp. 58).

Northeastern Tanzania

The northeastern highland areas of Usambara, Pare, Kilimanjaro, Meru and the Maasai steppe or plains bordering the eastern arm of the Rift valley form the northeastern region of what would become Tanzania. We have already seen how parts of this region were inhabited by iron-using Bantu agriculturalists, Nilotic postoralists and Cushitic mixed farmers since the beginning of the first millennium A.D. The region continued to attract immigrants long after 1000 A.D. In fact many people appear to have settled there between 10th and 18th centuries. Most of these later immigrants mainly settled on highlands of Usambara, Pare and Kilimanjaro where climatic and environmental conditions were more favourable. The spread and development of banana farming in these highland regions after 1000 AD increased the attraction of the region, as banana plantations provided more secure stable supplies of food than relying on grains and cattle alone. Here again (like northwestern and ntemi region) state societies appeared after 1000 A.D, Stahl (1964), Isaria Kimambo (1969) and Steven Feierman (1974) have shown that the Chagga, Pare and Shambaa states arose between 15th and 18th centuries. They were not a product of military conquest According to existing oral traditions in the region, iron working clans were the groups of people responsible for establishing these states. In Upare, for example, the Shana iron making clan is said to have established the Gweno state just before the 16th century. The Suya clan later succeeded the Shana as the royal clan.

The beginning of the Shambaa kingdom was initiated by the Wakina Tui iron producers in the Vugha-Bumbuli area of southern Usambara. But the centralization and expansion of the kingdom was carried on by Mbegha and his successors in the 18th and 19th centuries. As in the areas ruled by batemi, the right to rule remained tied to the ability to "heal the land" with its explicit requirement of reciprocity between royals and subjects (Feierman, 1990). The Chagga on the slopes of Mount Kilimanjaro formed states. Here evolution of many small states was partly due to broken up environment of ridges which were separated from each other by streams and valleys. These states were established by different clans which came from different places and settled on the ridges. In semi-arid areas bordering the northeastern highlands such as the Maasai plains, Handeni, Kondoa, the Tatoga area and Unyaturu, both unfavourable environmental conditions favoured more emphasis on livestock and as a result, population densities remained lower. Their social organisation was based on age-grades and age-sets.

The Southern Highlands

The southern highlands region consists of Iringa, Mbeya and Rukwa today. With the exception of Fipa plateau, the population remained small and as did political organisation before the Ngoni invasion of southern Tanzania in the 19th century. One possible explanation is the shortage of metals in the region. It seems that only Ufipa and Ukinga had iron-ore. The Nyakyusa got their tools from Ukinga. This means that they and their neighbours continued to use wooden hoes for cultivation until the early 19th century. This factor must have reduced their ability to expand agriculture and to clear the thick natural vegetation for settlement. Another factor which may have hindered growth of big population is the cold weather found there during the dry season. Finally, in the lower elevations, the presence of tsetse fly limited the ability to keep livestock. Even though the region receives more than 1016 milimeters of reliable rainfall every year, its soils are not that fertile except a few places. "These factors, however, did not make the southern highlands a hardship region. On the contrary, its small population was well fed with bananas, millet, beans and cattle products" (Itandala, 1997, p. 60).

Because the population was small and land fairly plentiful between 1000 and 1800 in the southern highlands, land was not owned by individuals but by village communities. This abundance of land appears to have influenced the pattern of social and political organisation of the Nyakyusa and others in the region. There was little basis for economic specialisation and social differentiation. The most characteristic of their social organisation was the age-village in which people of the same age or generation lived together as equals. As their children began to marry, they lived in their own villages which were officially established every 30 years. These age-villages were headed by elected headmen known as *amafumu*. These amafumu had political and ritual powers. From about 16th century, however, a new form of political organisation was introduced in Unyakyusa by cattlemen from Ukinga. The control of cattle and iron tools enabled the invaders from Ukinga to get more political influence in the area. But the political system they established did not lead to emergence of centralised society into antagonistic classes. Instead, they established many petty political units. So did their Nyiha neighbour in Mbozi and the Bena in Njombe.

Itandala (1997, p. 61) also describes that the only people who established states in the southern highlands before the 19th century were the Fipa of Rukwa Region. It was about 1700 when the Milansi kingdom was established by the Milansi iron-smelters. This kingdom is said to have covered the whole of Ufipa. Then in about the middle of the 18th century, this kingdom was invaded and taken over by a group of people known as Twa from the north After the takeover of Ufipa by the Twa, the Milansi kingdom was divided into two kingdoms known as Nkasi in the north and Lyangalile in the south.

References

Abrahams, Raphael. *The Peoples of Greater Unyamwezi, Tanzania (Nyamwezi, Sukuma, Kimbu, Konongo)*, London: International African Institute, 1967a.

_____. *The Political Organisation of Unyamwezi*, Cambridge: Cambridge University Press, 1967b.

Feierman, Steven. *The Shambaa Kingdom*, Madison: University of Wisconsin Press, 1974.

_____. *Peasant Intellectuals: Anthropology and History* (Madison: The University of Wisconsin Press, 1990.

Iliffe, John. *A Modern History of Tanganyika*, Cambridge University Press, 1979.

Itandala, Buluda A. "History of Tanzania to 1890", Dar es Salaam: The Open University of Tanzania, 1997.

Kimambo, Isaria N. "The Interior before 1800" in Kimambo, Isaria N., and Anold Temu. eds., *A History of Tanzania*, Nairobi, EAPH, 1969.

_____. *A Political History of the Pare of Tanzania, C.1500-1900*, Nairobi: EAPH, 1969.

Koponen, Juhani. *People and Production in Late Precolonial Tanzania: History and Structures*, Helsinki: Scandinavian Institute of African Studies, 1988.

Mbwiliza, Joseph F. "The Kimbiri Dynasty of Heru Kingdom" in Paul Ruzoka, et.al. eds., *The Baha and Related Peoples of Kigoma Region: History, Tradition, Culture and Development*, Kigoma: Kigoma Development Association, 2001.

Ogot, "B.A. "The Great Lakes Region" in Niane, DT, ed., General History of Africa: *Africa from the Twelfth to sixteenth Century*, Vol. IV. UNESCO, 1984.

Sheriff Abdul, M. H. "Tanzania societies at the time of partition" in Kaniki M.H.Y, ed., *Tanzania under Colonial Rule*, London: Longman, 1980.

Stahl, K., *History of the Chagga People of Kilimajaro*, 1965.

Schmidt, Peter R. *Historical Archaeology: A Structural Approach in an African Culture*, Westport, CT: Greenwood Press, 1978.

Scherer, Johan H. "The Ha of Tanganyika", *Anthropos*, Bd. 54, H. 5/6, 1959.

Wagner, Michelle. Environment, Community, and History 'Nature in the Mind' in Nineteenth and Early Twentieth-Century Buha, Western Tanzania" in Gregory Maddox, James Giblin and Isaria Kimambo, eds., *Custodians of the Land: Ecology and Culture in the History of Tanzania*, London: James Currey, Athens: Ohio University Press, Dar es Salaam: Mkuki na Nyota Publishers, 1996.

Webster, J.B. Ogot, B.A and Chretien, J.P. "The Great Lakes Region, 1500-1800", in Ogot, Bethwel A., ed. *General History of Africa*, Vol IV, UNESCO, 1984.

Chapter Six

Commodity Production and Exchange to 1800

Introduction

A commodity is a product produced primarily for sale. It is differentiated from a product produced mainly for consumption or use. Communities that existed in Tanzania between 1000 and 1800 A.D produced commodities mainly for consumption in order to survive. Food crops as millet, sorghum, bananas, beans and sweet potatoes, for example, were produced for consumption. In modern Tanzania, cash crops like cotton, coffee and sisal are commodities because they are produced for sale. Of course, food crops can also function as commodities if a market for them exists, but in times when human porters served as the main means of transport away from the seacoast, lakes and rivers in most cases transport of staple food stuffs did not justify the costs. A porter can only walk so far before he or she eats all the food being carried. Two principle factors drove the increase in commodity production in the long run. Environmental endowments created natural reciprocity as regions with sources of salt, metal ores, and different animal populations found it possible to exchange their surpluses. The development of regional networks that linked different communities together then expanded the opportunities for exchange in even more products. This chapter will consider the development of production and exchange in the four great regions of modern mainland

Tanzanaia: the Great Lakes Region, Western and Central Tanzania, Northeastern Tanzania, and Southern Tanzania.

The Great Lakes Region

We have already seen that before 1000 AD specialisation of production existed between livestock producers (Bahima or Batutsi) and agricultural producers (Bairu and Bahutu). The interdependence between these two groups in society helped encourage local trade in the region. People did not think of it as exchanging commodities but expressed it socially as dependence in the exchange of surpluses of their animal products such as milk, meat and skins with agricultural products such as bananas, millet, beans and sweet-potatoes. Unequal distribution of resources could also lead to development of local trade and eventually to commodity production and regional exchange. Salt was one of these important resources. People could produce most of their food, but high quality salt could only be found in certain areas. Throughout the region, poor quality salt could be obtained from surface salt pans and saline grasses. But because they normally preferred high quality salt for seasoning their food, they could only get it through exchange with those who produced it or at particular sources.

In the Great Lakes region, such salt was only produced from the shores of Lakes Kitwe, Kasenyi and Albert in western Uganda and at Uvinza on the Malagarasi River in what would become Tanzania. Salt producers specialised in salt production and got everything else which they needed for existence in exchange for it. From these production centres salt was carried in baskets by porters to different parts of Uganda, Rwanda, Northeastern Congo, Burundi and Northwestern Tanzania where it was exchanged for other goods.

Iron ore was another unevenly distributed item in the Great Lakes region. Bunyoro had the richest deposits, but deposits also existed in Karagwe, Buhaya, Buzinza and Buha. For this reason, northwestern Tanzania was one of the main suppliers of iron tools to other parts of the region as well as to communities in western Tanzania. Like high quality salt, specialist smelters produced iron from iron ore. In addition to iron and salt bark-cloth came from Buganda and the Haya states, tobacco from the Nkore kingdom and coffee beans from the Haya kingdoms. Well before the 19th century regional exchange networks linked many states and communities throughout the Great Lakes region.

Western and Central Tanzania

Western and Central Tanzania has generally poor soils and irregular low rainfall. Communities survived in the region by producing grain, root crops and livestock and well as exploiting other natural resources. They generally adopted shifting cultivation in order to maintain marginal production of their main food crops (millet and sorghum). Second, they utilised forest, river and lake resources of their region by hunting wild animals, collecting honey, making wooden crafts and fishing in rivers and lakes. Thirdly, they developed an exchange system which enabled them to share their scarce resources among themselves and to obtain other products from neighbouring regions, especially during times when the rains failed and crops did not produce enough food for the entire year. The variable nature of the environments in this broad region meant that often some areas would have surpluses even in years when others faced food shortages. Exchange played a key role in people's survival strategies

One of the common characteristics of this region was its uneven distribution of resources. People in western Unyamwezi near Lake Victoria-Nyanza, for example became fishermen and pot makers. They exchanged dried fish and pots for grain and other things with their northern neighbours. Similarly people produced goods from forest resources such as bark-boxes, honey and wooden products in southern Unyamwezi and Ukimbu and exchanged them for grain and other products. Livestock, especially cattle from northern Unyamwezi and Usukuma were exported to southern Unyamwezi and Ukimbu in exchange for crops, iron goods and salt. Iron and high quality salt were the most attractive commodities in this region. Iron deposits were only found in neighbouring areas. The Walongo in the former kingdom of Buzinza in the north, Buyungu kingdom in Buha in the northwest, Ukimbu and Ufipa in the south. In order to obtain iron tools people in many parts of western and central Tanzania had to travel to different production centres. The trade in iron tools used to take place during the dry season when people were free from agricultural work and travelling was easier. Expeditions of 30 or more men used to travel to the iron centres every year. They used to take necessary goods for exchange. Only men engaged in both trade and production, because iron smelting was associated with taboos which forbade women to come near iron smelters.

As in the Great Lakes, salt also served as an important item of trade. Salt production sites included Uvinza on lower Malagarasi River, Ivuna near western end of Lake Rukwa, Kanyenye, Ugogo, on the shores of Lake Eyasi, Lake Balangida, Lake Kitangiri, and Bukune to mention just a few. Notwithstanding the wide spread salt works in Tanzania, Uvinza stood as the most important salt works with a reputation for high-quality salt. Its springs produced exceptionally good salt. Its high quality made Uvinza salt expand trading networks within and beyond Tanzania. Consequently, by 1850 Uvinza had been integrated into the long-distance trade of the East African interior (Sutton & Roberts, 1968, p.68). Like the trade in iron tools from its sources, the salt trade took place during the dry season for the same reasons. But unlike iron-smelting, which in most cases was undertaken by men belonging to special families and clans, salt production could be undertaken by anyone who wanted to specialise. Even the trade in salt from the centres of production could be undertaken by both men and women. This trade led to caravans carrying heavy loads of food and on the return salt from places like Usukuma to Lake Eyasi.

Trade caravans became the networks that linked communities. Traders carried salt and iron from production centres to villages and exchanged it for other goods. The Wanyamwezi and Wasukuma developed the practice of organising caravans from this participation in trading iron and salt. They became the most active people in long distance trade between the coast and the interior in the 19th century. What was originally local exchange in basic goods like iron goods, salt, foodstuffs, livestock and crafts, gradually expanded and connected western and central Tanzania with other regions in the interior of Tanzania and even beyond to Zambia and the Shaba or Katanga region of Congo and to the East African Coast.

Northeastern Tanzania

As an economic region, this includes the Muheza and Handeni plateau, the highlands of Usambara, Pare, Kilimanjaro, Meru and the Maasai steppe. The region is known by scholars as the Pangani Valley because it is drained by the Pangani River. Centralised states evolved in the highlands. Economically, all peoples of the region established networks of local trade and regional exchange before 1800. The people involved in this regional exchange included the pastoral Maasai, the agricultural Maasai (Arusha and Parakuyo), Meru, Chagga, Pare, Shambaa, Bondei and Zigua. Most of the exchange was carried out in ordinary customer goods such as foodstuffs, livestock, crafts, pots, animal skins, medicines and tobacco. Iron goods were produced by certain families or clans in a few places. Because of the specialised production necessary and scarcity or iron ore, iron tools became important items of trade. The Chagga, Maasai and northern Shambaa obtained their iron from Pare smelters. Similarly, the Shambaa were the greatest producers of tobacco in the region. They exchanged it for other goods with the Zigua, Maasai, Pare, Bondei and Digo neighbours. They also exchanged ghee, livestock and tobacco for sea-shells and imported goods with the Swahili at the coast.

Unlike iron goods which were exchanged throughout this region, the exchange of salt was less important in this region. There was no major source of high quality salt in this part of the country. Most of the salt which was exchanged in this region was produced by the Zigua on the plains of Mombo. The Zigua also brought iron goods and game to markets on the border with Usambara which they exchanged for bananas, tobacco and other things. One special note about the exchange network is the existence of regularly rotating marketing system which facilitated possibility of exchange in all neighbourhoods.

The Southern Interior

This is a varied region extending from the Makonde plateau in the east to the Fipa plateau in the west and from the highlands of Iringa and Mbeya in the north to the Ruvuma River and Lake Nyasa in the south. Among the peoples found in the region include the Makonde, Makua, Yao, Kinga, Kisi, Nyakyusa, Bena, Sangu, Hehe, Nyiha and Fipa. A large variety of goods were produced and exchanged in this region. Apart from livestock and food stuffs, the main items of exchange were: iron goods, salt, cotton cloth and pots. Itandala and Mapunda report that the Fipa were famous for their iron industry which was probably biggest in the region. Their iron goods were traded in many parts of the southern highlands, western Tanzania, northeastern Zambia and northwestern Malawi. They were well known for their cotton-cloth and their smoked fish (Itandala 1997, Mapunda 1995, 2010). Other important iron producers were the Nyiha, Kinga and the Yao. The Nyiha and Kinga (like the Fipa), supplied their iron goods to people in the highlands, while the Yao supplied to people living southeast of the highlands.

The Nyiha and their western neighbours, the Nyamwanga, were also known to be famous tobacco and cotton-cloth producers. They exchanged these products with all their neighbours for other products. Most of the salt in the region was mostly produced by the Wanda at Ivuna salt pans, near the southern end of Lake Rukwa. Some of this salt was exchanged as far as western Tanzania, northeastern Zambia and northwestern Malawi. A good amount of salt was also produced by the Bena at Saja. This salt was exchanged for grain, livestock and other goods form Uhehe, Usangu, Ukinga and Unyakyusa. Areas lying southeast of the highlands such as Undendeule, Umatengo, Umakua and Ungindo received some of their salt form the Swahili coast. Other specialised producers included Kisi pot makers of the northern shore of Lake Nyasa. The pots were widely exchanged on the highlands and northwestern Malawi. Another group, the Ndali of Ileje district, were skilled makers of bark-cloth. One can therefore conclude that several individual patterns of exchange developed in the Southern Region between 1000 and 1800, Iron and salt were the most important items exchanged in the region as in other regions. But they were followed importance by cotton cloth, tobacco and pots.

References

Alpers, Edward. "Trade, State and Society among the Yao in the Nineteenth Century" *Journal of African History*, Vol. X, No. 3, 1969.

Feierman, Steven. *The Shambaa Kingdom: A History*. Madison: University of Wisconsin Press, 1974

Itandala, A.B. "History of Tanzania to 1890", Dar es Salaam: The Open University of Tanzania, 1997.

Kimambo, Isaria N. "Environmental Control and Hunger in the Mountains and Plains of Nineteenth-Century Northeastern Tanzania" in Maddox, Giblin and Kimambo, eds., *Custodians of the Land*, 1996.

Mapunda, Betram B. "An Archaeological view of the History and variations of Iron Working in South-western Tanzania" University of Florida, PhD Dissertation, 1995.

Contemplating the Fipa Iron Working, Kampala: Fountain Publishers Ltd, 2010

Roberts, A. "Nyamwezi" in Gray, R and Birmingham, (1), (Eds). *Pre-colonial African Trade: Essays on Trade in Central and Eastern Africa before 1900*. London, OUP, 1970.

Sutton, John E.G. and Andrew D. Roberts, "Uvinza and its Salt Industry" *Azania*, Vol. 3, 1968.

Chapter Seven

The Development of Swahili Civilisation

Introduction

By early in the first millennium AD, iron-working agricultural communities had reached the East African coast. Along the coast, these communities exploited maritime resources such as fish and learned to sail along coast in small fishing vessels. The biggest difference in these communities and their neighbous further inland lay in the presence of foreign traders that began to call on the coast from Red Sea, the Persian Gulf and further afield. Gradually, starting in the north along the coast of what is now Somalia and then extending south into today's Kenya and Tanzania, settlement consolidated into larger towns in advantageous places, especially on islands just off the coast. There they collected products from the interior – ivory, rhinoceros horn, and other products – and traded them for imported goods such as ceramics, metal goods, and beads. The people of these settlements began to build larger and larger boats and learned to sail along the coast, extending their trade networks as far south as present day Mozambique and into the Indian Ocean as far as the Comoros Islands and Madagascar. These settlements came to share a language and culture called Swahili. The basis of this maritime civilisation were laid by the last half of the first millennium.

The amount of trade between towns in what is now Tanzania remained small until the twelfth century. The most important early trading cities lay in Kenya and Somalia. The Swahili language developed as a means of communication between the people of these coastal settlements.

Even before the growth of what may be called "Swahili civilisation" coastal society already had undergone differentiation. As trade with southern Arabia, Oman, Persia and India expanded in about 11th century, settlements and villages formed towns of varying sizes such as Mtang'ata, Utondwe, Kunduchi, Kisiju and Kilwa Kisiwani including (of course) Zanzibar and Pemba. Greater wealth came to be concentrated in the hands of few leading families.

What was the "Swahili Civilisation?"

The theory of development of the "Swahili civilisation" is built on actual existing structures which at present are merely witnessed by ruins which can be studied and some of them have been studied by archaeologists. The explanations which have been given also include legends which have been discredited. There are therefore two distinct explanations about the Swahili civilisation. Swahili Civilisation as the work of Persians and Arabs who either built towns, introduced Islam and spread their own culture which was superior to that of the Africans or paved the way for and fostered such development. This theory was first put forward by J. Strandes at the end of the 19th century. It was based on Hegel's philosophies of history according to which peoples of the world are divided into those who have historical influence and those who are passive, have no creative powers and are condemned to be led by activists (Matveiev, p. 1984, p. 475). A number of variants of this theory can be seen in a number of writings written by colonial scholars.

Nationalist and materialist scholars have given a more acceptable explanation which sees Africans being involved in the whole development. Even the question of Shirazi dynasties claimed by a number of chronicles of the Swahili towns has to be understood in terms of evolution of Swahili culture built on a tradition of expanding communities which were becoming more complex as they incorporated people from many directions. New ideology provided a way of solving problems created by complexity. The Shirazi element should be seen as one of the absorbed ethnic components of a community seeking to solve existing problems such as influential groups in Swahili society competing for power with old aristocracy.

The Role of Islam

The penetration of Islam may have begun as early as 8th century, especially in the northern side of the East African coast. al-Masudi in the 10th century reports of Islam in the islands and by the 13th century

Islam is said to have spread to the coast. There is no evidence of organised effort to spread Islam in this region as it happened in North Africa. So conversion was gradual through economic and social contacts. As trade and contact expanded from the last decades of 12th century and into the 14th and 15th centuries Islam expanded greatly. But even then, this was a gradual process: Muslim titles such as Sultan still co-existed with local ones, like *Mfalme* and were used side by side as mentioned by *Ibn Batuta* in 1331. In fact in Zanzibar, the title of *Mwinyi Mkuu* for the ruler of the Island remained unchanged (see Itandala, p. 65). The first to adopt Islam were perhaps the rich merchants. Their example was followed by the old aristocracy and only later on followed by sections of the common people. Adoption of Islam was bound up with assimilation of cultural attainments. This was accompanied by much borrowing from Arabic and Persian, particularly terms used in trade, religion and law. The existence of kadis in some of the coastal towns would indicate the legal borrowing, though not the whole *sharia*. The highest example of this selective adoption was that of Kiswahili written in Arabic script.

Swahili Architecture

The spread of Islam to the coastal settlements and towns led to the construction of mosques and other buildings in stone. The earliest stone architecture began in 12th century especially at Gedi, Zanzibar and Kilwa. The initial construction was simple consisting of laying coral blocks on red clay. The only building surviving to this day is the Great Mosque of Kilwa. From 13th century, the building method changed: large and rather crudely shaped cubic blocks of coral measuring 25-30 across were laid in mortar, the lime of which was obtained from calcination of the coral. There are a number of ruins of this type: Mosques in Kisimani Mafia and the northern part of the Great Mosque of Kilwa among others.

By the 14th century, the main trading centre of Kilwa underwent a period of growth and prosperity with increased trade and higher development of its architecture. The use of undressed stone of more or less uniform size placed in mortar became common. This method simplified and facilitated the process of building although the masonry was naturally of lower quality than the 13th century. More carefully worked stone was used only for finishing mihrabs and door and window casings. A remarkable monument of the time is the palace of fortress or palace trading centre of Husuni Kubwa in Kilwa. In the course of the 15th century Kilwa became a large town; many stone houses were built there which reflected growing wealth. Views of this architecture differ. The views of colonial scholars on outside origins are almost entirely rejected by archaeologists and historians. Freeman-Grenville points to similarity in the ground plan of certificate buildings in Kilwa and that of the ordinary mud-walled houses which suggest the stone buildings were of local African origin. Kirkman and Chittick point that the spur to development was provided by Arabs and Persians while at the same time concluding that materially and especially architecture, people of the coast evolved a civilisation which is best to refer to as early Swahili. John E. G. Sutton expresses similar view arguing that ceramic lamps were used in the Swahili towns for lighting dark rooms. The rich made use of many luxurious imported items such as pottery from Iran, Egypt and Syria.

At the height of the 14th and 15th centuries, wealth came to be concentrated in the hands of a few leading families known as *Waungwana* or *Mamwinyi*. These families became very influential and powerful in different towns because of their wealth, family traditions and control of religious affairs. The main basis of their wealth was land ownership and control over labour and trade. But it should be noted that the Swahili coast remained fragmented up to the first three decades of the 19th century. Every settlement and town-state produced its consumer goods and commodities such as sorghum, millet, rice, coconuts, fruits, vegetables, iron, salt, ivory, rhino-horns, mangrove poles and tortoise shells. Each coastal town operated as a separate economic unit and sold its own commodities to visiting foreign traders. They remained dependent on each other as part of a trade network linking them to the broader Indian Ocean world. Kilwa became by the 15th century by far the wealthiest of the states as the main terminus of the gold trade from Zimbabwe, but dependent in part on more northern cities for access to traders coming from the Indian Ocean.

In the early 16th century, a Portuguese fleet sacked Kilwa and began the process of trying to control all trade along the East African coast. The Portuguese garrisoned many of the Swahili cities, including Kilwa, Zanzibar, and Pemba. Trade and economic prosperity of all coastal towns declined drastically during the period of Portuguese occupation in the 16th and 17th centuries. The Swahili responded with constant resistance, attempts to find allies, especially in the expanding Turkish Empire, and moving settlements away from the Portuguese. By the middle of the 18th century, several other towns such as Tanga, Pangani, Sadani, Bagamoyo, Mbwamaji [Mbuamaji], Kilwa Kivinje, Lindi and Mikindani emerged in response to the gradual development of caravan trade between the coast and the interior. One of the reasons for the recovery of the Swahili coast since the second half of the 18th century was the establishment of sugar cane and coffee plantations by the French in the islands of Mauritius and Reunion. These plantations started importing slaves from the southern interior. Another factor was the discovery of the coast and its commerce by the people of the interior such as the Yao, Nyamwezi, Zigua, Shambaa and the Kamba. These people paved caravan routes connecting their areas with the coast. Omani commercial activity began at the end of the 18th century. As the power and wealth of Oman in the Persian Gulf increased, there was corresponding growth in commercial activity in Zanzibar and the Mrima coast. It was in response to this new and rising demand for the wealth of East Africa, especially ivory and slaves that many dormant towns in the Mrima coast were revived and new ones sprang up.

References

Itandala, Buluda A. "History of Tanzania to 1890". Dra es Salaam: The Open University of Tanzania, 1997.

Matveiev V.V. "The Development of the Swahili Civilisation", in D.T. Niane, ed., *General History of Africa: Africa from the Twelfth to the Sixteenth Century, Vol. IV* UNESCO, 1984.

Nurse Derek and Thomas Spear, *The Swahili: Reconstructing the History and Language of an African Society, 800-1500*. Philadelphia: University of Pennsylvania Press, 1985.

PART THREE

The Nineteenth Century

Chapter Eight

The Integration of the Tanzanian Interior in the Capitalist System

Introduction

While trade had reached deep into the interior of East Africa for centuries from the Swahili settlements on the coast, its intensity remained low until the late 18th century. The rapid expansion of demand for tropical goods and for labour to produce them increased this intensity throughout the region. The Omani Sultanate eventually based in Zanzibar became the agent for this increase. Large trade caravans left from the coast intent on bringing back ever more amounts of ivory and increasingly captives to work as slaves on plantations on the East African coast, on islands in the Indian Ocean, and even further away. It involved communities in the East African interior in trading relations not only with coastal communities but also with traders from Britain, France, Germany and the United States of America. Oman had offered military assistance to communities on the East African coast and offshore islands to drive the Portuguese out of East Africa at the end of the 17th century. The Omani ruler (*imam*) appointed Arab governors to represent him in each of the important town and island. But political conflicts at home prevented him to consolidate the political power in East Africa. When the Yarubi ruling family was overthrown by the Busaid dynasty in 1741, many of the Omani governors in East Africa refused to accept or acknowledge the new ruler and declared themselves independent. Zanzibar was one of few places that accepted the change of dynasty while Mombasa led those who resisted.

It was only after Seyyid Said came to power in 1806 that Oman started asserting her overlordship over East African coast more effectively. By then the only places on the coast in which Oman ruler had great influence were Kilwa Kisiwani and Mafia. Seyyid Said came to power in Oman with the help of British East India Company which was then based in Bombay. Unlike other earlier rulers of Oman who were known as imams because they were also regarded as religious leaders of their communities he (like his father before him) used the non-religious title of Sultan Seyyid Said because he had seized power instead of being elected by different sections of Omani community. Behind his political success there was a strong economic ambition which enabled him to use all opportunities before him to build the commercial empire which took almost the whole first half of the 19th century to be seen internationally.

Establishment of the Omani Zanzibar Sultanate, 1810-1840

The role of the British East India Company

Having helped him to consolidate his political control in Oman, the East India Company urged Seyyid Said to assert his country's claim of overlordship of the East African coast. It did so because it feared that the French, who were since the 1770s buying slaves form Kilwa and Zanzibar for their sugar-cane and coffee plantations on the islands of Mauritius and Reunion and for export to West Indies, might take over the region as a colony. This would endanger British commercial interests in Western Indian Ocean. By supporting Omani claim of sovereignty over the region, the British East India Company hoped that Seyyid Said would protect its interests not only in the Persian Gulf but also in East Africa. This means that the Arabs of Oman, under the leadership of Seyyid Said, were not acting entirely on their own when they claimed their right to rule the East African coast. They were partly acting as agents of European capitalism which was at that time looking for secure markets for its manufactured goods and secure sources of raw materials for its factories.

The Process of Occupation

With the help of the East India Company, Seyyid Said was able to establish his political control in all important towns and offshore islands on the East African coast between 1810 and 1840. The first towns to be taken over were those of Kenya coast mainly Lamu (1813) and Pate (1822). In 1823, his forces occupied Pemba and in 1825 took control of Wasin, Vumba, Tanga, Mtang'ata and Pangani. His forces brought under control all major towns in the northern Swahili coast except Mombasa. Seyyid Said's influence extended along the Mrima and Mwera coasts as well. He was already represented by loyal governors in Zanzibar, Kilwa Kisiwani, Mafia, Kilwa Kivinje and Lindi. Control towns in the Mrima (the coast from the Umbar River to Rufiji River) and Mwera (the coast from the Rufiji to Ruvuma River) coasts came easier because they had already established close commercial connections with Zanzibar, where his influence and support were greatest on the East African coast.

The main problem which Seyyid Said faced was the opposition of the Marzrui rulers in Mombasa. Not only were they determined to retain their independence and to exercise control all over Kenyan coast, but also they wanted to maintain their control over Pemba which was their main source of food. Seyyid Said made several attempts to capture Mombasa, but not until 1837 that his troops eventually succeeded in capturing it. After the capture of Mombasa Seyyid Said became the undisputed master of the East African coast and the offshore islands. In order to make his control more effective, he moved the headquarters of his government from Muscat in Oman to Zanzibar town in Zanzibar in 1840. He decided to locate his new capital in Zanzibar island for several reasons. First, island's great fertility which promised the development of a successful agricultural economy. Second, its good insular climate and its excellent harbour that attracted many ships and dhows. Third, its strategic position directly opposite the Mrima coast in mainland Tanzania for which it had already become the main outlet of its ivory and slaves. And fourth, good revenue which the Sultan had started getting from ivory and slave trade of Kilwa and other towns in the southern Swahili coast through Zanzibar before the transfer of the capital. From 1840 until his death in 1856, Seyyid Said was the ruler of an Omani-Zanzibar Sultanate which extended from Oman in the Persian Gulf to cape Delgado on the East African coast. This state became divided into two separate independent states after Seyyid Said's death in 1856. The Persian Gulf part became known as the Omani Sultanate and the East African part as the Zanzibar Sultanate. Politically, the Zanzibar Sultanate was confined to the coastal strip and the offshore islands. Its influence in the interior was only commercial.

Establishment of the Zanzibar Commercial Empire

From previous chapters, it should be clear that Tanzania did not operate as one economic unit until prior to the establishment of the Omani Zanzibar Sultanate. The coastal towns each had market oriented economy of its own and the interior had a number of separate regional subsistence-oriented economies. After the establishment of the Oman Zanzibar Sultanate, however, the whole of Tanzania, and East Africa in general started operating as one economic unit. At the coast, for example, instead of each port-town exporting and importing its own goods independently, most exports and imports to the area went and came through Zanzibar.

We have already mentioned factors which contributed to revival of economic prosperity on the Tanzanian coast in the late 18th century (previous chapter). The French slave trade in Kilwa and the involvement of the Yao led to rapid development and economic prosperity at Kilwa Kisiwani and Zanzibar in the late 18th century and the rise of Kilwa Kivinje and other towns at the beginning of the 19th century. The arrival of other European and American traders in the region increased economic prosperity in all important trading towns at the beginning of the 19th century. The Omani governor in Zanzibar however monopolised the trade with Europeans and Americans and prohibited them from dealing directly with the coast on the mainland. In fact, it was because of their desire to make Zanzibar their main trading base on the Swahili coast that the Omanis had captured Kilwa Kisiwani and placed a governor there in 1785. Having gained control of Kilwa and directed its trade to Zanzibar, they were able to do the same with the trade of other towns (previously many of the other towns were connected with Mombasa). This means that Mombasa was commercially overtaken by Zanzibar by the beginning of the 19th century.

The formation of Omani-Zanzibari Sultanate by Seyyid Said created favourable conditions to the expansion of commerce and economic prosperity. The signing of commercial treaties or agreements with representatives of American, British, French and German governments in 1830s and 1840s intended to get secure markets for the main products of the region such as ivory and cloves. Seyyid Said encouraged Omani Arabs to move to Zanzibar and establish clove and coconut plantations even before transferring his capital there. Since these plantations needed a large labour force, which the local Muslim population in Zanzibar and Pemba refused to provide, it became necessary to import slave labour from non-Muslim peoples of the East African mainland. As a result, many Arab and Swahili traders from Zanzibar and the Mrima coast started penetrating the Tanzanian interior and other parts of East Africa in search of slaves for the clove plantations. They were also looking for ivory and other products.

To provide access to capital needed to finance the expansion of trade and plantations, Seyyid Said invited Indian merchants to come to Zanzibar in order to facilitate development of trade. These Indian merchants played a double role in the Zanzibar Sultanate. Some worked as customs officials of the Sultan in different ports; while the richest among them became money lenders. These money lenders gave loans in the form of trade goods to Arab and Swahili merchants who wanted to lead caravans in the interior of mainland Tanzania and other parts of East Africa. This lending of trade goods enabled many more Arab and Swahili traders in Zanzibar and the Mrima coast towns to lead caravans and penetrate the interior in search of ivory and slaves than ever before. Seyyid Said removed obstacles to trade at all the coastal ports by introducing a uniform five percent duty. Before each port had set its own rate. He also introduced Indian currency known as *pice* in order to facilitate the flow of trade from its base in Zanzibar. This new money joined the American dollar and Maria Theresa dollar from Austria which were already in circulation in Zanzibar. As a result of these measures, there was a spectacular expansion in Arab and Swahili economic activity in the Tanzanian interior and other parts of the East African interior between 1830 and 1880s. More and bigger caravans were organised; they followed or used trade routes which had been paved earlier by traders from the interior such as the Nyamwezi and the Yao. The main ones were those running form Bagamoyo and Sadani to Tabora and Ujiji and other parts of the western and northwestern interior. From Kilwa Kivinje, Lindi and Mikindani to Lake Nyasa and other parts of the southern interior. From Tanga and Pangani to Usambara, Pare, Kilimanjaro and Maasailand in northeastern interior. Tanzania and the rest of East Africa was crisscrossed by many trade routes and had fully been integrated in the capitalist trading system operating from its regional base in Zanzibar during the 19th century.

Consequences of Arab-Swahili Commercial Activity

The main effect can be summarised as subordination of the different subsistence economies of the interior to the capitalist system or international trade. This affected Tanzanian societies economically, socially and politically. Economically, many people from different parts of the interior were either employed as porters to carry ivory to the coast or were taken to Zanzibar and Pemba as slaves to produce for the capitalist world. Instead of producing for their subsistence in their home areas, they were made to serve for the capitalist market. Manpower was taken from the traditional economies in the interior. Some areas bordering the coast became suppliers of food to Zanzibar and Pemba in order to feed the labour force in plantations and the ruling and merchants classes in towns. For examples Usambara became the leading exporter of sorghum; Uzigua exporter of millet and rice; many other coastal communities became producers of food for export to Zanzibar and the coastal ports, while areas bordering trading centres and caravan routes in the interior had to supply food to resident coastal traders and to caravans. People around Tabora, for example, found it necessary to produce more food than before in order to feed coastal traders and their large number of porters and slaves residing there. Similarly people living near stopping stations in all routes had to produce more food to meet requirements of these caravans. In order to produce the extra food for export to Zanzibar and for feeding resident coastal traders and passing caravans in the interior, many communities in the interior resorted to using slaves for this purpose. Some had to supply livestock for meat.

There was also a replacement of the system of trade in essential or basic goods (such as iron tools, salt, pots, handicraft, foodstuff and livestock) with trade in luxury goods (such as cotton cloth, beads, looking glasses, copper wire, alcoholic drinks and guns). The coastal traders were not looking for traditional products of the interior. They were mainly looking for ivory and slaves; items which had no commercial value before the penetration. This led to the establishment of trade centres or towns in the interior. Mamboya, Puge, Msene, Ujiji all formed in 1840. Tabora was established in about 1852. Socially, the integration of the Tanzanian interior led to the conversion of some people to Islam particularly among the Yao in the southern interior, the Digo and Segeju in the nearby hinterland of the northern Mrima coast. Conversion also occurred more modestly among the Zigua, Bondei and Makonde. Arab and Swahili traders also married women from the interior and took concubines among their slaves. As a result of this intermarriage and conversion of some people to Islam, a small Swahili speaking community came into being in some parts of the interior. Swahili became the language of trade along the trade routes and beyond reaching throughout what would become Tanzania and even across Lake Tanganyika into the future Congo.

Slave trading, slave raiding, and slavery also intensified in the interior. Some chiefs began to conduct their own wars and raids to gain captives to trade with the caravans. The caravans themselves, always heavily armed, both raided and intervened in local conflicts to gain captives. In some cases new powerful warlords arose who created new political structures based on their access to wealth and arms from this trade. Considerable changes also occurred along the coast. As Africans from different parts of the interior were taken to the coastal towns and the islands of Zanzibar and Pemba as slaves, the population of these towns and islands became bigger and more ethnically mixed than before. Moreover, use of African women as concubines by Arabs produced a relatively large Swahili speaking Afro-Arab group. This mixing had started centuries earlier, but increased very much in this period. Even the Omani ruling family was greatly involved in this racial mixing.

Politically, there were several changes in the basis for political power or authority in all societies which had formed states before 1800. Originally descent and religion served as the dominant justification for political power; descendants of families which had been instrumental in the formation of these states or had conquered them claimed the right to rule. In other cases rulers were descendants of ritual experts or rain makers. After the development of the 19th century trade, economic and military power became the main path to power. For example in Yao country, a number of merchant rulers or princes set up new states. Political change went hand in hand with intensification of competition for succession to kingship between different ruling families in each state. In Western Tanzania, the best example is the acquisition of foreign goods like guns by the Batemi and other members of the ruling families intensified struggle. Powerful rulers in this area included Fundikira, Makasiwa, Nyungu ya Mawe and Mirambo.

While other states emerged, a number of existing states collapsed or lost power in the face of the increase in violence. The best examples in Western Tanzania include the Ha and Zinza kingdoms in the Lakes region. In the Pangani valley the Shambaa kingdom and the various Pare and Kilimajaro states were broken up into smaller entities. The only people who seem to have been positively affected in the Pangani valley were the Zigua. Some Zigua individuals accumulated wealth and guns which enabled them to establish states in Uzigua and neighbouring areas. A good example is Bwana Heri who in the 1880s resisted Germans with Abushiri. Another example is Kisabengo who established a state in Uluguru.

References

Alpers, Edward A. *The East African Slave Trade,* Nairobi: EAPH, 1967.

──────. "The Coast and the Development of Caravan Trade" in Kimambo and Temu, eds., *A History of Tanzania,* Nairobi: East African Publishing House, 1969.

Bennett, N.R. "The Arab Impact" in B.A. Ogot, ed., *Zamani: A Survey of East African History,* Nairobi: East African Publishing House, 1973.

Gray, Milner John Sir. *History of Zanzibar from Middle Ages to 1856.* London: Oxford University Press, 1962.

Itandala, Buluda A. "History of Tanzania to 1890", Dar es Salaam: The Open University Press, 1997.

Roberts, Andrew. "Political Change in the Nineteenth Century" in Kimambo, Isaria and Arnold Temu, eds., *A History of Tanzania,* Nairobi: EAPH, 1969.

Salim, A.J. "The East African Coast and Hinterland, 1800-1845", *General History of Africa: Africa in the nineteenth Century, until the 1880s* Vol. VI, ed., J. F. Ade Ajayi, UNESCO.

Sheriff, Abdul. *Slaves, Spices and Ivory in Zanzibar.* Dar es Salaam: Mkuki na Nyota, 1987.

Chapter Nine

The Ngoni Invasion and Its Impact

The Ngoni and their Society

Disruptive influence in what would become Tanzania came not only from the East African coast in the 19th century but also from southern Africa. In the southern region of the territory, a people known as the Ngoni came from South Africa where they had been part of the Nguni speaking peoples of northern Zululand. Having fled from their homeland in about 1820 to escape the rising power of Shaka as he was creating the Zulu kingdom, Ngoni warriors moved northwards under their leader Zwangendaba. They brought with them Zulu style military tactics based on massed infantry using stabbing spears and shields that usually overwhelmed their opponents. For about 15 years they wandered in southern Mozambique before crossing the Zambezi in 1835 on their march northwards until they reached the Fipa plateau in western Tanzania early in the 1840s. By this time what had started as a group of warriors had become an armed nation of over a hundred thousand people on the march as they absorbed conquered communities. The most intriguing question that we need to address is as to how this spectacular growth of Ngoni people accomplished? In order to answer this question we have to go back to the Zulu homeland. Shaka had built up a highly centralised military state organised according to two overlapping principles: one based on lineage and the other on military regiments. According to the first principle the king was at the pyramid of authority and below him there were segments of lineages consisting of the king's wives and their children and dependents. The segments tended to split and multiply at each generation as they grew larger. The youth on the other hand, were organised into age-regiments cutting across territorial and lineage lines and directly controlled by the king. This meant that a foreigner could easily be absorbed as he gradually entered into the dynamic structure of the society through both the lineage and the age-regiment. Shaka also introduced changes in military techniques, the most important being the use of the short stabbing spear which made the age-regiments very efficient fighting unit.

Having inherited this dynamic system, the Ngoni built up a well unified people out of the people they encountered on their movement northwards. Their superior military organisation enabled them to survive by raiding other people as they moved. They began their journey when Shaka defeated the Ndwandwe army from which three leaders (Soshane, Zwangendaba and Nqaba) and their followers moved northwards. Soshane succeeded in establishing the Gaza kingdom in southern Mozambique. Soshane's success prevented other Ngoni groups from settling in Mozambique. Zwangendaba and his followers after trekking to Zimbabwe then followed the northern route to the Fipa plateau. Nqaba's group known as Msene Ngoni roamed to Zimababwe and Zambia and was finally dispersed by the Kololo. Another group, Maseko Ngoni under Ngwane crossed the Zambezi in 1839, passed through southern Malawi and moved northwards crossing the Ruvuma River and settled in southern Tanzania. There they established a state under Ngwane's son, Mputa or Mputo, in what is now Songea District in the 1840s. They were later expelled from there by the Gwnagwara Ngoni (Zwangendaba's group).

Zwangendaba and his followers on their movements through Zambia and Malawi, avoided having major conflicts with powerful states such as the Bemba and Nkamanga kingdoms. Instead, they frequently raided defenseless groups such as Chewa and Tumbuka clans. Many captives were adopted into the Ngoni community. They continued with northwards march until they reached Mapupo in Ufipa in the early 1840s. They were attracted by the fine long-horned red cattle found there which were similar to those they used to have in the northern Natal. By then their size had been greatly increased by fresh recruits from many communities which they had fought against or raided for cattle during their long journey.

Ngoni Expansion in Tanzania and Neighbouring Areas

The Ngoni remained in the Fipa plateau until Zwangedaba died in 1845. After his death, the Ngoni community felt the great loss of their leader and this led to the problem of succession. His two sons Mpezeni and Mombera or Mbwela were still too young to succeed him. His junior brother, Ntabeni took over and declared his preference for Mpezeni as Zwangendaba's successor. But Ntabeni too died soon afterwards. Zwangendaba's cousin, Mgayi became acting leader and declared support for Mombera. As a result of these differences on succession, the Ngoni community split into five groups. Two of these groups remained in Tanzania and the rest settled in Malawi and Zambia. These groups were the Tuta, Gwangwara, Mpezeni, Mombera and Ciwere. A short discussion of each group follows here.

The Tuta Ngoni

After Ntabeni's death, his followers broke away from the main Ngoni community because they feared persecution for their leaders' support of Mpezeni as successor of Zwangendaba. They escaped northwards and became known as Tuta. Led by his two sons, Mtambalika and Mtambara, they established their camp at the northern end of the Rukwa valley. From this base they raided eastern Holoholo on the eastern shores of Lake Tanganyika. The Holoholo eventually adopted the war tactics of the Ngoni and fought on equal terms with the Tuta, whom they defeated. After this defeat by the Holoholo the Tuta turned to the Nyamwezi and neighbours whom they started harassing in 1850s. In so doing, they sometimes upset the trade route between Tabora and Ujiji. They captured many Nyamwezi and other people whom they incorporated in their group. Finally the Tuta settled in Runzewe in western part of Kahama District. From there they carried out frequent raids as far as the southern shores of Lake Victoria in the 1870s and 1880s until they were defeated by the Germans in 1890. After that, they were gradually assimilated by the Sumbwa and Nyamwezi.

The Gwangwara Ngoni

The Gwangwara were led from Ufipa by Zulu-Gama and travelled southwards to a place called Mlangala in what is now Songea District. Zulu-Gama died in about 1858. Mbonani became the new leader of the group. At Mlangala, the Gwangwara came into contact with the Maseko Ngoni who had established a kingdom there in the 1840s under the leadership of Mputa or Maputo Maseko. The Maseko were much stronger than the Gwangwara. Maputo was accepted as ruler of both groups for some time. But when he tried to strengthen his political position by killing Mbonani and other Gwangwara leaders the Gwangwara rose up in rebellion and killed him. After the death of both leaders, the Gwangwara staged a surprise attack and drove away the Maseko Ngoni from Songea. The defeated Maseko fled southwards across the Ruvuma in 1862 and eventually settled in southern Malawi.

When the Maseko Ngoni fled in 1862, they left behind many of their newly recruited members. Most of these people had been recruited from the Ndendeuli ethnic group. Because they had become part of the Maseko Ngoni community, the Gwangwara continued attacking them after departure of the main group. To escape these attacks, most of them fled to the Kilombero valley where they settled and became known as Mbunga. After the departure of the Mbunga from Songea, the kingdom which had been established there by the Maseko Ngoni came to an end. Having destroyed the Maseko Ngoni kingdom, the Gwangwara became the dominant community in Songea. But old disagreements between Mbonani's and Zulu-Gama's followers re-appeared and led to separation between them. The Mbonani group established its own kingdom known as Mshope in northern Songea under the leadership of Chipeta. The Zulu Gama group established a kingdom of their own known as Njelu further south with Hawagi as the first ruler.

The Mpezeni, Mombera and Ciwere Ngoni

The groups led by Mpezeni and Mombera left Ufipa soon after their separation from the Gwangwara. Mpezeni and his followers travelled southwards into the Bemba country in northern Zambia. After failing to conquer the Bemba, they continued southwards and re-entered Nsenga country in southern Zambia where they finally settled and founded a kingdom. Mombera and his followers marched southwards and entered Tumbuka country in northern Malawi. They established a kingdom of their own after conquering the Nkamanga kingdom of Tumbuka. Ciwere Ndhlovu and his warriors decided to settle in the highlands of modern Dowa District because they found good grazing land there. As a result, Ciwere and his followers established a Ngoni kingdom in this part of Malawi.

Ngoni Impact on Tanzanian Societies

The Ngoni invasion led to the creation of the Ngoni ethnic group consisting of people from several indigenous groups and a small Nguni speaking core group. The invasion led to introduction of Ngoni military techniques which were adopted by various Tanzanian communities in self defence against the Ngoni themselves or to enable political reorganisation and state building in the case of Sangu, Mirambo and Nyungu ya Mawe. It also weakened and disrupted many communities in western and southern Tanzania. As a result, it made it easier for coastal slave traders to obtain captives during the second half of the 19th century.

In Western Tanzania, the Tuta broke away and carried their raids up to Lake Victoria. The Tuta harassment touched the Nyamwezi, Kimbu, Konongo, Bende, Tongwa, Vinza, Ha and Sumbwa. We have seen how they disrupted caravan routes. Their raids disrupted normal life in western Tanzania. In this way they made it easier for Mirambo and Nyungu ya Mawe to build their empires and for coastal slave traders to get their captives. Moreover, because they lived by plunder, the Tuta provided an example or model to be imitated by rulers and robbers alike. Mirambo was one of the people who learnt Ngoni fighting method when he was captured by the Tuta. After escaping from them, he established a Ngoni-type of army made up of displaced young people and war captives from different areas of western Tanzania who came to be known as Balugaluga or Ruga-ruga.

In Southern Tanzania, the Gwangwara clashed with the Maseko Ngoni and the Mbuga. Then the Gwangwara became the most dominant ethnic group in southern Tanzania. From their two kingdoms, Mshope and Njelu, they terrorised a wide area lying between Lake Nyasa and Indian Ocean in southern and southeastern Tanzania between 1860s and 1880s. They are said to have met very little or no resistance from many of the small segmentary communities of the region. Many areas of this region were almost depopulated by their warriors as they seized captives both for their armies and for sale to the Arab and Swahili traders of Kilwa. At the same time brigands called Mafiti or Maviti, who learnt Ngoni military methods and acquired guns, started raiding many parts of southern Tanzania with the intention of capturing people for sale to coastal traders as slaves.

Ngoni-inspired states developed in Usangu and Uhehe too. The Sangu lived in the area bordering Ufipa until they retreated eastwards into western Uhehe. But when the Ngoni left Ufipa, they returned to their former areas and began to organise themselves on Ngoni military lines. Moreover, one of their leaders Mwahavangu, united all Sangu political units into one kingdom. His grandson, Merere succeeded him in 1860 and dominated most of southern highlands for some time from his capital in Utengule. After the 1870s, the Sangu were overshadowed by the Hehe who also were origainally organised on segmentary clan lines. During the 1860s, their different political units united to form one kingdom under one of their leaders known as Munyigumba. Many people accepted Munyigumba's authority because he was able to protect them from the harassment of the Ngoni attacks. Just as the Sangu had adopted Ngoni military techniques, so did the Hehe learnt these techniques form the Sangu. By 1877, the Hehe had taken over some of the Sangu territory. As the Hehe expanded, they came into conflict with the Gwangwara Ngoni of Songea. They fought two major wars (1878 and 1881), in which none of them won. As a result an agreement was reached by king Chabiruma of Mshope and Mkwawa, the new Hehe leaders not to fight again. Together with the Gwangwara Ngoni, the Hehe remained the most powerful states in southern Tanzania until imposition of German rule.

References

Gulliver, P.H. "A History of Songea Ngoni", *Tanganyika Notes and Records*, No.41, December, 1955.

Itandala, Buluda A. "History of Tanzania to 1890", Dar es Salaam: The Open University of Tanzania, 1997.

Kimambo, I.N. "The East African Coast and Hinterland, 1845-1880", *General History of Africa*, Vol VI, UNESCO, 1989.

Sheriff, Abdul M. H. "Tanzanian Societies at the Time of Partition" in Kaniki, ed., *Tanzania under Colonial Rule*, London: Longman, 1980.

Omer-Cooper, John D. *The Zulu Aftermath: A Nineteenth-Century Revolution in Bantu Africa*. Evanston: Northwestern University Press, 1966.

Chapter Ten

The Expansion of European Influence to 1890

Introduction

During the 19th century Europeans expanded their presence in East Africa, just as they did throughout much of the world. While people from Europe had visited East Africa as far back as classical times, and the Portuguese had dominated parts of the coast in the 16th and 17th centuries, but their power faded, and East African and Omani forces drove them from their position north of Mozambique. The decline of Portuguese power coincided with the rise of sea-borne trade by other European nations. The Dutch, English, and French all became to challenge Portuguese monopoly on African trade in the 16th century and by the beginning of the 18th had begun to set up their trading bases across the Indian Ocean. While vessels from many nations began to call on the East African ports, Europeans focused their efforts on controlling bases in India and Southeast Asia. They made little effort to establish permanent trading posts, control of the coast, or directly trade with the peoples of the mainland.

European Activity in the Nineteenth Century

Increased European activity in Tanzania started when the French established a base on the islands of Mauritius and Reunion. They considered attempting to annex the whole East African coast in the 1770s (Itandala, 1997, p. 118), but abandoned these plans and concentrated on buying slaves at Kilwa and Zanzibar in the 1770s for export to the West Indies and for their sugar cane and coffee plantations in Mauritius and Reunion. The British and American traders joined the French on the coast and established branches of their commercial companies in Zanzibar beginning in the 1830s.

Direct European involvement in Tanzania and other East African countries was a result of social, economic and political changes which occurred in Europe starting in the 18th century. The Industrial Revolution began in Britain in the 18th century and spread to other European countries and the United States of America in the 19th century. This revolution led to improvement in the tools and methods of production which made slave labour less profitable on plantations and therefore produced new attitudes towards the slave trade. In fact, the success of industrialisation persuaded European countries to abolish the Atlantic slave trade at the beginning of the 19th century. These changes awakened the interests of traders, missionaries and travelers or explorers to carry out their activities outside Europe. The rapid increase in technology gave European and American traders both the ability to provide greater amounts of the goods Africans (and others throughout the world) wanted and more power weapons and faster ships. By the 19th century this combination created the ability for Europeans to expand their power across the globe.

European Traders

In the 19th century Britain began to dominate trade in the Indian Ocean. Shortly after becoming directly involved in the region at the British navy began to explore its coast and offshore islands. Between 1809 and 1824, for example, the navy completed four surveys of the region: one by Lt. Tomkinson in 1809, two by Captain Philip Beaver and Captain Thomas Smee in 1811, and the fourth by Captain W. F. Owen in 1824-1826. British interest drew in part on their growing control of India. The East India Company, the chartered company that ruled India for the British Crown until the mid-19th century, dominated British policy towards East Africa. Traders from India represented British interests in much of the region. Some of these Indian traders had settled there permanently and established branches of trading houses based in India. They bought ivory and other goods in Zanzibar and the mainland coast which they then sold to the East Indian Company in India, as well as providing financing for the development of the caravan trade to the interior.

Early in the 1830s, however, a British firm known as Newman Hunt and Christopher started trading directly with Zanzibar and established a depot there. Competition between British traders and those of other nations increased. The Americans, for example, who had started trading with Zanzibar in the 1820s, overshadowed the British and French commercially by the 1830s. In order to make it easier for the traders to do business in the region, the American government signed a commercial treaty with the Sultan of Oman in 1833 and established a consulate or trade mission in Zanzibar in 1837. The Sultan of Oman on his part signed this treaty with the Americans in order to get a guaranteed market for East African products.

Fearing the development of an even greater American share in the trade of the region as a result of the 1833 treaty, the British Government signed a treaty of its own with sultan Seyyid Said in 1839. It also appointed a commercial representative or consul to his capital in Zanzibar in 1841. Similarly, the French signed a treaty with him in 1844 and appointed a consul to Zanzibar in the same year. Thus, these nations stimulated each other into greater commercial relations with Zanzibar in the first half of the 19th century. The competition between them became even greater when more European companies or firms such as the British firm Henderson and Co. and the German firms W. M. O'Swald and Co and Messers A.J. Herz and Sons established branches in Zanzibar in the 1840s. In doing so they provided a wider market for East African products.

As trade grew between East Africa and western capitalist countries in the second half of the 19th century, many more European and American firms as well as individual traders took part in it. One outstanding example of this group of traders was the British ship owner, William Mackinnon. He began to run his shipping line known as the British India Steam Navigation Company between Britain and Zanzibar in 1872. All these European and American commercial companies bought their goods from Africans and Arabs in Zanzibar partly because they preferred to do so there and partly because the Sultan and his Arab and Swahili subjects did not want them to go to the source of goods on the mainland. The Sultan's government tried to ensure foreign traders only traded at Zanzibar both to protect the sources of trade and to ensure that all traders paid the required duties. A few individual European traders attempted to penetrate the mainland interior only after European travelers and missionaries had done so in the 1860s and 1870s. Many of them however, failed to establish themselves successfully. A French trader named Legere for example was driven away from Unyanyembe, and one unidentified German trader was killed in 1886. Only one European trader is known to have established himself successfully on the mainland. Charles Stokes, allied with the Nyamwezi of Busongo and kept away from trading centres dominated by Arab-Swahili traders.

As trade in ordinary commodities or "legitimate trade" as it was often referred to, expanded in Zanzibar and the rest of East Africa in the 19th century, so did the slave trade or "illegitimate trade". Before any treaties restricting it were signed between the British government and the Sultan of Zanzibar in the early 19th century about 10,000 to 15,000 slaves were exported a year from the East African mainland. Many were traded throughout the Indian Ocean winding up in Arabia, India, and all the islands in between. Others were put to work on the plantations that developed along the coast and on the islands of Unguja and Pemba. The British Government signed a series of treaties with the Sultan Seyyid Said and his successors between 1822 and 1876. By the 1860s, when the British ships were patrolling the sea along the East African coast to prevent slaves from being exported from the region had risen to about 20,000 a year. Even after 1873, when all shipment of slaves by sea was made illegal, slave raiding and trading within the region reached new high levels. The slave trade was so important to the Zanzibar economy as a source of labour and revenue that none of the treaties to restrict or abolish it were implemented fully by the Sultan and his government.

European Travellers

Until about 1850, European knowledge of East Africa was still limited to what the traders could obtain from Roman, Greek, Arab and Portuguese sources and from recent sources such as reports of British navy, European trade missions based in Zanzibar and Church Missionary Society (CMS) stations at Rabai, near Mombasa.

The first missionaries in East Africa were Germans working for the British CMS. They were J. L. Krapf, J. Rebman and J. Erhardt who established a mission station at Rabai in 1844 in what is now Kenya. While at Rabai, these missionaries visited some parts of the interior and gathered a lot of information about the region. That is why they are partly regarded as having been the first European explorers in the region. Rebman, for example, travelled to Kilimanjaro and saw the snow-capped mountain there in 1848. His colleague, Krapf, saw Mount Kenya in 1849 when he visited the Tana River headwaters area. At the same time both of them obtained information about existence of a big inland lake variously known as Unyamwezi, Ukerewe, Ujiji or Nianja. Their colleague drew a sketch map in 1850 showing what he thought was the location of this inland lake. Both the map and the information about existence of snow-capped mountain on the Equator caused a lively debate among European geographers.

In 1856, the Royal Geographical Society sent Richard Burton and John Speke to find out whether indeed there were snow-capped mountains and a big inland lake or not. They were also asked to look for the source of the Nile River in the Lakes of East Africa. When they arrived they stayed in Zanzibar for some time and explored the northern Mrima coast. Then they travelled from Bagamoyo to Ujiji via Tabora in 1857 and Speke visited Lake Victoria, near Mwanza in 1858. They confirmed existence of snow-capped mountain and at least two big inland lakes in the region. Lake Nyasa was visited by a German traveller named A. Roscher and David Livingstone in 1859. What remained to be discovered was the source of Nile.

After the initial penetration by Burton and Speke, what would become mainland Tanzania was visited by many European travellers from the 1860s to 1880s. The best known included John Speke and James Grant (1860) to find whether Lake Victoria was the source of the Nile, David Livingstone who explored Lakes Nyasa and Tanganyika between 1866 and 1873, Charles New who climbed mount Kilimanjaro to its snow line in 1871, Henry M. Stanley who explored northern part of Lake Tanganyika and western Tanzania with Livingstone in 1871 and then sailed around Lakes Victoria and Tanganyika in 1875 and 1877, J. F. Elton who explored southern highlands in order to gather information on slave raiding in 1877, Joseph Thompson who surveyed the region between Dar es Salaam and Lake Nyasa from 1878 to 1880 for construction of a road by the Sultan of Zanzibar, and William Mackinon and also surveyed the northern interior in 1883 for the purpose of opening up short route from the coast to Lake Victoria and Maasailand. The accounts of these explorers' journeys when published back in Europe generated tremendous interest in support Christian missions, fighting the slave trade, and even led some in Europe to think of colonizing the East African interior.

European Missionaries

The penetration of the interior of mainland Tanzania and other parts of East Africa by European travellers went hand in hand with the spread into the region of Christian missionaries. In fact, some of the best known European explorers of the region such as John Krapf, Rebman, Livingstone and Charles New were missionaries. Missionary activity in East Africa started with the establishment of CMS station at Rabai in 1884. Following the CMS example were the Universities Mission to Central Africa (UMCA) – both Anglican – and the Holy Ghost Fathers – Roman Catholic – which both established stations in Zanzibar in 1860s. The Holy Ghost Fathers established another station in Bagamoyo in 1868. Up to mid-1870s, these missionary bodies confined their work to converting freed slaves in Zanzibar and the coast. Most of these freed slaves were given to the missionaries by British patrol ships which had rescued them. After acquiring Christian principles and manual skills the freed slaves were usually married and set up what were called Christian villages. These settlements helped to spread Christianity across the coastal region. By 1885, the Holy Ghost Fathers had villages of this kind which extended as far as Morogoro from Bagamoyo.

The work of Protestant missionaries in the interior was the result of Stanley's appeals during his second journey to East Africa. In a letter to the Daily Telegraph newspaper of 15th November 1875, he challenged the British churches to send missionaries to Buganda. In response, the CMS sent a group of missionaries to Buganda in 1877. Mission stations were also established at Mamboya, Mpwapwa and Busambiro to link up the Buganda mission with Zanzibar. Not content to be left behind in missionary work in East Africa, the Catholic White Fathers (Missionaries of Africa) sent missionaries to mainland Tanzania and Buganda soon after the British CMS. The first group went to Tabora in 1878 where they established a station. From there five of them went to Bukumbi near Mwanza which became the second station in 1883. Three members of this group remained at Bukumbi while two went to Buganda. Some of the White Fathers missionaries left Tabora and went to Lake Tanganyika where they established stations at Ujiji in 1879 and Karema in 1885.

Apart from the CMS and the White Fathers, other missionary groups which established stations in mainland Tanzania in 1870s and 1880s were the London Missionary Society (LMS) at Urambo and Ujiji and the UMCA at Magila, near Muheza, and Masasi. Missionaries were the first group of Europeans to reside in the interior on long term basis. They had to learn the people's language and customs. They provided the first direct permanent link between East Africa and Europe. Although they regarded Africans as fellow human beings who should be made Christians, they brought with them many misconceptions about about

Africa and Africans They often regarded Africans as barbaric or wild people and sinners who had to be converted to Christianity. Some regarded Africans as inferior to Europeans. They wanted to "civilise" them. And finally, they regarded themselves as humanitarians who were to save the Africans from the evil deeds of the Arab traders.

Significance of European Activities

By the late 19th century the increasing wealth and power of Europe compared to the rest of the world had made itself felt in what would become Tanzania. European commercial interests aligned with "humanitarian" interests to create a demand for increased intervention in East Africa as it did elsewhere on the continent. The power expressed by modern weapons and ships gave Europeans the ability to dominate even the strongest African states and societies.

Travellers such as Speke, Stanely and V. L. Cameron for example, campaigned openly for British annexation. Their speeches and writings often contained exaggerated reports of riches to be gained and the human misery to be ended. Unlike travellers, who supported colonisation mainly for economic and political reasons, the missionaries campaigned for European intervention mainly on humanitarian and religious grounds. These included the suppression of slave trade, the suppression of local wars and the spread of Christianity and "legitimate" commerce. In order to achieve them, their experience convinced them that they needed a European administration. It is evident, therefore, that the partition of East Africa into European colonies between 1885 and 1890 was a logical outcome of the efforts made earlier by traders, explorers and missionaries to "open up" the African continent for commerce, Christianity and European control.

References

Itandala, Buluda. "History of Tanzania to 1890", Dar es Salaam: The Open University of Tanzania, 1997.

Oliver, Roland. *The Missionary Factor in East Africa*, London: Longman, 1965.

Gray, Milner John Sir. *History of Zanzibar from Middle Ages to 1856*. London: Oxford University Press, 1962.

Kimambo, Isaria N. "The East African Coast and Hinterland 1845-1880", *General History of Africa*, Vol.VI, UNESCO, 1989.

PART FOUR

The Colonial Period

If the 19th century brought great changes to East Africa as it and its peoples were integrated more closely into the world economy, the hundred years beginning about 1885 brought even greater ones as the region was portioned into colonies by European powers, conquered, and remade into colonies. This section covers that tumultuous period. Chapter twelve is divided into two sections. The first section discusses the relationship between imperialism and colonialism from a number of different viewpoints. As the chapter asserts, the establishment of a colonial economy destroyed the balance between local communities and their environments without changing either the technology or the method of production. The forces of imperialism required Africans to produce their own food and at the same time produce cash crops for export to metropoles. Consequently, two economies were created in the new territory, the first was the traditional economy which was commonly called the subsistence economy for production was mainly for subsistence. The second was a cash-based economy producing for export. To meet the needs of imperialism and colonisation, the infrastructure created (roads and railways) was intended to connect areas with potential minerals and plantations producing for export to world commodity markets. As a result, sharp regional economic differentiation occurred in the colony.

The second section deals with the scramble for and partion of German East Africa. Before the Berlin Act, European nations established spheres of influence in Africa, including that of German East Africa, through settlement (South Africa), exploration (Burton and Speke, Grant, Stanley, Barker), commercial posts (West Africa, Zanzibar, and Indian Ocean islands), missionary outposts, the occupation of strategic areas like the Nile valley and treaty making with African leaders. All of these actions brought European nations into conflict with each other as well as with African states and societies. The Berlin conference that brought European powers together to negotiate means of settling their disputes in Africa. Two of its acts (article 34 and 35) were of special importance in the colonisation process because they defined the two doctrines of "spheres of influence", and "effective occupation". Resistances to occupation and conquest occurred across what would become Tanzania as it did across Africa. The first section of chapter thirteen provides a general overview of African resistance against the imposition of colonial rule. The second section provides case studies of African resistance both along the coast and in the interior. Despite the determined efforts in fighting against the imposition of colonialism, all African resistance failed due to the fact that Europeans had a pronounced advantage in technology. The failure of African resistance led to the effective establishment of colonial economy in German East Africa. Both the two sections of chapter fourteen provide a thorough description of peasant, settler, and plantation agriculture established during the German and British colonial periods. The establishment of peasant, settler and plantation agriculture corresponded with the establishment of transportation infrastructure. On the whole, railway construction was the main focus during the German period and road construction for motor vehicles became main concern during the British period. The chapter ends with the accounts of methods used to ensure labour stability, and labour supply on one hand, and the emergence of peasant societies on the other.

The establishment of colonial rule in Tanzania involved the institutionalisation of the state. Chapter fifteen examines the German and British administration systems in the colony. The two powers that colonised Tanzania, Germany (1890-1918) and Britain 1919-1960 designed two different administrative approaches: the Germans preferred direct administration and the British used indirect rule. This chapter provides different viewpoints as far as the effects of colonialism are concerned. Supporters of colonialism saw it as beneficial to Africans with the introduction of hospitals and modern medical care and education as well as railways. Critics saw it as exploitive and as denying Africans the right to self-determination. Radicals argued that it created dependent economies that led to underdevelopment.

Chapter sixteen covers the unique case of Zanzibar. The chapter begins with an account of the transition from slavery to wage labour, followed by the period when Zanzibar was under the rule of the British Foreign Office from 1890 to 1913. Control over the Protectorate was transferred to the Colonial Office in 1913 which controlled the Sultan's government up until independence in 1964. The last chapter in this part deals with nationalism in both parts of what would become Tanzania – Tanganyika and Zanzibar. The first section of chapter seventeen deals with nationalism in Tanganyika. The emergence of Tanganyikan nationalism benefited from the use of Kiswahili as a common language throughout the colony, the lack of dominant ethnic groups in the colony, and colonial policies under mandate. The creation of the Tanganyika African Association (TAA) and its successor the Tanganyika African National Union (TANU) gave the colony a more unified anti-colonial movement than in many African nations. Unlike Tanganyika, independence in

Zanzibar was accompanied by a revolution that overthrew the Sultan's government which Britain had granted independence. The chapter ends with the union of two countries to form the United Republic of Tanzania, a union that exists to date.

Chapter Eleven

Imperialism and Colonialism: The Scramble and Partition of Africa

Section I: Imperialism and Colonialism

Introduction

European activity in East Africa increased in the 19th century as a result of changes in western economies introduced by the Industrial Revolution. Thus, traders, travellers and missionaries consciously or unconsciously opened the way for the imperialist invasion. In one sense, European imperialism in the late 19th century was just the example of imperialist expansion that dated back to ancient times and included such examples as the rise of Rome, the expansion of the caliphate in the early days of Islam and even Portuguese and Omani expansion in East Africa before the 19th century. However, the late 19th century expansion of European power was different. As Marx first argued, imperialist expansion in the late 19th century grew out of the development of the capitalist system. In Marx's view, capitalism developed through three stages: merchant capital or primitive accumulation, competetive capitalism, and monopoly capitalism. Merchant capitalism or primitive accumulation was characterised by European adventurism and expansionism to other continents in search of wealth especially bullion (i.e. gold and silver). The concept can be applied as well to the competition before the 19th century between powers such as Persia and Oman in the region. In East Africa we have seen how the Portuguese followed by the Dutch and English have played part in the trading system of the Indian Ocean. We have also seen how Europeans used the Persians and later the Omani groups in their struggles to control the system.

As European countries came to industrialise competitive capitalist ideas dominated the trading system. This was the period of growing commodity exports from East Africa. Products of European industry were to be marketed freely and raw materials required by industries in Europe were also to be obtained where they were found. Britain being the first to industrialise had a lead in this competitive structure. In East Africa, by the time we come to the 19th century, the Omani Arabs under Seyyid Said increasingly came under the control of the British. But by the 1840s the Americans, French and Germans were all competing in the system which drew the huge hinterland into the capitalist trading system. By the 1870s Europeans started to compete for control against each other. Capitalism had been transformed into the monopoly phase because of crisis created by industrial expansion. As capital (and hence wealth and power) became more concentrated and centralisation in a few countries, so the returns to finance capital declined. Capitalist nations saw the world not just as a place for trade but also as places for investment and hence sought to divide the world.

Penetration Under Imperialism

Despite economic connections between Europe and Africa since the 15th century, the creation of colonies and colonial economies in Africa came towards the end of the 19th century when, after military conquest, forces of imperialism proceeded to reshape local economies into ones suitable for capitalist exploitation. Whether the conquering power was British, French, German, Portuguese, Spanish or Belgian they all tried to establish colonial states to supervise the establishment of a capitalist system subordinate to that of the mother countries. Of course, Africans resisted this process throughout the colonial period. John Iliffe, in his book entitled *The African Poor* argues that the pre-colonial African economies were poor; African peoples had to continuously struggle to make sure that they themselves and their dependents would not fall into a physical want. This contingent poverty resulted from relatively low levels of technology. African pre-colonial economies were basically self-sufficient. They were in that sense balanced to take care of the subsistence requirements of their societies both in relations to their environments and socially.

The establishment of a colonial capitalist economy destroyed the balance without changing either the technology or the method of production, especially during the early decades of colonial rule. The forces of imperialism required Africans to produce their own food and at the same time produce cash crops for export to metropoles or work for wages, often on mines or plantations. While some have described the results in terms of two economies created in each colony: one a traditional economy producing for subsistence and a second a modern economy producing for export. In reality, however, there were not two economies. They formed one articulated structure in which the labour of the colonised with its poor technology was utilised to produce raw materials for capitalist industries in the metropole while at the same time having to reproduce itself. In the settler dominated economies of eastern and southern Africa, migrant labour was used to avoid the cost of feeding families on wages. Elsewhere peasant agriculture was used as a means of producing export crops.

Generally, the infrastructure created by colonial states (roads and railways) was intended to connect areas having minerals and the potential for the production of cash crops with sea ports in order to link them to the world commodity markets. There was no intention of opening up regions of countries for internal and external communication. Therefore this emphasis led to sharp regional differentiation in economic development. In this system, the development of food production for trade was often neglected. Technical inputs into agriculture such as extension services, fertilizers and credit facilities, all went to cash crops. It is no wonder that Africa emerged into independence with an economy that devoted most of its resources to the production of export of commodities for which there was little domestic demand and depended on outside countries for the support of its basic requirements, including in many cases its food. The destruction of balance in the subsistence economy was signaled by recurrence of famines including ones that caused mass numbers of deaths. Above all, there was a deliberate discouragement of industrialisation. Even industries and crafts which existed were almost entirely destroyed as all African colonies were turned into markets for the consumption of manufactured goods from the metropoles. The little industrialisation which took place was applied in the processing of agricultural products for export. Towards the end of the colonial period some import substitution industries were established, but within the general guidelines of the colonial economic system in which manufacturing activities were discouraged. African economies were expected to support those of the metropoles and not to compete with them. It was this externally oriented economy which post-colonial African states inherited and attempted to transform without success. It does not matter the strategies they chose; they all failed to achieve the expected result.

Section II: The Scramble For and Partition of East Africa

The term "scramble" refers to the sudden rush for control of territories towards the end of the 19th century. As Uzoigwe argues, "what is most remarkable about our period is the co-ordinated manner, speed and comparative ease from the European point of view, with which the occupation and subjugation of so vast a continent was accomplished." (Uzoigwe, 1985, p.19).

Traditionally, scholars have argued that the British occupation of Egypt in 1882 triggered the scramble as other European powers sought to avoid being shut out of access to markets and investments in Africa. Recent studies (see Uzoigwe, 1985 pp. 27-29) have argued that the actions of three other nations, Belgium, Portugal and France in the period between 1876 and 1880 had helped spur British action. Their actions drew in part of the discovery of gold and diamonds in South Africa and the expansion of white control there under British rule. Belgium convened a Geographical Conference in 1876 in Brussels which set up the international African Association and employed Henry Morton Stanley to explore the Congo in 1879. Portugal sent a flurry of expeditions from its outposts along the coasts in Angola and Mozambique starting in 1876 and by 1880 had annexed what were then independent states in Mozambique. The French expansionist mood between 1879 and 1880 was exemplified by the work of Savorgnan de Brazza in the Congo basin and his treaties with chief Makole of Bateke. Thus it was not the British occupation of Egypt in 1882 which triggered off the scramble as argued by Robinson and Gallagher but rather by events of the period between 1876 and 1880 in different parts of Africa.

The Berlin Conference
The idea of holding an international conference to settle territorial disputes arising from European activities in the Congo region was first suggested by Portugal perhaps out of fear of being pushed out of

Africa. Later the idea was taken up by German Chancellor Otto von Bismarck who, after sounding opinions of other powers, encouraged its implementation. The Conference occurred in Berlin between 15th November 1884 and 26th February 1885. The calling of the conference intensified the scramble. Initially the Conference was not intended to attempt a general participation of Africa but it "nevertheless, ended up disposing of territory, passing resolutions pertaining to the free navigation of the Niger, Benue and their affluent; and laying down general rules to be observed in future with regard to occupation of territory on the coast of Africa" (Uzoigwe, 1985, p. 29)

Two articles of the Berlin Act were of special importance in the colonisation process: these were Articles 34 and 35. According to Article 34, any European nation which, in the future, took possession of an African coast or declared "protectorate" there, must notify such action to the signatory powers of the Berlin Act in order to have its ratification. This is the so called "doctrine of the spheres of influence". Article 35 stipulated that an occupier of such coastal possessions must also demonstrate that it possessed sufficient "authority" there "to protect existing rights, and as the case may be, freedom of trade and of transit under the conditions agreed upon." This is the so-called "doctrine of effective occupation" that was to make the conquest of Africa such a murderous activity.

Prior to the Berlin Act, a sphere of influence in Africa had been acquired in variety of ways: settlement (South Africa), exploration (Burton and Speke, Grant, Stanley, Barker), commercial posts (West Africa, Zanzibar, and Indian Ocean islands) and missionary settlements. Others were occupation of strategic areas like the Nile valley and treaty making with African leaders. In the German sphere, treaty making had started before the Berlin conference. For example, July 1884 Johnston's made treaties in Kilimanjaro. In March 1884 the Karl Peters formed the Society for German Colonisation to push Germany into competing for colonies. By December 1884, Karl Peter's had "negotiated" treaties in Usagara, Uluguru and Ukami which he claimed showed that local leaders recognized the authority of Germany. His colleagues the Denhardt brothers in Witu (Kenya coast) concluded treaties in the same period. At the time the Berlin Act was closing on 26th February 1885, Bismarck granted a Royal Charter to Peters' organisation to govern the territory he claimed by treaty in the name of the German state. After the conference, Germany had to negotiate not with African leaders but also with the British over their competing spheres of influence in East Africa.

African-European Treaties

The British first negotiated treaties with the Sultan's government in Zanzibar, primarily over the ending of the slave trade. These agreements gradually resulted in the establishment of a British Protectorate over Zanzibar and gave the British the ability to negotiate with the Germans in the Sultan's name over the fate of East Africa. Other African rulers either purportedly surrendered sovereignty in lieu of protection or undertook not to enter into treaty obligations with other European nations. Many of these agreements were deceptive. The crosses they put over their names may have meant nothing to them. While the treaties between the Africans and Europeans defined the latter's sphere of influence, the bilateral treaties, conventions and agreements between Europeans concluded the paper partition practically by the end of the century. With the Anglo-German Delimitation Treaty of 1st November, 1886, the islands of Zanzibar, Pemba, Mafia, Lamu and towns of Kisimayu, Brava, Merca, and Mogadishu were defined as dominions of the Sultan of Zanzibar [British sphere]. Furthermore, the country between Mogadishu and Ruvuma River was divided by a line from the Umba River to Lake Victoria. The northern half was to be a British sphere while the area to the south was to be German sphere. Germany also acquired the coastline of Witu which they eventually surrendered to the British. The two powers agreed to maintain the integrity of the Sultan's dominions and to settle their rival claims in Kilimanjaro area peacefully. The European powers sought to avoid conflict with each other over their claims.

While Germans benefited from the Delimitation treaty, the British gained more in the Anglo-German Treaty of 1890. In 1890, Germany recognized Uganda as within the British sphere of influence. This put an end of Anglo-German rivalry and wrangling in the area. Germany also abandoned her claim over the territory of Witu, Germany accepted the British Protectorate over Zanzibar and Pemba, and Germany got the island of Heligoland in the North Sea. Britain gave up her claim of a strip of land on Lake Tanganyika. And the coast of Tanganyika had been given to Germany through payment to the Sultan of Zanzibar. Italy had claimed that by the virtue of the treaty of Ucciati, signed with Ethiopia in 1889, the latter was her protectorate. This was regarded by Britain as a threat to the sources of the Blue Nile. The Agreement of 1891 was an attempt to remove this threat: while Britain recognized Italy's claim to Ethiopia, the latter was excluded from the main Nile River. Italy further undertook not to interfere with the Atbara, a tributary which would affect the water level of the Nile.

References

Betts R.F. ed. *The Scramble for Africa: Causes and Dimensions of Empire.* London: D.C. Heath, 1972.

Brown, Michael B. *Economics of Imperialism.* England: Penguin Books Ltd, 1974.

Hobson, J.B. *Imperialism A study.* Ann Arbor: MUP, 1965.

Iliffe, John. *The African Poor: A History.* Cambridge: Cambridge University Press, 1987.

Itandala, Buluda A. "The Anglo-German Partition of East Africa, 1885-1895", *Tanzania Zamani*, Vol.I, January 1992.

Lenin, Vladmir I. *Imperialism the Highest stage of Capitalism.* New York: International Press, 1969.

Langer, WL. *The Diplomacy of imperialism 1890-1902.* Vol II. New York: Knopt, 1935.

Mwanzi, I.T. "African Initiatives and Resistance in East Africa", *General History of Africa*, Vol VII, UNESCO, 1985.

Nabudere, Wadada D. *The Political Economy of Imperialism: Its Theoretical and Polemical treatment from Mercantilism to Multilateral Imeprialism.* London: Zed Press, 1978.

Penrose, E. ed., *European Imperialism and Partition of Africa.* London: F. Cass, 1975.

Robinson R. and J. Gallagher. *Africa and the Victorians.* London: Macmillan, 1961.

Nabudere, D. W. *The Political Economy of Imperialism*, Chapter 12

Uzoigwe, G.N. "European Conquest and Partition in East Africa: An Overview", *General History of Africa*, Vol.VII, UNESCO, 1985.

Chapter Twelve

Colonial Conquest and African Resistance

Section I: German Conquest and Resistance

Introduction

The paper partition of East Africa was followed by military conquest and occupation as required by the doctrine of effective occupation. Britain used Zanzibar as a base for the conquest of the rest of her empire in East Africa after the formal declaration of protectorate over it in November 1890. Germany as the main competitor had taken action to declare a protectorate over much of her sphere even before the end of the Berlin Conference.

German Military Conquest

German aggression had begun with Karl Peters supposedly treaty-making ventures in 1884. As we had already seen, the German Chancellor had recognised the treaties and had given an imperial charter to Karl Peters' organisation. Between 1884 and 1887 treaties had been concluded with many more communities' groups. Peter reorganised his society in 1887 to become the German East Africa Company (DOAG) which ruled what became known as German East Africa until 1905 in the name of the German Crown. The company both served as a government and sought to make profits for its investors. On the coast German traders sought to control the ivory trade and trade in agricultural products produced on slave plantations. They faced great competition from local traders who had long experience operating in the region. The personnel and capital of the company were too small, and they worked in a new country whose soil and crops, seasons and rain, they did not know very well. Ivory served as the only large scale export, but by 1885 the source of ivory lay deep in the interior and Arab-Swahili caravans controlled most of it. Under such circumstances prospects for extortion, exploitation and maladministration loomed large. Actual German occupation by the company started in May 1887. The following year 1888 the Sultan of Zanzibar agreed to cede to the Germans the coastal strip for half a century. Despite the agreement, effective occupation required the arrival of warships to intimidate the people. Very shortly, leaders of some coastal communities rose in revolt against company efforts to collect duties on exports and control trade. The Germans called this "Arab revolt" and labelled it a rebellion of slave traders frightened of losing their economic position. However, the revolt gained the support of many people along the coast who fought to preserve the autonomy of their communities.

In the aftermath of the revolt in 1889 the German government took over the company. The company retained a near monopoly on trade. However, company personnel remained the administration of the colony, and old rascals thrived. Peters himself was a case in point. Military operations under the German Government to extend effective control and suppress resistance went on for a number of years. The Abushiri rising was suppressed. There was confrontation with Mkwawa of the Wahehe from 1891-98. There was confrontation in Kilimanjaro, Tabora and all across the territory. Many Africans in the territory began to recognise the opportunities opened by the new era, but military conquest involved a brutal suppression of African resistance. Many communities fought to resist surrendering their sovereignty.

Resistance to Imposition of Colonial Rule

Colonial histories tended to both downplay resistance to conquest and to suggest that when it did occur fear and superstition drove it. They often claimed most Africans willingly accepted incorporation into new colonial societies in contrast to the perceived constant warfare and slaving of the pre-colonial era. Such views both underrepresent the amount of resistance that actually occurred and belittle the motivations and organisational skill with which Africans resisted conquest. African resistance did face the inherent difficulty of having many autonomous communities and states with little to no history of common action. Such division also meant that conquerors, the Germans in this case had to face many incidents of resistance. Some communities and individuals more quickly saw opportunity in the coming of European power. Europeans often made a distinction between naturally war-like and peaceful societies. Such distinction, as well as later efforts to label some as resisters and others collaborators, mask the common interests of people and communities in the era of conquest. All states and communities had crucial interests or values which they were prepared to defend, if necessary by armed resistance. Even non-centralised societies had interests they were ready to defend. Virtually every sort of African society resisted and there was resistance in virtually every region of European advance. Colonial scholars stressed that armed resistance was irrational and desperate. They claimed that it was often a result of "superstition" and that people otherwise content to accept colonial rule had been spurred to action by "witch-doctors". Even many critics of European colonialism sympathetic to African protest nevertheless argued that Africans had little in their "traditional" social organisation or thought which could help them mount an effective or practical response to attacks on their way of life. The ideologies of revolt, in this view, consisted of "the magic of despair", bound to fail and incapable of pointing to the future. In such a view the resistance, no matter how heroic, became a tragic dead end. In recent years historians of resistance have challenged this sort of interpretation. They have done this in two ways, by showing that African resistance had its underlying ideology and by reexamining its religious origins.

Ajayi argues that "the most fundamental aspect of the European impact was loss of sovereignty…Once people lose their sovereignty, and they are exposed to another culture, they lose at least a little of their self-confidence and self-respect; they lose their right of self-steering, their freedom of choice as to what to change in their own culture or what to copy or reject from other cultures" (Cf. Ranger, 1985, p. 48). A similar point is made by Walter Rodney with greater emphasis: "The decisiveness of the short period of colonialism…springs mainly from the fact that Africa lost power…The power to act independently is the guarantee to participate actively and consciously in history. To be colonised is to be removed from history…Overnight, African political states lost their power, independence and meaning" Defense of sovereignty clearly provided an ideology of resistance. The question remains as to whether all African rulers were "guardians of the sovereignty of their people" (Rodney, 1972, pp. 245-246).

Religious beliefs and symbols often bore very directly on the question of sovereignty and legitimacy. Rulers gained legitimacy through ritual. When a ruler and his people were determined to defend their sovereignty they naturally drew heavily on religious symbols and ideas. It was out of such crises of legitimacy that the great movements which attempted to redefine sovereignty often emerged. The Maji Maji uprising of 1905 against the Germans exemplifies this pattern.

In so far as resistance sought to defend sovereignty, it anticipated the recovery of sovereignty that became the main goal of African nationalism. In so far as resistance movements relied on a prophetic ideology they attempted to create new concepts of community. Some of them even resulted in improving the position of the peoples who had revolted. Otherwise threw up an alternative leadership to the officially recognised ones. Terence O. Ranger argued that resistance movements were connected with later anti-colonial nationalism. Resistance movements mobilised large numbers of people in mass mobilisation. They created a range of symbols and ideas which later mass movements used to mobilize support against colonialism. Nationalists would draw from the memory of heroic past in the struggle for independence (Cf. Ranger, 1968, pp. 437-453, 631-641).

Section II: Resistance to the Imposition of Colonial Rule in German East Africa

Resistance occurred all across East Africa. In German East Africa resistance by force of arms was more general than in Kenya and was concentrated in the period between 1891 and 1898. The Germans wanted economic exploitation immediately unlike Kenya where the British's initial economic interest lay more in Uganda. With this intention and with their small forces being in constant fear of attack, irrational actions by colonial representatives tended to stimulate greater resistance. A period of comparative peace followed until the Maji Maji uprising of 1905-1907 seemed to challenge the whole imperial purpose. After the brutal suppression of this uprising, colonial rule was firmly established by the time World War I broke out in 1914.

The Coastal Region

In this region there were two major resistance movements, one led by Abushiri and Bwana Heri sparking fighting along the whole coast up to 40 miles inland. The second based in Kilwa did not spread very far because "it was almost nipped in the bud" by the Germans. The Abushiri uprising occurred when the German government took over from the company. Abushiri bin Salim al Harth – the leader of the uprising – was born in 1845 of an Arab father and Galla (Oromo) mother. He was a descendant of one of the first Arab settlers on the coast who came to regard themselves as local people. Like many others, he opposed the influence of the Sultan of Zanzibar on the coast and even advocated independence. As a young man, he had organised expeditions into the interior to trade in ivory. From the profits he bought himself a plantation in Pangani and planted sugar cane. He also engaged in campaigns against the Nyamwezi. This experience enabled him to assemble warriors who would later fight against the Germans. Having been outlawed in Zanzibar, he had by 1888 established himself around Pangani. Bwana Heri, the second leader of the uprising, came from Uzigua. He had previously been in the service of the Sultan of Zanzibar. He had become independent of the Sultan after he defeated a force sent to consolidate the Sultan's control of the coast in 1882. By 1888 he too wielded considerable power around Sadani. The outbreak of the resistance seemed to be spontaneous; trouble began in August 1888 when the Germans arrived in Pangani to establish their authority there. The company flag could only be hoisted after the arrival of a German warship, the Moewe. After it left trouble broke out again; Baluchi troops sent by the Sultan of Zanzibar, under General Mathews to assist the Germans proved of no avail.

When Bagamoyo joined against the Germans, the Liwali of that town tried to use his influence to stop the rebellion but failed. On September 25, 1888 fierce fighting took place around Bagamoyo; company officials were imprisoned but later were rescued and sent to Zanzibar. On 20th September, the rebels sacked Mikindani was sacked and a company official named von Bulow escaped death by sailing until rescued by Moewe off Kilwa Kivinje. In Kilwa itself, the company representatives were given 48 hours to leave. When they did not comply, they were killed and their heads hung on poles outside the German station. By October 1888 the remaining German officials were penned in Dar es Salaam and Bagamoyo. Describing this as "the Arab revolt" the Germans sent out Hermann von Wissmann to suppress it. Major Von Wissmann recruited 600 Nubians, 50 Somalis, 350 "Zulus" from Mozambique and 20 Turkish police to serve as his force. The British assisted the Germans in a naval blockade of the coast. Then the Germans also secured Portuguese cooperation. Between May and December 1889 von

Wissmann was engaged in suppressing resistance in the north. Starting from Pangani, he quickly captured towns in the north of Dar es Salaam. Abushiri himself escaped inland. During his last days Abushiri attacked Mpwapwa. One of the two officials, Nelson, was killed; his colleague, Griese, escaped to the coast to tell the story. In the end Abushiri was betrayed by Jumbe Magaya of Usagara. He was hanged at Bagamoyo on 15th December 1889. In the south Wissmann moved to Kilwa which he quickly took, then Lindi and Mikindani. By January 1891 Wissmann was convinced that there would no longer be trouble. Meanwhile Bwana Heri of Uzigua had failed many German attempts to capture him since January 1889.

After bombardment of Sadani on 9 June, 1889 Bwana Heri escaped inland and built a series of forts as one after another was destroyed by the Germans. Bwana Heri obtained about 600 troops from Mohamed bin Kassim in Tabora and Ujiji. Later Bwana Heri capitulated in March 1894, but he soon tried to rise again but was defeated by the Germans and fled. His place and manner of death remains a mystery. Both of these leaders rose in revolt because of the German threat to their positions as local powers. While they acted independently of each other, both benefited from their simultaneous action. They drew support from peoples and communities across the coastal region because they represented an attempt to retain sovereignty against foreign domination.

In 1894 Hassan bin Omari Makunganya led an attack on Kilwa. In June, two Germans led a campaign against him; his fort was destroyed and he fled inland where he planned a second offensive. German troops were engaged in Uhehe, and Kilwa was quite vulnerable. Hassan's forces were repulsed. In October 1895 four companies of troops attacked him; Hassan escaped but later was captured. On November 15, 1895 he was hanged in Kivinje on a mango tree--later used for mass hanging and up to today known as Mwembe-Kinyonga. Other small resistance movements involved Matumbi (1898), Usagara, Machiga (1890-91); and Masitu (1889) which continued to harass Dar es Salaam and Bagamoyo from 1891 to 1893.

The North

The Germans in Kilimanjaro had great difficulty in subduing the Chagga kingdoms; but the chiefs failed to unify and eventually they were defeated one after another. Rindi (or Mandara) had suffered from attacks from Sina, probably the strongest rulerin Kilimanjaro in the

1870s. When the Germans arrived Rindi welcomed them as he had welcomed Johnston and General Mathews; he was a shrewd diplomat. He had managed to prevent Europeans from reaching Sina's kingdom at Kibosho. He invited C.M.S missionaries from Mombasa and was in correspondence with the British consul in Zanzibar as well as with Queen Victoria and with Kaiser Wilhelm II. His capital became that of first the Germans and later the British who moved it to the present site on the plains.

Rumours circulated that Sina had pulled down their flag as a sign of defying the Germans. Wissmann quickly decided to punish him. In February 1891 Rindi played a host to a German expedition against Kibosho. The German expedition had 500 Nubians and Zulus. On February 11, 1891 they invaded Sina's fort. For 4 days Sina's men fought, and Sina escaped. He was later induced into a treaty with the Germans who guaranteed Sina peace on two conditions: give two districts to Rindi, and release the king of Uru. Marealle of Marangu, another great diplomat, took advantage of Rindi's death in 1892 and the succession of a weak son to play a traditional trick on the Germans. He posed as a big man of Kilimanjaro. The murder of the company agent Bulow was arranged in such a way that Rindi's successor would be held responsible. A messenger sent to Moshi from Marangu was killed on the Moshi-Kirua border. The killing was attributed to Meli, Rindi's successor. Von Bulow led an expedition accompanied by Lt. Wolfrum. The expedition was ambushed and Wolfrum and Bulow plus a large number of askaris were killed. Survivors returned to Marangu the headquarters had moved; they packed and evacuated Kilimanjaro. Later Marealle wrote to the Germans asking them to return and restore peace and order. Von Schele led the second Kilimanjaro expedition against Meli; 800 Sina's men joined and Meli was defeated. In 1900 Marealle had convinced the Germans that the chiefs of Moshi, Kibosho and his other rivals were plotting against them, precipitating the execution of 19 chiefs.

Pare intrigues were of similar model. The Wasangi solicited assistance against the Wambaga. Petty warlords presented themselves as rulers so that the Germans would give them flags. In 1896 a German force under Johannes attacked the Wameru and people of Arusha because two missionaries were killed there. In 1898 the Wameru and Waarusha attacked the Germans in Moshi and consequently Johannes in 1899 attacked them and built a post in Arusha. In Mbulu further south, The Iraqw were not subdued until 1906.

The West

Resistance in this area was localised and scattered all over the region. The main resistance centre was Tabora. By 1885 Isike had built a large army and levied *hongo* (duty) from passing caravans. In 1886, Giesecke, a German trader was killed in Unyamwezi because of fraudulent trade transactions. Isike confiscated Giesecke's property and also forced the White Fathers out of Kipalapala in 1889. Later in 1890, Emin Pasha entered Tabora with two Germans and over 1,000 troops. In August 1890 Emin Pasha concluded a treaty with the Arabs of Tabora. They retained the power to choose their own Wali if they accepted German suzerainty. Isike was forced to surrender Giesecke's property and pay indemnity in ivory.

In April 1892 Isike's son intercepted a Gernman column; in retaliation they attacked Isike's stronghold at Ipuli; the Nyamwezi were defeated. In June 1892 the Germans attacked Isike, but he inflicted heavy casualties on them. A punitive German expedition sent in August was nearly annihilated. Isike ordered all caravan routes in his country closed. There was fierce German-Nyamwezi fighting. On 9-12 January 1893 Isikes fort was destroyed. Many versions say that Isike blew himself up and his family in his gun powder magazine. Shorter in his *Nyungu ya Mawe*, however, says Isike did not die in the explosion; he was hanged by the Germans. There were many other confrontations in throughout the central and western regions in Ugogo, Kilimatinde, Mwanza, and Bukoba.

The South

The southern region of the territory saw some of the largest resistance movements. Machemba, a Yao leader, defeated the Germans several times between 1890 and 1899. Eventually when his fort was occupied by the Germans he escaped to Mozambique. The greatest challenge, however, came from the Hehe under Mkwawa. Before he was defeated in 1894, the Germans suffered a serious defeat in 1891 at Lugalo. The Germans sent a force under Tom von Prince to subdue the Hehe. His force eventually laid siege to the Hehe capital at Kalenga. After the Hehe defeat Mkwawa hid himself and continued to harass the Germans until, when his position became insecure, he committed suicide in 1898. There were many other resistance movements in Upogoro (1898) and Unyakyusa (1899). The Wangindo initially welcomed the Germans as protecting them against Wangoni, but later many of the leaders of the Maji Maji rebellion came from among them.

The Maji Maji Uprising

The most serious challenge to colonial rule in East Africa occurred in southern German East Africa beginning in 1905. The Maji Maji rebellion was different from previous wars of resistance. It united people from across the region into a single movement against the Germans. Earlier, Mkwawa when he had realized the need to expand beyond the bounds of a single community or state. He had invited Isike and Chabruma to join an alliance but to no avail. By 1905 colonial rule had been in practice for a while and the meaning of lost sovereignty was clear. Religious ideas were used to overcome the ethnic barriers. Forced labour, taxation, harassment and harsh conditions of work all combined to create the conditions for the Maji Maji uprising. The immediate cause was the introduction of a communal cotton scheme. People were required to work on this scheme for 28 days in a year, but the proceeds did not go to the workers. They were paid such low sums that some of them refused to take their wages. This African response was not against cotton as such; it was a reaction against this scheme which exploited their labour and threatened their own economy. They had to leave their own farms to work on the communal projects. To unite the people of the southern regions in their challenge to the Germans, the leader of the movement, the prophet Kinjikitile Ngwale used the religious beliefs familiar in the southern region. He preached that the unity and freedom of all Africans was fundamental principle, they were to unite and fight the Germans in a war which had been ordained by God, and they would be assisted by their ancestors who would return to life. To understand and give concrete expression to the unity of the African people, Kinjikitile Ngwale built a large shrine which he called "House of God" and prepared medicinal water – *Maji* – which he said, would make his followers who drank it immune to European bullets.

The movement which lasted from July 1905 to August 1907 spread over an area of 10,000 square miles of the southern third of German East Africa. The first victims of the war were the founder and his assistants who were hanged by the Germans on August 4, 1905. His brother picked up his mantle and assumed the title of "*Nyangumi*", one of the three divinities in the area, and continued to administer "*maji*". But the "*maji*" was ineffective; bullets did not turn into water, the ancestors did not return as promised, and the movement was brutally suppressed by the Germans. The Maji Maji uprising was the first large scale movement in East Africa. According to John Iliffe it was "the final attempt by Tanganyika's old societies to destroy colonial order by force" (Iliffe, 1979). It was truly a mass movement of peasants against colonial exploitation. It took a lot of effort on the part of the German colonial regime to suppress it; but at the same time the Germans were also forced to abandon communal cotton scheme. There were also reforms in the colonial structure, especially with regard to recruitment and use of labour which were designed to make colonialism more acceptable to Africans.

References

Gwassa, G.C.K. "The German Intervention and African Resistance in Tanzania" in Kimambo I. N. and Arnold Temu, eds. *A History of Tanzania*, Nairobi: East African Publishing House, 1969.

Gwassa, G. C. K and John Iliffe. *Records of Maji Maji Rising*. Dar es Salaam: Historical Association of Tanzania, Paper No. 4, 1968.

Iliffe, John. A *Modern History of Tanganyika*, Cambridge: Cambridge University Press, 1979.

Mapunda, O. B and Gaudence Mpangala. *The Maji Maji War in Ungoni*. Maji Maji Research Paper, No. 1. Dar es Salaam: EAPH, 1969.

Mwanzi, H.A. "African Initiatives and Resistance in East Africa, 1880-1914" in *General History of Africa*, Vol VII, UNESCO, 1985.

Ranger, T.O. "African Initiatives and Resistance in the Face of Partition and Conquest" in A. Adu Boahen (ed.), *General History of Africa: Africa under Colonial Domination*, Vol. VII, UNESCO, 1985.

Chapter Thirteen

The Colonial Economy

Section I: The Colonial Economy in German East Africa

The German colonial state set out to reorient the economies of German East Africa towards the benefit of Germany, German firms, and German settlers. In the 1880s and 1890s the DOAG and then German state sought first to control the existing export trade in ivory and other natural products. Part of the struggle to control the coast stemmed from their effort to take control of that trade. Gradually other natural products such as wild rubber and beeswax, cultivated products such as copra from coconuts, and even hides from livestock began to be produced. Missions played an important role in encouraging the first commodity production by African farmers. The Germans also sought to encourage settlers to come and establish plantations. Many came from Germany and a few from the Afrikaners of South Africa. Transport remained the greatest roadblock to the growth of the colonial economy. Until the completion of the first railways, caravans employing porters remained the main means of moving goods around the colony.

Transport Infrastructure

The Germans like other colonial power focused on the building of railways as a means of solving the transportation issues of their colony (Iliffe, 1979, p. 135). In 1891 the German East Africa Company undertook to build a line inland from Tanga through a projected plantation area around the Usambara Mountains to Mount Kilimanjaro and possibly to Lake Victoria. John Iliffe tells us how a private company built the Tanga line slowly, inefficiently and with much forced labour. By 1899 only 40 kilometers had been completed. Then the Government took over; but not until 1905 did the line reach Mombo, 129 kilometers inland. The stimulus for railway building came rather from the British side. The Uganda railway had reached Lake Victoria in 1901 and quickly transformed a hinterland which included the German lake posts. Between 1903 and 1906 Mwanza's export rose from £3,559 to £97,898. Mwanza attracted long-distance trade from the central caravan route and encouraged commodity production around the Lake. The Germans were losing their hinterland (Iliffe, 1979, p.135). Thus railway transport policy was transformed with the decision to build a central railway along the caravan route from Dar es Salaam to Kigoma. The building of the railway began in 1905 in Dar es Salaam; it reached Morogoro in 1907 and by 1914 it had reached Kigoma.

Apart from railway construction, the colonial government sought to aid European settlers by extending the northern route from Mombo to Moshi, which it reached in 1912. Later the British extended the line to Arusha. It reached Usa River and Tengeru in 1929 and Arusha in 1930. The Germans also sought to build in 1914 a railway westward from Tabora to densely populated Rwanda, but only 40 kilometers had been completed before the war. The British completed it to Mwanza. Unlike the Uganda railway, the Tanganyika lines were built by African labour working in huge gangs with only simple tools. At its peak the central railway employed some 20,000 men. About 100 died each month in the marshes east of Kilosa. The railways affected many spheres of life: it ruined the Zinza iron smelters who had produced hoes used by caravans as currency. The immigration of Europeans and Asians was accelerated. By 1912 there were 8,698 Asians in the colony, and they had better access to imported goods, export markets, credit facilities and commercial skills. Asian shopkeepers commonly drove out African competitors.

The Development of the Settler-based Economy

From the point of view of the colonial state, increasing white settlement measured the advancement of the colonial economy. Between 1904 and 1913 the European population in German East Africa grew from 1,390 to 4,998. Of those settlers, 882 were male adults engaged in agricultural production (Iliffe 1979, p.141). Between 1901 and 1906 the colonial state supported schemes to establish Afrikaner refugees from the Boer war and impoverished Germans from Russia on the foot of Mount Meru, but considered this as an experiment. Early 1900s most settlers in West Usambara were hoping to combine mixed farming with coffee plantations. By 1911 there were 41 farmers in the mountains. The District Commissioner had a land commission consisting of himself and local akida or government agent and headmen. They decided to concentrate Africans on part of the land and alienate the rest for European owned estates. The common practice was to leave about 4 hectares per family. The land vacated was declared crown land and leased for 25 years. In 1912 a shortage of land and labour forced the government to close West Usambara to further European settlement. European farming did not prosper in the area. Coffee failed, dairying and vegetables lacked sufficient market, and most settlers grew African cereals to feed sisal plantations in the plains (Iliffe 1979, p.143). Settlers also sought land around Kilimanjaro and Meru. In 1907 the German government decided to alienate only apparently unused land in the *Shamba* belt and foothills, leaving gaps between farms to allow access to lowlands by African herders and farmers. The Germans wanted explicitly to limit Chagga expansion so that population growth would provide settlers with a sufficient labour force growing parallel with needs. Alienation produced localised land hunger as Africans sought to expand their own production and create new households and farms. Such land hunger struck both Mt. Kilimanjaro and especially around Mt. Meru.

The government policy of encouraging settlers in northern German East Africa meant that very large areas around the base of Mt. Meru bordering immediately African holdings became almost a European reserve. Thus in 1914 slightly less than 10% of the land of German East Africa had been alienated- mainly in Usambara, Kilimanjaro and Meru as main centres. Early plans to support settlers in Uhehe and Unyakyusa highlands and other parts of Southern highlands were frustrated by transport. A few coffee planters obtained land in Buhaya. The only other settlement area was Morogoro district where the central railway enabled 82 plantations to be opened by 1911.

Rubber – as plantation crop – created a boom which collapsed in 1913. There were two reasons for collapse of rubber plantations. One was the fact that only a poor variety (manihot) could grow well in East African soils while good varieties had been developed in other areas, especially Southeast Asia. Manihot could not compete with these other varieties. Thus, rubber from German East Africa was considered the worst in the world. Two, plantation growth outran labour supply and pushed up production cost. By 1914 many rubber plantations were abandoned. Sisal emerged as a plantation crop better suited than coffee, cotton and rubber. It could grow well in shallow laterite soils of the northeast, central railway area and southern coast. It could withstand unpredictable rainfall. Its A DOAG manager introduced the crop by getting the first plants from Florida in 1893 and experimenting with planting them near Pangani. Investment rose rapidly. By 1912 it was the dominant export crop. About 57% of the crop came from European owned estates, and those settlers began to seek a voice in the running of the colony.

As early as 1898, Europeans who had settled in certain districts were nominated to advisory councils administering "communal" funds. In 1904 the governor's council (made up of all Europeans) was created as advisory body. During last decade of German rule settlers attempted to control these advisory councils, make them elective and giving them decision making power. By 1914 the settlers possessed a degree of political power which European settlers were never to exercise again in Tanganyika. There were as many Europeans in German East Africa as in Kenya, they were better organised, better represented in public bodies, more influential in metropolitan politics, far more important economically, and able to ignore Asian political demands which Europeans in Kenya had to heed.

The Struggle for Labour

Settler and plantation agriculture appropriated vast quantities of African labour by a mixture of economic and political means. Most workers were migrants from distant regions, since the economic and environmental conditions which made plantations possible in the north-east also enabled Africans in the region to commercialise their agriculture. The result was differentiation between labour importing and exporting regions. In the importing regions African societies tended to develop towards peasant production. By contrast, the labour exporting regions tended to stagnate or even retrogress. Many labour importing regions were high-rainfall areas, which could easily get into the cash crop producing system for the colonial capitalist system.

After disastrous experimentation with Chinese and Indonesian "coolies" employers began in 1895 to recruit Nyamwezi and Sukuma workers. By 1900 they numbered between 4,000 and 5,000. Taxation was introduced in 1898 and people were forced to sell labour in order to get money to pay taxes. European employers however, continued to need workers. They demanded political action because economic measures proved inadequate in producing the number of workers they wanted at the low wages they could pay. Before 1910 areas were divided into labour divisions, each attached to a plantation to which headman had to supply labour. The governor Rechenberg prohibited this arrangement in 1910, but by then of 14,000 workers in European plantations in Tanga district, 1,200 were local men. Compulsion was through a card system where each male had to carry a card stating how many days he had worked. By 1914 labour compulsion still existed in Lushoto, Dar es Salaam, Rufiji, Morogoro, and Lindi districts.

On Kilimanjaro the situation was complicated by several Chagga who had themselves become coffee producers. Most of them were catechists. For example, Sawaya Mawala (Marealle's advisor) became the first coffee farmer. He obtained seeds from an Italian settler. Then chiefs followed. Growers were exempted from labour recruitment but not allowed to employ labour and compete with settlers. Settlers insisted "we don't need black capitalists; we need black workers" (Iliffe, 1979, p.155). Between 1909 and 1913 Mwanza's export of cotton lint rose from 123 bales to 3,735 bales. It enabled some Sukuma to abandon labour migration. Haya coffee production also increased in Bukoba. Robusta coffee existed in pre-colonial period. When the Uganda Railway reached Lake Victoria in 1901, local German officers encouraged commercial production. Between 1906 and 1912 exports grew from 214,556 to 681,245 kilogrammes. The main beneficiaries were chiefs. They extended the *Nyarubanja* land tenure system to include many areas either planted with or suitable for coffee. As Iliffe contends, "ancient agricultural skills and pre-capitalist forms of exploitation were absorbed intact into colonial structure" (ibid, p. 156). Plantations had more difficulty than other enterprises in attracting labour. Plantation conditions of work had harsh discipline. Planters used "task" system. Eventually migrant labour became a lasting solution. The great expansion of migrant labour around 1908 continued until the war. Supply of Nyamwezi and Sukuma workers diminished during the depression caused by the war.

Section II: Development of Settler and Peasant Production During the British Period

The Effect of World War I

German East Africa served as a battle field during the war (see Iliffe, 1979, pp. 240-261). The war affected many sectors of life. For civilians, primary emotion was fear. Both the German state and the allied invaders led by the British sought labour, food and local knowledge. They sought to win Africans to their side without being able to guarantee protection. This competition offered opportunity for intrigue similar to those at the time of conquest. Wartime plunder left local populations suffering from famine. By 1918 famine struck in Dodoma, Singida and Kondoa where the Germans had ransacked 26,000 cattle and five months later the British took 5,659 beasts plus 24,000 porters and 100 tonnes of flour. The spread of diseases also created suffering and death. Smallpox broke out, and Spanish influenza killed 50,000 to 80,000 between 1918 and 1921. Tsetse fly expanded their range and led to an increase of tsetse borne disease to human beings and animals.

The war saw many Africans recruited as *askaris* and porters. Apart from loss of life by *askaris* and porters, this group suffered the greatest frustration after the war. *Beni* societies expressed these frustrations. High status *marini* groups and low status *Arinoti* kept alive the *askari* and the porter memories. Many more men served as porters than as soldiers. The British had formed the Carrier Corps in Kenya early in the war; the Belgians also created their own corps in the Congo and Central Africa. By 1917 German East Africa provided most of the porters. In March 1917, the British commander-in-chief controlled 125,000 porters, 44,000 from Kenya and 81,000 from German East Africa. The porters experience was terrible. They suffered a death rate of 100,000 to 300,000 out of estimated total of 1/2 – 1 million men serving. Dysentery killed most; but also sheer cold on the Livingstone Mountains.

During the war the colonial economy ground to a halt. German personnel either retreated with German forces or faced capture and imprisonment by the allies. The allies as they slowly occupied the territory sought to revive African production and even some plantations, but a lack of certainty about the status of the colony inhibited both government and private investment for many years. At the end of the war, the British received the bulk of the territory as a Mandated Territory under the new League of Nations. Rwanda and Burundi were separated from the rest of the colony and give to Belgium as mandates. As a result in part of the mandate which stated that the colony must be governed for the benefit of its inhabitants, the British Colonial Office declared in 1921 that the newly named Tanganyika Territory "must be primarily a black man's country." While the British sought to create a governing system similar to that in its other African colonies and implemented "Indirect Rule" as its means of governing its subjects, in fact very little changed for most Africans in Tanganyika immediately.

Economic Restoration

British imperial firms sought to take advantage of the new colony. British banks stepped in (the National Bank of India and later Standard Bank of South Africa as government bankers). Big sisal estates were auctioned, and British investors bought the most profitable ones. Mombasa and Durban Companies handled the restoration of the Dar es Salaam Harbour. Most ex-German plantations were bought by European investors and many mixed farms went to British settlers, but many medium sized properties such as urban estates and smaller sisal and coffee plantations were sold at low prices to Asian merchants. The Karimjee Jivanjee family became major landowners. Greek settlers also invested in Tanganyika estates. George Arnautoglu became the most successful of them. In the 1920s, the British allowed German settlers to return to their properites in order to complete re-establishment of the colonial economy to the levels before the war.

European Enterprises and African Labour

Despite the new investment, stagnation followed the war. Then in the 1920s quite rapid growth occurred. The economy collapsed between 1929 and 1932 during the Great Depression, and an analysis of exports shows two important changes. In early 1920s peasant production gained over the production of plantation crops and natural products which had dominated during German times. The later 1920s and the 1930s saw revival of plantation enterprise now almost wholly dominated by sisal. Between 1921 and 1932 colonial state borrowed £8,693,350 to spend on public buildings, renovation of German railways and extension of branch lines to Arusha 1930, Mwanza 1929 and Kinyangiri (Unyaturu) 1932. One planned to Northern Rhodesia (now Zambia) never materialised.

The deportation of Germans during the war reduced the white population from 4,998 in 1913 to 2,447 in 1921. After 1921 British settlers bought ex-enemy properties but no new land was alienated for white settlement. By 1939 there were 6,514 European unofficial residents in the territory, including 2,100 Britons and 2,729 Germans. Most Germans were small farmers, often financed indirectly by the Reich. They gained much land on Kilimanjaro and dominated in Southern Highlands and Oldean in Mbulu District. Altogether the period added 400,000 hectares of newly alienated land bringing total peak of 1,157,246 hectares in 1937. The official view was that Tanganyika must be predominantly an African territory; the British colonial state gave less indirect aid to settlers (freight subsidy, technical assistance etc.) than had the Germans. Between the wars sisal became chief export crop. Exports rose between 1921 and 1938 from 17,057 to 103,428 tonnes. Even the international depression had little effect on sisal. The interwar period intensified the earlier trend of recruiting migrant labour. In the early 1920s the largest group of migrants were still Nyamwezi, Sumbwa and Sukuma. During the depression many Sukuma became cotton growers and the Nyamwezi area was closed for labour recruiting because of sleeping sickness. Migrants came increasingly from remote peripheral regions: Nyaturu, Nyiramba and Irangi from Central Province (Kondoa, Mkalama, Singida) for plantations in Moshi and Arusha; Bena and Nyakyusa from Southern Highlands. Many Nyakyusa travelled to northeast in 1920s until the Lupa goldfield offered a closer market for food and labour. The Ha from Kigoma had travelled to north-eastern plantations beginning around 1925. The Makonde and Makua (from Mozambique), Rundi, Mabwe and Bemba (from Zambia) also sent large numbers of migrants. New migration was stimulated by tax whose collection increased almost by 155% when compared 1912 and 1939. Wage earners increasingly used the money they earned to buy imported goods, to pay school fees, to obtain cattle for bride-wealth and even to invest. When profitable crops, transport facilities, or markets became available, men usually abandoned migration—as Sukuma cotton growers, Ndendeule tobacco and Matengo coffee planters. Plantation labourers expressed their ideas and experience most vividly in the forms of protest, but normally lacked leadership. The most common protest was desertion and the typical response to a breach of contract by an employer was to down tools. Sisal strikes became common in 1930s.

Peasant Agriculture

Two processes emerged between the wars; the first was the continuing integration of local economies into international capitalist economy, until capitalist relationships among the Africans appeared and peasant societies emerged in certain areas. The second was clear regional differentiation. Iliffe holds the view that, regional differention "was a peculiarity of sub-Saharan Africa that capitalism and peasant societies evolved together. Peasants live in small communities, cultivate land they own or control, rely chiefly on family labour and produce their own subsistence while also supplying larger economic systems including non-peasants" Iliffe (1979, p. 273). According to this definition "coastal peoples were probably Tanganyika's only peasants before European invasion." European control, taxation, acceptance of world regions and production for the market began to extend peasant status in German times; but it was in the 1920s that peasant societies appeared inland notably in Kilimanjaro, Buhaya and Usukuma. Political eruptions consequent on the successive peasantisation of Tanganyika's societies powered much of the country's political development. Cash crop areas joined towns and European plantations as regions most integrated into world capitalist economy. But they in turn drew resources from peripheral regions supplying migrant labour and from intermediate regions supplying food and other services.

Emergence of Peasant Societies

Kilimanjaro

During the 1920s coffee transformed the Chagga into peasants. In 1916 they owned 100,000 trees. Rising prices after 1921 spread the popularity of coffee cultivation quickly. By 1925 there were 6,716 Chagga coffee growers with 987,173 trees; five years later, the number of coffee trees had almost reached 6 million trees. Differentiation among individuals also grew. In 1930 only one man in three grew coffee and of these 96% had less than 1,000 trees. The remainder (about 500) owned a hectare or more often in distinct plantation farms rather than planting trees in *Kihamba* and these largest farmers used hired labour. Two groups supplied most of these successful farmers Established leaders including chiefs and other prominent men possessing often possessed several vihamba. Educated Christians, like Joseph Merinyo made up the second group of wealthy planters. Around 1927 some Chagga began to buy and sell land. Local trade flourished, and in 1925 a Native Shopkeepers Association was formed. "Settlers protested that African coffee would spread disease, devalue the local product, and encourage theft from European farms. Privately they feared that it would harm their labour supply" (Iliffe, 1979, p. 276). In 1923 the settlers formed Kilimanjaro Planters Association. In 1925 the Kilimanjaro Native Planters Association was formed with Joseph Merinyo as President and Stefano Lema as Secretary. In 1927 KNPA became the nucleus of a marketing cooperative. The farmers' interests brought them into conflict with the colonial state, settlers and chiefs. In 1927, under settler pressure, colonial state decided to discourage cultivation of Arabica coffee by "natives". In 1928, it reopened Kilimanjaro's lower slopes for alienation.

Conflict also arose between the KNPA and chiefs who wanted to control marketing. Crisis eventually came during the depression when between 1929 and 1931 prices fell from £70 per ton to £29. In 1931 many Chagga sold coffee to private traders (Chagga and Asians). A government investigation alleged Merinyo had embezzled KNPA funds. During his imprisonment the colonial state transformed KNPA to Kilimanjaro Native Coffee Union. KNCU was seen at first as government institution. It was a target of Chagga hostility which reached a climax in 1937 when they wanted to destroy their primary societies.

Buhaya

In 1937 witnessed riots in Buhaya as well. The expansion of coffee growing had also taken place in the 1920s. In 1923 2 million trees had been planted. By 1928 more than one-half of the 80,000 tax payers in Bukoba district grew coffee. Their 7,873 tonnes marketed dwarfed the 314 tonnes sold by the Chagga. By 1936 several major coffee areas were no longer self-sufficient in bananas. Education, Islam and Christianity spread rapidly. Buhaya differed from Kilimanjaro in three ways: Wage-labour was more common. By 1924 there were least 20,000 *bashuti* – migrant workers – from Burundi, Bugufi, Biharamulo and Karagwe. Large coffee farmers were more numerous. Capitalist relations were accompanied with weakening of feudal relations- at the same time emerging capitalist relations strongly coloured by pre-capitalist survivals. Feudal relations were weakened by abolition of tribute. Buhaya hierarchical traditions made its peasant society more sharply differentiated.

Peasant agriculture was established in other parts of Tanzania too. For instance, in 1923 Sukuma cotton production exceeded 1913 figure of 3,714 bales. 1926 coffee spread among the Nyakyusa who had grown very small quantities during the German period. It also spread during the 1920s to Shambaa (1921) Hangaza of Bugufi (1924-25) and Nyiha and Matengo in 1928. Tobacco was pioneered in Ungoni (1928) and Buzinza (1931). By late 1930s Tanganyika's economy had developed both a settler based sector and a peasant based sector. Both were integrated into the western capitalist economy. The African peasantry sector had been articulated without raising the level of technology. It was part of the colonial periphery economy serving the interests of capital in the industrial sector. Differentiation had taken place among the peasants individually as well as regionally.

References

Iliffe, John. *Tanganyika under German Rule, 1905-1912*, Cambridge: Cambridge University Press, 1969.

_____. *A Modern History of Tanganyika*, Cambridge: Cambridge University Press, 1979.

Kaniki M. H.Y. ed., *Tanzania under Colonial Rule*, London: Longman, 1980.

Chapter Fourteen

Colonial Administration in Tanzania From the Germans to the British

Introduction

The establishment of colonial rule in mainland Tanzania as well as Zanzibar created new political structures on top of existing societies. Colonial rule meant the institutionalisation of the state. On the mainland, the Germans created the state but lost the colony at the end of First World War. The allies divided the former German East Africa into three colonies. The densely settled former kingdoms of Rwanda and Burundi became separate colonies ruled by Belgium, while the bulk of the colony became the new League of Nations Mandated Territory of Tanganyika ruled by the British. As the British took over administration they sought to both integrate their new possession into their existing imperial system, and to establish a system of administration internally consistent with their practice in other colonies. This change meant the replacement of the system of direct rule under the Germans with a system of Indirect Rule that tried to govern people through "traditional" authorities.

German Administration in Tanganyika

In the early 1890s governors Julius von Soden and von Schele constructed the framework of an administrative structure for German East Africa. At its head was the Governor, who enforced the laws, imperial edicts, and chancellor's instructions in the colony. He had the power to issue local decrees. The civil administration at Dar es Salaam was organised in separate departments. The first department was the Finance Department. Rudolf von Bennigsen was the head from 1893 to 1899. He realised that a new colony needed public works and welfare services. In the 1890s this department was the most important in the administration and it handled many problems of a general nature. The second department was the Department of Surveying and Agriculture. This was set up in 1893. Franz Stuhlmann was in charge and encouraged the collection of information concerning the topography of the colony and the demarcation of lands to be alienated for settlers or retained by local communities. Other Departments included the Department of Justice, the Medical Department, and the Public Works Department. All these were set up in early 1890s. In the interior, German authority was generally established in three stages. In a number of areas treaties had been signed with local chiefs and German influence depended upon the extent to which the chiefs fulfilled their obligations. The colonial military, the *Schutztruppen*, initially made up of African troops recruited from outside the colony, grew over time as the German administration used it to quash resistance and stage punitive expeditions against recalcitrant leaders and communities.

The second stage in the establishment of German authority was to set up military posts on caravan routes, at centres of maritime trade, at places from which European merchants and missionaries already existed and exercised influence and at headquarters of agents of the Sultan of Zanzibar or of local chiefs. In the third stage civilian district officers replaced the military government. These officers exercised both executive and judicial functions. In some places the Germans relied on existing rulers who collaborated with them to administer local populations, collecting taxes and ensuring that local men supplied labour. In other areas the Germans imposed the coastal structure of the Sultanate, Akidas and Jumbes to administer local populations. Jumbes were local men named to rule villages and territories while akidas were men literate in Swahili who served as clerks and oversaw tax collection from jumbes. In 1891, four administrative districts were established on the coast and by 1903 the colony had been divided into 12 civil and 16 military districts. The Swahili and Arab Jumbes and Akidas were used to collect tax and recruit labourers. By 1914 the number of districts had changed from 16 to 24. District Officers had a great deal of autonomy given the difficulties in communication. He commanded a small police force or a company of one to two hundred troops. He collected taxes, appointed and dismissed African jumbes and akidas, judged cases, and administered punishments. Often he ruled with a strong and ruthless hand. Yet the government's power was limited, for it lacked staff and money. The Germans feared African up-risings and suppressed the slightest discontent with great brutality.

The Establishment of British Administration in Tanganyika

Under the supervision of the League of Nations, British administration in Tanganyika Territory was formally established by the Tanganyika Order in Council of 22 July 1920. By the terms of the order the title of the chief representative of His Majesty's Government was changed from that of Administrator as it had been during the war to Governor and Commander-in-Chief. Subject to the Colonial Secretary's general power of disallowance, the Governor was then empowered to make ordinances for the "good government of the country", provided he respected existing native laws and customs. He was to be assisted in this work by an Executive Council consisting of the Chief Secretary, the Attorney General, the Treasurer, and the Principal Medical Officer. A High Court also existed and possessed full criminal and civil jurisdiction over all persons in the Territory. In all other cases, with the exception of a special tribunal which dealt with civil cases, the Indian Civil Procedure, Criminal Procedure and Penal Codes formed the basis of jurisdiction. The twenty-two administrative districts into which the Germans had divided the territory were retained. So too, where possible, were the services of akidas whom the Germans had formally employed in some areas. New British administrative officers, in many cases men who had served in the British military during the East Africa Campaign, were left a remarkably free hand in the formulation of their own local policies and in changing those of their predecessors.

Indirect Rule

In 1925, the British introduced a form of government called indirect rule into Tanganyika. The system, used in many British colonies, including Nigeria, relied on "traditional" authorities to administer local populations according to "Native Law and Custom." Governor Sir Donald Cameron arrived from Nigeria in 1925, after setting up the Legislative Council turned to drastic changes in local government. The new policy intended that African "tribes" should be administered by their chiefs and elders under British supervision. The British hoped this system would encourage political and economic development without leading to "detribalisation" or nationalist politics. The effort of creating local authorities was a complicated one. It created conflicts even within "tribes. J. D Graham argues that in some instances it involved creating tribes even where they did not exist before. Within well-established ethnic groups conflicts could arise between privileged chiefs and their unprivileged subjects as it happened in Buhaya. To ensure uniform application of this system of administration it was proposed that the 22 districts should be grouped into provinces under senior officials and that the office of the Secretary for Native Affairs should be created. The British hoped the new system would lead to greater control over local populations, increase the collection of taxes and improve the delivery of public services such as the construction of roads. In public projects, for example African chiefs became responsible for recruiting labour for the construction of roads. As the Germans before them, British administration had relatively few European officials given the size of the territory. The British government of Tanganyika through African leaders kept costs low.

The Effects of Colonial Rule in Tanzania

The most important effect of colonial rule in mainland Tanzania was the linking of the African communities of the area to the global capitalist system. Both German and British administrations took as their first priority the production of exports and the payment of taxes by local populations. Both German and British home governments required the colonies to pay their own way for the most part, and large expenditures such as colonial pacification and railroad building under the Germans and the extension of transportation networks under the British had to be recouped as much as possible from local resources. Administration also sought to limit the ability of Africans to make common cause against the colonial regime. The Germans used brutal tactics to suppress any sign of resistance, while the British system of Indirect Rule served explicitly to combat the rise of a nationalist anti-colonial movement.

References

Graham, J.D. "Indirect Rule: The Establishment of 'Chiefs' and 'Tribes' in Cameron's Tanganyika", *Tanzania Notes and Records*, LXXVII, 1976.

Henderson, W.O. "German East Africa, 1884-1918"in Harlow and Chilver, eds., *History of East Africa*, Vol. II, Oxford University Press, 1965.

Iliffe, John. *Tanganyika under German Rule*. Cambridge: Cambridge University Press, 1969.

_____. *A Modern History of Tanganyika*, Cambridge University Press, 1979.

Ingham, Kenneth "Tanganyika: The Mandate and Cameron, 1919-1931" in Harlow and Chilver, eds, *History of East Africa*, Vol. II, Oxford University Press, 1965.

Lugard, Frederick D. *The Dual Mandate in British Tropical Africa*. London: Frank Cass, 1965.

Chapter Fifteen

The Political Economy of Zanzibar

From Slavery to Wage Labour

Colonial rule in Zanzibar both differed from that of other East Africa colonies and resembled it in many ways. In technical terms, the Sultan of Zanzibar remained sovereign over the Isles and after 1892 the British advised his government and handled all foreign relations. In reality, the system resembled that of Indirect Rule used on the mainland. British officials determined the shape of policy, remade laws they found inconsistent with their interests, and administered the local population through authorities technically appointed by the Sultan but in reality nominated by the British. The British sought the same aim as they did on the mainland, the integration of Zanzibar into its colonial system and the world economy as a commodity producing area. The most important change they insisted on was the abolition of slavery on the isles.

Jacques Depelchin provides two levels of analysis in studying the transition from slavery to wage labour Zanzibar. First, he examines the transformation of slave-based economy into one based on the use of free labour, the transition from a merchant-dominated formation to one dominated by productive capital, and a process of peasatisation and proletarianisation where self-sustaining agriculturalists were forced to produce cash crops for sale or to work for a wage, since labour itself was being transformed into a commodity. Secondly, he examines the social relations of production that reveals three issues, exploitation of slaves by slave masters, the emergence of merchant capital leading to the decline of the land-owning class, and the antagonism between different forms of capital especially European based capital against Indian capital (Depelchin, 1991, pp. 11-12). Before the nineteenth century, Zanzibar was dominated by merchant traders of ivory and slaves. During this period, the dominant mode of production as Sheriff argues, was feudalism but did not preclude the use of slave labour. The introduction of clove plantations in the 1800s altered relations of production in Zanzibar as slaves formed the source of labour on plantations (ibid, p. 15).

The emergence of slavery and a plantation economy meant the shift of the ruling class from supporting itself—through trading activities-- to depending on plantation labour for survival. It also meant that slave owners' survival depended on the supply of cheap labour in the form of captives or sold from the mainland to the cloves plantation in the island. The transition from feudalism to a mode that relied on slave labour was prompted by the increasing activities of Great Britain in the Indian Ocean that gave rise to merchant capital. The influence of Great Britain and other European powers corresponded with the Sultan's loss of political and economic hegemony. The loss of Sultan's power was attributable to series of "Amity and Commerce" treaties with the United States (1833), Great Britain (1839), and France (1844) that favoured the activities of those nations and weakened the power of Sultan in the island (ibid, p. 15). The signing of treaties occurred in the crucial period when the United States and Europe advocated for the abolition of slavery. The move against slavery in Zanzibar was evident too. It was characterised by constant debates that were determined to get rid of slavery in the island (ibid).

Under Foreign Office 1890-1913

Efforts to stop slavery began in August 1, 1890 with the Anti-Slavery Decree that had the following provisions: prohibition of sale or exchange of slaves; closing all markets; slaves of childless masters free or death; forbidding wives of Indians to hold slaves; punishment for ill-treatment of slaves; and permitting slaves to purchase their freedom. In order to effect control of the Protectorate, Gerald Portal succeeded Euan-Smith as Consul-General in 1891. Under Portal, the British assumed control of finances and administration and began appointing Europeans to take charge of the treasury, army, police, customs and post office. Mathews was made First Minister to coordinate Sultan's affairs. The Sultan was left only with a salary from the civil list fixed at 250,000 rupees per annum. In 1892 Sultan Ali died. The British sought to nominate his successor. One of the members of the royal family, Seyyid Khalid ibn Barghash, attempted to install himself in the palace. The British objected and instead nominated Seyyid Hamid ibn Thuwain as the new Sultan. He became a cooperative agent of the British. In 1896 when there was another succession and Khalid again wanted to seize power, the British bombarded the palace; 500 defenders were killed or wounded. Seyyid Hamoud was nominated and ruled as a total dependent of the British.

Abolition of slavery itself began with very gradual provisions in 1897. While the British had justified their intervention in Zanzibar in the name of combatting the slave trade and slavery, they moved very slowly to actually abolish slavery. Their concerns once assuming responsibility for governance lay in ensuring peace and continuing production of export commodities. Hence, the process of abolition proceeded slowly. The Decree of 1897 put the onus on the slave to claim his freedom by applying to district courts. Owners could receive compensation from the British each slave freed. Concubines could only apply if they could prove cruelty. This difficult and slow process gradually succeeded. By giving powers to the slave to free himself/herself improved the status of the slave. Masters had to compete to retain their services often willingly giving plots of land to transform slaves into tenants. The Sultan led the way in this process. By 1901 critical labour shortages had arisen in the plantation sector. The colonial state assisted by encouraging the migration of labourers from the mainland, especially the Nyamwezi. By 1909 the state was able to carry through the final measure of abolition. After December 31, 1911 slave owners could no longer receive compensation for slaves. Even concubines could claim their freedom although they had to forfeit their rights over their own children. Plantation owners often claimed that the abolition of slavery led to heavy indebtedness, often to Indian merchants, but such a claim ignores the fact that many were in debt even before 1897 (Flint, 1956, p. 650).

Transfer to Colonial Office in 1913

In 1913, the British reorganised their administration in Zanzibar. They created the new post of British Resident which combined the functions of the Counsel General and the First Minister. The British Resident was to be under "general supervision" of the Governor of the East African Protectorate (Kenya). Appeals of court decisions were heard by the East African Court of Appeal in Mombasa rather than Bombay as they had been before. In 1925, the Governor of Kenya was deprived of his position as High Commissioner for Zanzibar and the British Resident reported directly to the Colonial Office. In effect these changes brought administration in Zanzibar more in line with the administration of the other East African colonies even though it retained the status of Protectorate.

Between the Wars, 1918-39

World War I had little effect on Zanzibar aside from the withdrawal of German firms from the Isles, but trade soon recovered. Over the next 10 years high prices of cloves and copra caused complacency among both the colonial state and growers. The global Great Depression caused great difficulties for the economy. Zanzibar continued to lose its position as the entrepot for East Africa as trade from the mainland shifted directly to mainland ports such as Mombasa and Dar es Salaam. Two types of changes occurred on the Isles. The Arab aristocracy faced windling economic power while mounting large debts to maintain accustomed standards of living. Indian merchants began to acquire land. The Pemba, Hadimu and Swahili also slowly began to gather up land from needy Arabs. The colonial state worried greatly about the decline of the Arabs. The British classified the population on racial lines: the Arabs owned land, Indians were traders and financiers and Africans were labourers. Colonial services were segregated by these classifications. The Education Commission of 1920 had upheld the concept of education separation rather than integrated schools. After separation from Kenya, in 1926 both Legislative and Executive Councils were created. The Executive Council included the Sultan and British officials while the Legislative included Officials and six nominated unofficial representatives appointed after consultation with local organisations. In 1927, growers (large and small) were organised along cooperative lines as the Clove Growers Association (CGA) and 9,000 people joined. Prices for commodities collapsed in 1929 with the price for one *frasila* (16kg) of cloves falling from 24 rupees in 1929/1930 to 15 rupees in 1931/1932, 7 rupees in 1932/1933 6 rupees thereafter. A slow recovery set in after that date. Already burdened by debts, growers now faced ruin. In 1934, the government instituted six reforms in an attempt to stem the crisis. Legislation forbade the transfer of Arab or African land to any non-Arab or non-African without the consent of the British Resident. Secondly, restrictions for mortgages on such land were passed. Thirdly, a moratorium on all debts owed by Arabs and African was applied to persons of other races. Fourth, the CGA was established as a privileged corporation authorised to levy a compulsory contribution on all exports. Fifthly, all clove exports had to be licensed, and the CGA became the licensing authority. These measures touched off acute and bitter controversy. The Arabs and the Swahili population strongly supported the colonial state. Indians supported by British merchants regarded it as frontal attack on their position. In September 1937 the Indian Association accused the Government of deliberately trying to drive Indians away from Zanzibar. Finally, the decree of 1937 gave the CGA a complete monopoly on the export of cloves. In August 1937 Indians in Zanzibar in collaboration with their agents overseas organised a boycott of clove trade. Government revenues were greatly depleted. By February 1938, the Resident had reached agreement with Indian dealers who called off the boycott. Indians merchants could again trade in cloves and the power of the CGA was reduced so that it could not to employ its own buyers nor to sell directly overseas except in abnormal situations. Two Indian merchants became members of the CGA Board and two to the advisory committee fixing prices. Again, in 1938, the Government dealt with the debt crisis through special courts that established amount of disputed debt and the value of mortgaged land. In this regard, the Government would pay the debt and the debtor would repay the Government by installments according to means.

World War II and It's Aftermath

Two decades after 1939 were of remarkable for the changes economically and socially on the Isles. The war had an unmixed blessing with the Japanese occupation of East Indies which temporarily eliminated the other main source of cloves in the world from markets. Wartime supplies passing through Zanzibar revived its port trade. Prosperity wiped out the debt burden. Expanded revenues allowed the colonial state to expand social services including medical services, education and teachers training facilities. In 1944 the state created town councils for Zanzibar and Ng'ambo with nominated individuals representing local interests and in 1947 Local Government Councils gained the power to raise revenue, make by-laws and spend money for improvements. In 1956 the colonial state wanted to appoint the first African unofficial member of the Legislative Council. The African Association suggested Ibrahim Saadala, but he was not accepted by the Government, instead Ameir Tojo of the Shirazi Association in Zanzibar was appointed. In the following year (1947) Ali Shariff Musa of the Shirazi Association in Pemba received appointment as the second African member. Thus the picture for unofficial members became: European, Arabs, Indians, and Africans (all from the Shirazi Association). Mass agitation began in 1948 starting with the dock strikes which became a general strike and necessitated the use of emergency powers by the colonial state. State authorities claimed that the trouble was caused by mainland Africans. At this time, the main political divisions had become established on the Isles, with Arab and Indian interests allied with the colonial state against African ones represented by the African Association and Shirazi Association. At the same time, Arab interest also sought allies in the newly independent Arab states to the north.

References

Flint, J.E "Zanzibar 1890-1950", in V. Harlow and E.M. Chilver, eds., *History of East Africa,* Vol. II, Oxford: Oxford University Press, 1965.

Jacques Depelchin, "Transition from Slavery 1873-1914" in Adul Sheriff & ED Ferguson, eds. *Zanzibar under Colonial Rule.* London: James Currey; Nairobi: Heinemann, Dar es Salaam: Historical Association of Tanzania; Athens: Ohio University Press, 1991.

Lofchie, Michael F. *Zanzibar: Background to Revolution.* Princeton, NJ: Princeton University Press, 1965.

Mosare, J. "Background to Revolution in Zanzibar" in Kimambo & Temu, *A History of Tanzania.* Nairobi: East African Publishing House, 1969.

Chapter Sixteen

Nationalism in Tanzania

Section I: Nationalism in Tanganyika

Introduction

Nations defined as social and political formations in which the members accept a commonality based most often on shared language and culture are never born but created by the acts of men and women. Nations as people usually aspire to autonomy and sovereignty as nation states. Of course not all states in history have been nation-states. Empires, kingdoms, and federations have united peoples of different communities in common states. European and other nation-states came into being not just as the expression of a desire for a common and autonomous future but also because states sought to a sense of commonality among all the subjects and citizens of their territories. In colonial Africa, colonial conquests created what would become national boundaries which divided some groups that shared a language, culture and history and united many others that shared none of those things. Thus the process of conquest and domination also gradually planted the seeds of a potential unity which grew to a national movement in the process of demanding decolonisation and self-determination. From very early during the colonial period, Africans in Tanganyika like in other African colonies created new associations that brought people together from across the colony to campaign for improved conditions for African people and eventually self-determination and independence.

Types of Associations

The farmers associations discussed in the previous chapter served as one model for communal organisation the Kilimanjaro Native Planters Association (1925) and the Bukoba-Buhaya Union (1924). Both groups represented the economic interests of cash crop producers and fought with the government appointed chiefs who sought to control them. In the 1930s and 1940s, the idea of such rural associations spread, sometimes encouraged by colonial agents who saw them as means to support increased agricultural productivity. The rural producers' associations or cooperatives became in turn important avenues for people to begin to question the legitimacy of colonial rule. However, they offered little means of linking people together across the territory as they remained focused on the issues facing particular groups of usually fairly successful farmers in specific locations.

Over the course of the colonial era emerged that would take the lead in challenging colonial domination. Beginning the German era, the colonial state sought to employ Africans literate in the dominant European language and in Kiswahili as clerks, tax-collectors, and eventually school teachers. The Germans also began to promote Kiswahili as an official language in the colony and taught it in their schools as well as encouraging mission schools to teach it. Missions also began to train catechists and teachers as well as medical assistants. The British, despite their policy of Indirect Rule which encouraged Africans to think of themselves as members of distinct tribes with their own languages and customs, continued the policy of requiring the use of Kiswahili in administration and education. This process gradually built up a group of men and women, often employees of the colonial state, educated in a common language who began to see themselves both as part of a larger community uniting the peoples of Tanganyika across ethnic boundaries.

Labour unions became the third source of unity linking people together across the colony. Early efforts to form workers' organisations occurred in urban areas, especially among dock workers in Dar es Salaam. These efforts spread to migrant workers, especially on the sisal estates. Workers faced common issues in wages and working conditions that enabled them to begin to build organisations, again crossing the ethnic boundaries the colonial state tried to build. The Tanganyika Territory African Civil Service Association, formed in 1922 in Tanga, was the first effort by mostly educated people to organise. In 1929 a branch was formed in Dar es Salaam. This organisation gave birth to the African Association-later Tanganyika African Association (TAA) in 1929 formed by a combination of civil servants and urban leaders in the city.

The TAA as an Early Nationalist Organisation

Between 1929 and 1945, the TAA began to create the idea of Tanganyika as a nation. TAA began to collaborate both with unions and with other anti-colonial organisations in other colonies. Gradually it concentrated more and more on territorial affairs, so that by 1945 it came to see itself as a Tanganyikan institution. TAA was non-tribal and non-religious in character. It sought to place itself above other regional and ethnically based organisations that also began to be organised in the years before and after World War II. World War II proved a great catalyst for the organisation. The year 1945 was the turning point for mass mobilisation as TAA began to expand countrywide and to campaign for mass support. In 1939 there were only 9 branches, mostly in urban areas, but by 1939 39 branches had come into existence with 1,780 members. During and after the war, African employment both in urban areas and on estates increased dramatically. Workers faced rising prices and shortages of necessary items including food, and began to both organise and stage strikes.

After World War II, the colonial state both sought to reassert its control over the territory and to promote greater development as a means of both justifying its continued control and supporting the British economy in its recover from the war. People across the territory in turn sought to assert control over their own lives, often against not only state actions but also against Native Authorities perceived as more as agents for the state than protectors of the people. The colonial state initiated a number of rural based development schemes that sought to transform agricultural practices in different parts of the territory. These schemes often included new restrictions on agricultural practices and on the number of livestock people could own. Examples include the Mbulu Development Scheme, the Mlalo Rehabilitation Scheme, the Uluguru Land Usage Scheme, the Iringa Dipping Scheme and the Groundnut Scheme in central and southern Tanganyika. For example, the Usambara TAA branch campaigned against the chief and the Mlalo Rehabilitation scheme. In Kilimanjaro, Joseph Kimalando led the Chagga Citizens Union (later called the Chagga Democratic Party) in a campaign against government chiefs in 1946. In Upare, in 1945 the

Mbiru uprising organised first by the Usangi Sports and Welfare Club led to the establishment of a TAA branch in the district. In 1947 strikes involving dock workers in Dar es Salaam and Tanga, teachers across the territory, salt workers at Uvinza and sisal workers in Tanga broke out. In 1949 the Lake Province Growers Association which later became the Victoria Federation of Cooperative Unions in Usukuma, under Paul Bomani, became an important force linked with TAA. On Mount Meru, the British sought to reorganise land allocation between settlers and the Meru. They want to force the eviction of 3,000 Wameru from Engare Nanyuki to give room to settlers. This led to the formation of the Meru Citizen Union, with Kirilo Japhet as leader and the presentation of the case to the United Nations. TAA sought to link both these protests and the local organisations they created into one national movement.

In 1953 TAA meeting in Dar es Salaam elected a young school teacher recently returned from post-graduate training in Scotland as its new president. Julius Kambarage Nyerere had moved in both anit-colonial and socialist circles while abroad, and he argued for the need to transform TAA into a true anti-colonial nationalist political party. On July 7, 1954 at its meeting in Dar es Salaam, TAA transformed itself to Tanganyika African National Union (TANU).

TANU Leading the Process of Decolonisation

TANU inherited the organisational structure of TAA which it continued to expand both by gaining new members and by bringing regional and ethnic organisations into its fold. TANU and Nyerere positioned the party as a nationalist, secular and non-tribal organisation. It drew support from both Christians and especially from Muslim urban dwellers. It took advantage of popular discontent with colonial initiatives across the colony. Sometimes, these local protests led the party and especially local leaders to support acts that seemed counterproductive by slowing down agricultural improvements, preventing dam building and stopping pest control schemes to mention just a few. TANU had to identify itself with the grievances of the masses, and in the long run it helped build its support throughout the territory. The colonial state attempted to stop TANU activities and proscribed the organisation in a number of districts between 1954 and 1958. By the end of 1954 because of disturbances in Malampaka, Maswa, Musoma and Bukoba, TANU had been proscribed in the whole of Lake Province. In 1955 because of the protests against the Uluguru Land Usage Scheme, TANU was banned in the whole of Morogoro district. A similar pattern occurred in

Kondoa Irangi in 1956, Usambara in 1957 and Iringa in 1958. By 1958 the ban of TANU had been extended to 11 districts.

TANU had to confront the issue of multi-racialism. During the 1950s, the British promoted the idea of multi-racialism as a method of promoting political development in its African colonies while retaining a privileged position for white settlers and British interests. The TAA had always fought against the racial discrimination. The British responded by expanded the membership of its Executive and Legislative Councils to include not only European and Asian members but also Africans chosen by the government itself. By 1951 the political picture was as follows:

Executive Council

Official members	Unofficial members
8	3 Europeans
	1 Asian
	1 African

Legislative Council

Official	Unofficial
15	7 Europeans
	4 Africans
	3 Asians

In the face of continuing agitation by TANU, by 1957 the state introduced the idea of racial parity in representation despite the large African majority in the population (Iliffe, 1997). Officially the colonial state supported formation of the United Tanganyika Party (UTP), mainly by unofficial members of Legico and some chiefs. About the same time multi-racial district councils were created that increased tension in the rural areas. By 1958, TANU had grown to a membership of over 200,000, and called for one-person, one-vote elections and a path to independence. At a January 1958 conference called to consider the question of multi-racial election the British adopted a policy of 3 candidates, one from each group, for each seat in the legislature. In response Zuberi Mtemvu started the African National Congress (ANC) to oppose both the multi-racial and TANU's willingness to work with the colonial government as a means of advancing towards the goal of independence. However, in the 1958-1959 election held under the system neither the UTP nor the ANC won any seats. TANU swept not only the African seats but also elected many Asian and European representatives who supported its cause. In

1959 a further threat to TANU's drive towards independence emerged when a petition in the name of all Muslim of Tanganyika proposed that Tanganyika should not become independent until Muslims in the country attained greater educational progress. While expressing a real concern of many Muslims in Tanganyika, most Muslim leaders, many among the earliest supporters of TANU, opposed any delay in independence. Under constant pressure, the British accepted another election for "responsible government" based on one-person, one-vote principles in 1960. TANU won an overwhelming victory and proceeded to negotiate independence which came on 9th December 1961.

Courtesy of the Tanzania Information Services

A number of factors contributed to the relatively smooth and peaceful progress towards independence in Tanganyika. Most importantly, the anti-colonial movement remained united under the leadership of TAA and then TANU, unlike in other colonies where competing movements often led to conflict among nationalists. This unity in turn had its roots in the lack of dominant ethnic groups and especially in the near universal acceptance of Kiswahili as a common language. On the British side, continuing pressure on their African colonies, especially in the aftermath of the Mau Mau uprising in Kenya, made them more willing to compromise. However, the unity of the nationalist movement in Tanganyika remains the single most important factor in the history of the struggle for *Uhuru*.

Section II: Nationalism in Zanzibar

Introduction

The politics of decolonisation in Zanzibar were more complicated than in Tanganyika for a number of reasons. Most importantly, colonialism had reinforced social and racial divisions within Zanzibar. In the fertile arable land, where clove and coconut plantations were established, most Africans living as squatters on land owned by Arabs or Indians. The British protected, nurtured and respected the Arab elite as the natural legitimate rulers of Zanzibar. By 1948, Africans formed a large majority of about 75% of the population. The African population included the Hadimu who were the indigenous inhabitants of Unguja occupying most of the southern part island, the Tumbatu on the northern part, the Pemba on Pemba and many descended from Africans who had come to the isles in the pre-colonial era or as migrants during the colonial era. The Hadimu claimed to be descendants of Arabs and Africans. The Pemba were indigenous inhabitants of Pemba. Others claimed the title of Shirazi, claiming descent from Persian migrants centuries before. By 1940 the term Shirazi came to be applied more widely to include all groups such as the Hadimu, Tumbatu and Pemba claiming to be indigenous to the Isles as distinct from mainland Africans who were regarded as descendants of slaves and infidels. The Shirazi not only distanced themselves from mainland Africans but also competed among themselves for political influence. Arabs political leaders took the advantage of this division and tried to draw the Shirazi closer to their cause which associated Zanzibar with the coming of independence to the Arab states of the Middle East. In 1948 the Arab population comprised of 18.2% of the total, the second largest group next to Africans. Indians and Goans also accounted for a small but significant part of the population.

Background to Party Politics

Political parties in Zanzibar grew out of ethnic associations organised early in the colonial era. The most significant associations were the Arab Association, the African Association and the Shirazi Association. The Arab Association was formed by rich and influential Arabs in the 1920s to press for compensation for the abolition of slavery; during the 1930s it sought to defend landowners against Indian creditors. Later on the association widened its scope to protect the general privileged position of the Arab community. The African Association was formed in 1934 with most of its supporters from the mainland Africans. It was closely associated with TAA in Tanganyika. It advocated for the welfare of Africans. The Shirazi Association was formed in Pemba in 1939 but later it spread its activities to the rest of the protectorate. It was intended to safeguard interests of indigenous Africans.

The Emergence of Political Parties and National Elections to Independence

The Zanzibar Nationalist Party

This was Arab dominated party, but had an African peasant background. It had its origin in 1953 when a small group of Swahili peasants in the village of Kiembe Samaki formed a political party which they called National Party of the subjects of the Sultan of Zanzibar (NPSS). The move was a protest against the arrest and use of violence against villagers who refused to obey colonial directives of cattle dipping and inoculation. The party advocated multi-racial ideology and demanded independence under the Sultan of Zanzibar. Soon the Arab elite discovered the potential usefulness of the party in advancing their interests in the protectorate. Some of the members of the Arab Association like Muhisin and Amour joined and hijacked NPSS in 1955. They renamed it Zanzibar Nationalist Party and transformed it from its rural peasant base at an Arab dominated urban nationalist movement. Right from the beginning ZNP promoted an ideology of Arab nationalism. Membership was open to all groups. Shortly before the 1957 election the party called for 'freedom now' as its central slogan.

The party stressed the unity of the peoples of Zanzibar but remained dominated by its Arab leadership. Although the party managed to win a good number of Africans' support, many others, both mainlanders and Shirazi, argued that it stood for continued Arab domination of government and organized against it.

The African Association

In 1951-1953 African nationalism on Zanzibar acquired a militant character. The African Association adopted a more militant stance. African civil servants who became active in nationalist politics led the more militant tendency. They formed a small club called Young African Union (YAU) in 1951. It became an affiliated league of the African Association. Its intention sought to move the AA (African Association) to adopt a more militant position towards the colonial government. YAU used its paper *Afrika kwetu* to educate and arouse African nationalist consciousness. The YAU and AA leaders attacked the existing socio-political structure which placed the African in the most disadvantageous position in Zanzibar. YAU attacked African domination by "alien" races and the denial of justice and civil rights on the Isles. It also attacked the system in which the Africans were unrepresented in the Legislative Council and other statutory bodies and government committees. It condemned the denial of education to Africans while favouring the Arabs and other Asians. It attacked the miserable condition of poverty and ignorance in which the Africans lived. YAU also attacked the colonial government policy of treating the Shirazi and the mainland Africans as distinct groups, and thus called for unity.

The YAU and AA's militancy was curtailed by the colonial government's move to prohibit civil servants from participating in politics in 1953. The AA entered a period of dormancy and the Arabs seized that opportunity to move quickly. They used ZNP to demand immediate self-rule under the pretext of multiracial ideology. The colonial government responded to this call by calling the first general election to be held in 1956. Many conditions were imposed upon the election process intended to make it practically impossible for the Africans to secure any seat. One of the restrictions required voters to be able to speak, read or write Kiswahili, Arabic or English. The second restriction required voters to be residents in Zanzibar and had to have lived in their constituency for at least one year. Thirdly, voters were duty bound to be over 25 years of age and must have property worth Shs. 3,000 or an annual income of Shs. 1,500 or property and income amounting to Shs. 3,000 or more. The fourth restriction required that voters have been in continuous government employment for at least 5 years or possess certificate or medals of good performance in war. These awkward conditions denied the vote to the African majority. Africans protested against these extreme unfavourable conditions led to postponement of the elections to the following year.

The Afro-Shirazi Party

As already seen, one serious weakness of the African nationalism in Zanzibar was the lack of unity between the Shirazi and mainlanders. Early in February 1957, in response to the formation ZNP and the scheduled elections in July 1957, the leaders of the African and Shirazi Association met to discuss possibility of forming a joint political party to compete with ZNP. The Zanzibar Shirazi Association branch under Sheikh Thabit Kombo and Ameir Tojo came out in favour of unity. The Pemba Shirazi branch objected the union. The result was formation of Afro Shirazi Union (ASU). This was simply a union of two parties and not a new party. The president of AA Sheikh Abed Aman Karume was elected its chairman while Sheikh Thabitt Kombo became its Secretary General. In July 1957, elections were held in Zanzibar for the first time. ASU won 3 seats (out of 6), Pemba Shirazi party won 2 seats, an Indian Independent one, and ZNP won no seats. Following the victory for ASU, a complete merger of the two parties was effected. It now became Afro Shirazi Party (ASP). The two members of Pemba Shirazi joined forces with ASP but retained a separate identity of as the Pemba Shirazi Union. The result of 1957 elections acted as a morale booster on the part of Africans and supporters of ASP. On the other hand, the Arabs realized that they had no support of the other classes, and thus could not win any elections fairly.

Zanzibar and Pemba Peoples Party

In 1959 internal conflicsct in the ASP's top leadership led to the expulsion of one of its leaders Mr. Ameir Tojo. The two Shirazi representatives from Pemba also resigned from the party. These three leaders formed a new party called the Zanzibar and Pemba Peoples Party (ZPPP). ZPPP sought to avoid the Arab domination ofthe ZNP and at the same time opposed African control in the ASP. 1960 Sir Hilary Blood was appointed Special Commissioner to make constitutional proposals for the future of Zanzibar. He proposed a full elected unofficial majority in an enlarged Legico with a ministerial system under a Chief Minister.

The preparations for the election to this new body caused an atmosphere of tension. The British threatened to ban political meetings.

In January 1961 elections were held and three parties contested with the ASP winning 10 seats, ZNP 9 and ZPPP 3. ZNP and ZPPP formed a coalition government, but two members crossed the floor to join ASP. Thus the two sides had equal numbers in the new body. As a result, the British called new elections in June. They were characterised by tensions leading to violence in the campaign and vote rigging in the counting all over the territory. ASP won 10 seats while the ZPPP and ZNP coalition won 13 seats. Thus the ZPPP and ZNP coalition formed government with Mohamed Shamte, the leader of ZPPP as Prime Minister. ASP complained about rigging and unfairness in the elections demanding its nullification. The British called fresh elections in 1963. In these elections the colonial state increased the number of seats in the areas under the influence of ZNP and ZPPP. ASP polled 87,082 votes (54%) won 13 seats, but because of the allocation of seants ZNP and ZPPP with 47,950 votes (45%) won 18 seats. The ZNP and ZPPP coalition again formed a government. The British granted Zanzibar independence on 10th December 1963. The Sultan became the Head of state and Mohamed Shamte the Prime Minister.

The Zanzibar Revolution and Union with Tanganyika

Frustration by being denied their rights in the elections, the ASP resorted to violence in order to restore African majority rule. While the ASP, led by Karume, tried to direct a movement against the government, popular violence increased. The ASP sought the support of the labour movement on Isles and its ally the Umma Party led by A. M Babu. On January 12, 1964 John Okello led a group of policemen in an attack on the government. The government crumbled, and violence broke out that led to the deaths of over a thousand, mostly Arab and Indian supporters of the government. Karume and a steering committee of 14 members from ASP quickly proclaimed themselves the revolutionary government of Zanzibar, and announced the end of the Sultan's rule. Karume appealed for support from the Tanganyika government. By April, Karume and Nyerere negotiated an agreement to form the United Repulbic of Tanzania on April 26. The Union created a Union government but left Zanzibar's revolutionary government in control of the Isles with wide autonomy.

President Julius Kambarage Nyerere of Tanganyika and President Abeid Amani Karume of Zanzibar handing over official documents of the Union at the State House in Dar es Salaam [Courtesy of the Tanzania Information Services and the National Museum and House of Culture]

President Julius Kambarage Nyerere mixing up soils of Tanganyika and Zanzibar to mark the union of the two countries on 26th April 1964 [Courtesy of the Tanzania Information Services]

Soldiers marching in support of the Union of Tanganyika and Zanzibar [Courtesy of the Tanzania Information Services]

Civilians in Dar es Salaam marching in support of the Union of Tanganyika and Zanzibar [Courtesy of the Tanzania Information Services]

References

Cliffe Lionell and John Saul, eds., *Socialism in Tanzania,* Vol I. Dar es Salaam: Tanzania Publishing House, 1972.

Iliffe, John A *Modern History of Tanganyika*. Cambridge: Cambridge University Press, 1979.

_____. "TANU and the Colonial Office", *Tanzania Zamani*, III, 2, 1997.

Kaniki M. H. Y. ed., *Tanzania under Colonial Rule*. London: Longman, 1980.

Minael-Hosanna Mdundo, *Masimulizi ya Sheikh Thabit Kombo Jecha*. Dar es Salaam: DUP 1999.

Mosare, J. "Background to the Revolution in Zanzibar", in Kimambo and Temu, eds., *A History of Tanzania*. Nairobi: East African Publishing House, 1969.

Okello, John. *Revolution in Zanzibar*. Nairobi: East African Publishing House, 1967.

Sheriff Abdul and E.D. Ferguson, eds., *Zanzibar under Colonial Rule*. London: James Currey, Athens: Ohio University Press, 1991.

Temu, Arnold J. "The Rise and Triumph of Nationalism", in Kimambo, Isaria N and Arnold J.

Temu, eds., *A History of Tanzania*. Nairobi: East African Publishing House, 1969.

PART FIVE

The Post-Independence Period

This last section surveys the post-independence history since the union of Tanganyika and Zanzibar in 1964. Chapter eighteen describes the struggles of the post-independence government situation up to the 1967 adoption of the Arusha declaration as a guiding policy. The early independent government had to rely not just on institutions inherited from the colonial government but also in many cases on personnel. The new government had to ensure the transfer of power and the security of the nation while forging new institutions and an ideology. Struggles over the pace of the process of Africanisation brought tensions among the nationalist leaders.

For the first six years, the government of independent Tanzania struggled to develop the country within the inherited model of development. However, building on the colonial model, plans to develop agriculture and manufacturing based on attraction of investment and aid from the the global north was hindered by political and diplomatic conflicts over Tanzania's support for African liberation, especially in southern Africa. The failure to achieve rapid change led Julius Nyerere to formalise a new set of policies known as the Arusha declaration as a means of extending the nation-building project. By and large, the declaration was a blue print of the nationalist paradigm whose primary goal was to change the direction of social development so that the whole country would advance together. Chapter seventeen describes the early years of independence up to 1967. It is followed by chapter eighteen that provides an analysis of the Arusha declarartion, its associated policies (Socialism and Self-Reliance, and Socialism and Rural Development) and sectoral development following the Arusha declaration including agriculture, industry, and education (Education for Self-Reliance).

Basically, the adoption of *Ujamaa* in 1967 was a way of bringing in a new hope based on ideology. Throughout the 1970s, the ideology seemed to have offered a solution, but towards in the end of the 1970s as series of crises brought the country to a critical point. The Kagera War with Iddi Amin's Uganda, the global oil crises, and recurring droughts led to economic crisis in the 1980s. In response to the crisis, the country adopted economic liberalisation and multi-party politics to meet the demands of global financial institutions in return for economic support for the country. In light of all these developments, chapter nineteen examines the evolution of the neo-liberal economy and multi-party politics in Tanzania from the mid-1980s to the 1990s. It is followed by chapter twenty that sheds light to the transition from neo-colonialism to globalisation. The chapter argues that although Tanganyika and

Zanzibar (now the United Republic of Tanzania) became independent in the 1960s they have nevertheless not abandoned their ties with their colonial masters in economic and political spheres. The current era of global integration makes the country open to multinational corporations, the transfer of technology, expertise, and culture.

Chapter Seventeen

The Early Years of Independence up to 1967

Introduction

Tanganyika achieved her independence on 9th December 1961 but political independence did not alter economic dependence. Generally, the nation lacked sufficient trained manpower to replace all the expatriates (usually former colonial officials) who held senior positions in government. The inherited economy was largely dependent on the developed countries as markets for export of cash crops, the source of critical imports and foreign investment. Rugumamu (1997) identified four problems which the nationalist government confronted soon after taking power. The first problem was that the country inherited not only a structurally weak and dependent economy, but more importantly, given a weak skilled manpower base, it came to rely on ex-colonial officers to administer the new nation. Secondly, the nationalist government inherited a colonial education system that did not encourage analytical thinking or provide the opportunity to train specialists for remedying the pressing national problems. Thirdly, the nationalist government administration started with a weak institutional and organisational capacity to define, defend, and develop comprehensive long term development plans, and strategies for the new nation. Finally, on attaining independence, the new government had to be run by politicians who lacked the necessary functional skills and experience to manage the various apparatus of the modern state.

Such problems could easily be noticed due to the fact that under British colonial rule, no government employees could join or participate in any political association, and more seriously, the senior administrative posts were restricted to white personnel. It was a neo-colonial state per se that still depended on the metropole to carry out its socio-economic and political functions. Such dependence on former colonial institutions carried within threats to independence and accountability of the new government. In the absence of national experts, former colonial officers influenced national policies, and plans and helped select and design projects and programmes. Independence brought the challenge of nation building where colonial policy had sought to keep the people divided by ethnicity. Nationalist leaders found themselves confronted with new tasks of nation building in a politically hostile and economically competitive international environment.

Nation Building

Lionel Cliffe (1969) identified securing the transfer of power, defending the security of the nation, forging new institutions, and developing an ideology and development strategies that promoted improved lives for all as the four most important issues facing the new nation. The transfer of power was the first and immediate task for the nationalist government. This process included the Africanisation of government and indeed many other institutions. Many in the new country demanded that administration, political system, civil service, commerce, industry and agriculture immediately replace Europeans and Asians with Africans in all positions. Those who could take new positions benefited greatly but sometimes became highly corrupt rather than being leaders who were politically and economically responsible to the people. The question of the security of the nation was the other issue which was at the heart of the nation building process. Serious concerns for security began in 1964 after an army mutiny by soldiers demanding more rapid promotion of Africans into the highest ranks of the military to replace British officers who had remained to assist with training the country's new armed forces. British troops were called in and disarmed the mutineers. A serious reorganisation of the army took place including replacement of both commissioned and non-commissioned soldiers with new men from the party and TANU Youth League. In 1964 the trade union movement was also restructured and as a result a single National Union of Tanganyika Workers (NUTA) was established to replace the independent unions and the TFL (Tanganyika Federation of Labour). The same year the government announced a policy of non-alignment to avoid cold war politics. On 26 April 1964 Tanganyika and Zanzibar united to form the United Republic of Tanzania. Tanzania became a leading supporter of the liberation struggles during this period. In recognition of this commitment OAU made Dar es Salaam the headquarters of the Liberation Committee, and Tanzania hosted representatives and even training facilities for nationalist movement in Mozambique, Namibia, Zimbabwe, and South Africa

The new nation had to forge new institutions to ensure all citizens had access to services and benefited from government action. In particular, TANU sought to establish itself as the sole representative of the people in the name of promoting development. In 1963 the government abolished the positions of local chiefs and the party extended its structures and organisation to the grass root level. In 1965 the government instituted a one party system and banned all other political parties. Nyerere worried greatly about the emergence of social differentiation in the years immediately after independence. Africanisation created new elites who used the wealth they had accrued from leadership positions to obtain a high standard of living and invest in more income generating activities such as rental property. They also acquired shares as well as directorships in private companies. A new bureaucratic class of African elite emerged. The Arusha Declaration of 1967 grew in part out of concerns about the inequity that had developed since independence.

Nyerere developed a new ideology based on the tenets of socialism and self-reliance called *Ujamaa na Kujitegemea*. There were three other challenges which pre-occupied leaders in the 1960s with respect to nation building. The first challenge stemmed from gaining the confidence of the people and restoring African dignity. This could be achieved by getting rid of discrimination in social services, economy and politics, but also by Africanising the civil service. The second challenge was about the differences that had developed between TANU and the labour unions was the other important challenge. TANU and the labour unions had worked mutually together in struggling for independence, but after independence clashes started to emerge particularly on question of wage increase. In 1964, the government suspended Tanganyika Federation of Labour and affiliated unions and in its place created the National Union of Tanganyika Workers (NUTA) with its executive was appointed by the President. Following the Union of Tanganyika and Zanzibar in 1964 the question of creating an effective means of managing the union became a central issue. The creation of the single party state meant that each side of the union initially had its own single party – TANU and ASP.

Eventually, Nyerere forced the two parties to merge into a new party, *Chama cha Mapinduzi* – CCM – The Party of Revolution. The third challenge to the nation building project concerned the question of nation's foreign policy. As stipulated by Nyerere the pillars of Tanzania's foreign policy included protection of the integrity and security of the country. The country embarked on supporting for African liberation and freedom from racist oppression, supported the United Nations in its search for peace and justice, promoted African unity, and non-alignment. The policy of non-alignment was geared towards promotion of peace, justice, and unity, as well as harnessing external resources for national development. Given the political concerns which the newly independent government became preoccupied with, Rugumamu (1997, p.110) argues that little time and efforts were devoted to assessing critically the forms and content of national economy and it relation to the national income system. There existed a strong and mistaken belief among the top state leadership which assumed that actors in the world economy played fairly and that the global economy worked in the interests of participants. These assumptions made leaders accept uncritically foreign advice on economic policies and development plans.

Development Planning

In 1961 the World Bank assessed resources available in Tanganyika and made recommendations on how to develop those resources and their financial implications. The World Bank report became the basis for the Three Year Development Plan (1961-1964) and the First Five Year Development Plan (1964-1969). The World Bank had begun this study at the invitation of Britain. The First Three Year Development Plan (1961-1964) represented an attempt by Britain to ensure that British colonial policies and interest continued to operate in the post-colonial period with as little interruption as possible. The plan was based on that traditional theory which stipulated that rapid economic growth and development in the South would only be through infusion and diffusion of capital, expertise and technology from the North. Foreign capital was also expected to reduce the gap between the North and South. The three-year development plan and others that followed were largely result of foreign advisors and consultancy reports. The report focusing economic development on agriculture and foreign investment. It also recommended the country embark on import substitution industrialisation and processing of raw materials. The report also recommended the institutionalisation of a liberal investment code, the promotion of private sector, and government focus on the provision of social and economic infrastructure. The plan assumed that improved socio-economic infrastructure would create a conducive investment climate attracting private investors to Tanzania. The new government did not have the capacity to generate comparable quality studies on which to base its alternative policy proposals or the requisite capacity to improve upon those made by foreign agencies (Rugumamu 1997, p. 114). The new government set about to create its own blueprint for development in its first Five Year Plan. This plan sought to end the country's reliance on the export of primary commodities by creating and promoting industry and agriculture. The plan depended heavily on foreign aid largely from Britain and Germany. This dependency proved a fatal weakness to the goals of the plan as diplomatic clashes between Tanzania and Britain and West Germany, and later with the United States severely curtailed the amount of investment in the country. Tanzania clashed with Britain over the Unilateral Declaration of Independence (UDI) in 1965 by the white minority government in Southern Rhodesia, supported by Britain. The British took no action to restore majority rule in the colony. Tanzania was one of the African countries that broke off diplomatic relations with Britain in reaction. Britain responded by cutting aid. Tanzania lost around 19.5 million dollars of aid (Rugumamu 1997, p. 120).

Tanzania clashed with West Germany over Tanzania's decision to recognise two Germany (East and West Germany) and her intentions to welcome both German governments to be represented in Tanzania. From those disputes Tanzania leadership learned at least three crucial lessons. First, it became increasingly apparent that relations among actors in the international system were chiefly government by distribution of power among them. The domination of the South by the North became obvious. Secondly, it became obvious that it is unrealistic to plan national development by relying on foreign aid and those donors and recipient interests are incompatible. Finally, aid was instrument of foreign policy and that unconditional reliance on foreign aid was bound to compromise national sovereignty.

References

Coulson, Andrew. *Tanzania: A Political Economy*. Oxford, Clarendon, 1982.

Cliffe, Lionel. "From Independence to Self-reliance", in Kimambo, Isaria and Anold Temu, eds., *A History of Tanzania*. Dar es Salaam: East African Publishing House, 1969.

Ghai, D.P. (1974), "Some Aspects of Social and Economic Progress and Policies in East Africa, 1961 to 1971", in Ogot B.A. ed., *Zamani: A Survey of East African History*. Nairobi: East African Publishing House, 1973.

Havnevik, K.J. *Tanzania: The Limit to Development from Above*. Dar es Salaam: Mkuki na Nyota, 1993.

Maliyamkono, T.L. et.al. *The Challenge for Tanzania's Economy*. Portsmouth, NH: Heinemann Educational Books, 1964.

Rugumamu, Severine. *Lethal Aid: The Illusion of Socialism and Self-Reliance in Tanzania*. Trenton, NJ: Africa World Press, 1997.

Chapter Eighteen

The Arusha Declaration and Sectoral Development

Section I: The Arusha Declaration

Introduction

Given the problems facing Tanzania in the immediate aftermath of independence and union, Julius Nyerere sought to find a way of mobilising the people of Tanzania in comprehensive strategy for promoting humane and equitable development. Drawing on his ready of political economy literature and seeking to adapt those ideas to what he thought of as Tanzanian and African reality, he developed the ideas that became *Ujamaa*. He articulated these in a policy document that became known as the Arusha Declaration, designed as a grand statement of the ideology and a guide for its implementation.

Birth of the Arusha Declaration

Nyerere presented his ideas to the National Executive Council of TANU in February 1967. The Declaration declared the intent to build a socialist society in Tanzania. It also contained a critique of the post-colonial situation the country found itself in. It aimed to challenge the capitalist development which Nyerere had already criticized since the early years of independence. It declared that the goal of the nation was socialism and self-reliance. By socialism, the declaration meant public ownership of the means of production, distribution and consumption. This required a greater interventionist role of the state. It also required mutual cooperation by people for their socio-economic survival. It argued that people in rural Tanzania should live in villages where they would have access to social services such as health and education and work cooperatively. The policy of self-reliance had internal and external dimensions. Internally it sought to mobilise domestic resources, land and people and minimise excessive dependence on foreign aid. Self-reliance would safeguard Tanzanian independence and freedom (Nyerere, 1968, p. 248). Externally it aimed at empowering the state and its institutions to establish international cooperation which would facilitate economic development as well as enhance political autonomy (Rugumamu, 1997, p. 123). So at the heart of the Arusha Declaration was the internalisation of socio-economic development. It did not however ignore the role of external aid. The government admitted that it was unable to provide the basic needs of people and the investment required for development. But it also stipulated that aid from foreign countries should not constitute the basis for Tanzanian development. The Declaration underscored that only aid that did not endanger the country's freedom to make key policy decisions and consistent with the policy of socialism and self-reliance should be accepted. The Declaration generally underlined the dangers of relying on foreign assistance, emphasised hard work and agricultural development. It put less emphasis on industrial and urban development (Havnevik, 1993, p.42). The party adopted the Declaration on February 4, 1967 as its official statement of principles and goals for the nation.

In September 1967 Nyerere and the party issued a second policy document known as *Socialism and Rural Development*. It aimed at promoting *ujamaa*. The concept of *ujamaa* implied a commitment to a collective way of rural production, life and society. Other related policy documents issued by Nyerere and the party included *Education for Self-Reliance* issued in March 1967, *TANU Guidelines* which set standards for persons in the leadership of the party and government in February 1971 and the decentralisation policy of May 1972. The main outlines of the Tanzania socialist programme were public ownership and control of the major means of production, self-reliance and elimination of exploitation, establishment of democracy and equality, the establishment of socialist agriculture in Ujamaa Villages, the reaffirmation of party supremacy and the spread of welfare services to all areas.

General analysis of the Declaration

Maliyamkono, (et al, 1986) argues that the Declaration was based on a broader nationalist paradigm and that its primary aim was to change the direction of social development so that the TANU leadership, the bureaucrats and the social base of the nationalist movement would grow closer together. It sought to control the use of political powers by the party and government and ensure that the people benefited. The policies that emphasised equality and self-reliance meant to open a space for consensus which Nyerere feared was disappearing. The Declaration appealed more to the people because its language was not only economic and political, but echoed religious and cultural chords (Frostin, 1988, p.1). Between 1967 and 1973 featured a great deal of experimentation in policy. The government sought both to continue to support Africanisation while at the same time moving towards a socialist organisation for the economy.

The second five-year development plan (1969-1974) aimed at translating the Declaration into concrete policy programmes. State intervention in the economy increased dramatically. The most significant initiative undertaken was the policy of villagisation. The government sought to expand social services such as health, water, transport and education and promote communal production. The government also moved towards the nationalisation of all sectors of the economy. It took over many businesses including banking, insurance, and manufacturing firms, creating parastatal companies to run them.

The TANU guidelines of February 1971 emphasised the role of the vanguard party. The party was to take the leading role in directing society and the economy. The party claimed the power to set national goals, organise people, supervise the implementation of party's policies, supervise conduct of leaders and guide people's actions. The party became the central authority and key player in economic and political as well as social life of Tanzania.

The youths who walked from Karatu to the State House in Dar es Salaam in support of the Arusha declaration and to praise Mwalimu Nyerere for detaining those plotting against the government, 18th September 1967 [Courtesy of the Tanzania Information Services]

Mwalimu addressing students of the University College, Dar es salaam, (now University of Dar es Salaam) at the State House on 29th September 1967 [Courtesy of the Tanzania Information Services]

Mwalimu, with a symphathising face, is greeting the old Haruni Hassan (75 years old) who walked for 38 days from Tabora to State House in Dar es Salaam in order to congratulate Mwalimu for establishing the Arusha declaration and for detaining those who were opposing it, 18th September 1967 [Courtesy of the Tanzania Information Services]

Students from three Primary Schools who walked from Kilwa to Dar es Salaam in support of the Arusha Declaration 22nd September 1967. [Courtesy of the Tanzania Information Services]

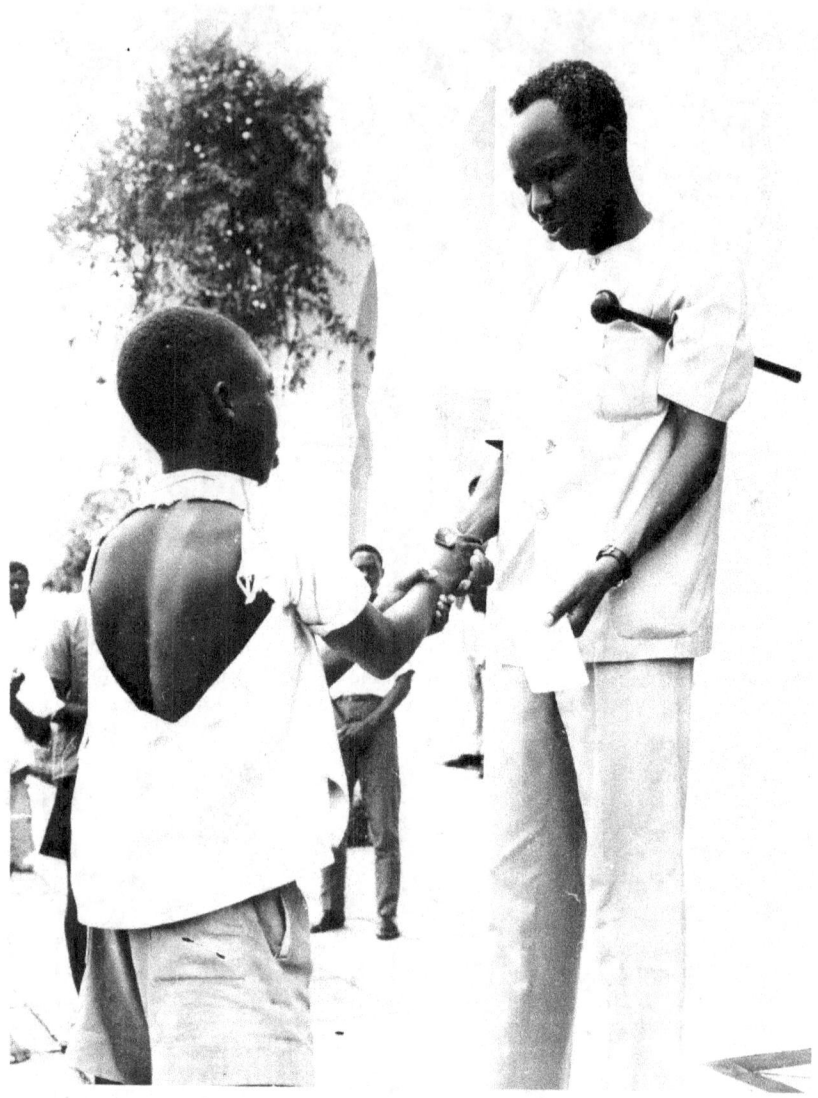

A primary school pupil was among the many youths who walked from Segera in Handeni, Tanga in support of the Arusha Declaration. [Courtesy of the Tanzania Information Services]

Section II: Sectoral Development After the Arusha Declaration

Agriculture

Socialism and Rural Development

This policy statement outlined the process of building socialism in rural areas and more importantly the formation of Ujamaa villages where people would live together and cooperate mutually in agricultural production. The Second Five Year Development Plan favoured Ujamaa Villages in allocating social services like health, schools, dispensaries and water. It aimed to encourage people to live in those villages. Movement into the villages was slow in many parts of the country. In 1973, state intervention in rural areas took a new turn. Between 1973 and 1976 there was intensive implementation of villagisation. The government used force and other coercive measures to require people to move into the new villagesw. Between 1973 and 1975 the number of people in nucleated villages jumped from 2,028,164 to 9,140,229. The villagisation process continued and by 1980 there were 14,179,299 people or 91.4 per cent of the rural population in 8269 villages (Maliyamkono et.al, 1986, p.42). Gradually, the state dropped the emphasis on communal production but continued to require people to register in villages.

New agricultural producer price policies were introduced in 1973. These aimed at influencing agricultural production raising producer prices for food crops so as to enhance food production. Prices for export crops remained low. Farmers' organizations had no say in price determination and the essence of this was the transfer of financial surplus from the farmers to the state (Havnevik, 1993, p. 48). Agricultural marketing also faced major new initiatives from the state. From 1972 government established crop authorities to control the marketing of almost all crops. In the process of villagisation, the government simply banned the cooperative unions in 1976. Instead, each village was made a primary society and authorities were responsible for crop purchases, processing and sale. The government also sought and received a fairly large flow of foreign aid directed at rural development. Instead of foreign capital being channelled through the government or its financial institutions such as Tanzania Rural Development Bank, as it used to be, now foreign capital began to be fell more directly and this emphasised intensive farming systems, crop rotation, soil conservation and integrated crop and animal production. These programmes also emphasised credits for farm implements and extension services. In 1976 National Agriculture Development Project (NAP) was established by the government. Kleemier (1981) argues that, to implement NAP, the government invited comprehensive development plan for regions from donor organisations. The country was thus parceled out to different donors, some of whom only participated either in the planning or the financing stage, while others participated in both.

Despite the increased attention and investment, many rural regions in Tanzania entered a crisis in the 1970s. Villagisation disrupted agricultural production in many areas as people were forced to move away from existing farm or range lands and into villages located by government officials near transportation. Drought followed which reduced grain production by as much as 30 per cent. Famine struck in some regions as the government destroyed existing marketing systems and could not always distribute food aid in adequate amounts. In 1974-1975 Tanzania imported 550,000 tonnes of maize, 210,000 tonnes of wheat, 130,000 tonnes of rice at a cost of over Tshs. 1.4 billion, ten times the amount of the preceding four years (Maliyamkono, et. al, 1986, p. 41). The tendencies towards agricultural stagnation in Tanzania during the 1970s were the only most serious of the economic problem emerging. Maliyamkono et al, show that by early 1980s, agriculture, hailed as the focus of the country's development effects, had been ignored. Exports declined. For example, sisal declined to 61,200 tonnes in 1983 which represented 31% of the 1961 volume. Basic food crops such as maize, rice and wheat also declined, and the country had to import food. These two decades after the Arusha Declaration (1967) agricultural output signified decline and stagnation.

Industry

The Arusha Declaration favoured nationalisation of the major means of production and exchange so that the state controlled them on behalf of the people. But nationalisation was to be associated with compensation for investors, retention of foreign management and the continuation of partnership arrangements between pubic parastatals and foreign firms in order to facilitate technology transfer and training of Tanzanians. What we can realise from nationalisation, therefore, is that it did not signal total disengagement from capitalism. The country embraced capitalist elements and this embrace indirectly translated in the continuation of the drain of surplus capital to the metropolitan countries. More importantly it signified the failure of government to establish total control over finance, production, distribution and consumption.

Industrially, the Arusha Declaration de-emphasised industrialisation as a path for development because Tanzania did not have the resources to invest in industrialisation and the country's foreign policy sought to limit external dependence. That is why the second five-year development plan contained no comprehensive plan for industrialization. However in 1973, the government established Small Scale Industry Development Organisation (SIDO) to support domestic industries. Such industries could essentially depend on utilising local resources, develop technical skills in the villages, emphasise self-reliance, providing extra economic activity in rural areas, using small capital and reducing rural urban imbalance. In 1973 the government invited economists from Harvard Institute of Industrial Development to make recommendations on the long term industrial strategy. The consultation resulted into a long term industrial strategy (1975-95). It emphasised the provision of basic need goods for Tanzania, thedevelopment of capital goods industries, the expansion of agro-processing industries, training and research and the promotion small scale industries especially in rural areas.

Foreign aid to industrial sector increased from 8% annually of total aid in the period 1974-76 to 29% in 1977-80 (Collier, 1987) and during the same period foreign aid to agriculture dropped from 18 to 11 per cent (Havnevik, 1993). Both Tanzania state and its donors progressively increased investment in industrial development at the expense of agriculture. Furthermore, private industrial capital continued to play a key role in Tanzania development even after the Arusha Declaration. Industry suffered from low productivity of labour and capital (Skarstein and Wangwe, 1986). An important factor for the problem in industry was agriculture's inability either to generate sufficient foreign exchange for imports of spare parts and raw materials required by industries, or to supply domestic processing factories with raw materials. For instance, the eleven cashew nut processing factories which were established (with World Bank and Italian support) in the 1970s had a rated annual capacity of processing 103,000 tons. This was below the actual collection figures at the time. By the end of the decade agriculture could only provide about 40,000 tonnes of cashew nut annually, which implied that six of the 11 factories never processed any cashew nuts at all (Havnevik, 1988, p. 32). Yet Tanzania had to repay the World Bank loans, if the country wanted to continue to receive international assistance and loans.

Assessing industrial development, Maliyamkono (et al, 1986) argued that the import dependence of industry and the lack of funds to pay for those inputs had severely retarded industrial production which in 1983 operated at only 30% of the capacity and contributed only 5.8% of GNP. The stagnation of industrial production helped increase the country's trade deficit which reached Shs. 5484 million in 1983, a 20 percent average annual increase over the preceding decade. Poor performance in the economic sector as reflected by agriculture and industry in the two decades after the Arusha Declaration meant that the country's autonomy, independence and viability were challenged. Its ability to provide social services was insecure. In the face of such constraints, dependence on borrowing from foreign multilateral organisations and private sources which had been considered undesirable seemed the only solution. The government embarked on heavy borrowing from external sources of capital. Thus, in 1967 foreign aid was only Shs 100 million. This figure grew at an average annual rate of 32 per cent between 1967 and 1983 when it reached Tshs. 6436 million (Maliyamkono et al, 1986). This signified a contradiction in the policy of self-reliance. Despite the struggles to be self-reliant economically, Tanzania was becoming increasingly dependent on foreign assistance.

Education

The direction of development posed by the Arusha Declaration required a change in the education system in Tanzania towards one which would prepare learners to acquire socialist values and be integrated to the community. Education for Self Reliance (ESR) was the ideological instrument legitimised the state policy of socialism and self-reliance as well as the Arusha Declaration at the political level. ESR published in 1967 was a reaction against colonial construction of the education system. It was an attempt by Tanzanian leadership to conceptualise its own educational agenda which was inward looking and tapping the vast knowledge of the people in the rural areas (Roy-Campbell, 1991). An important aspect of ESR was the attempt to make agriculture an integral part of the curriculum. Recognising that Tanzania remained basically a rural country, based mainly on agricultural production, the leadership sought to produce individuals with healthy attitudes towards agriculture. ESR was egalitarian and demanded the provision of basic education for all members of the society. The document analysed the system of and attitudes towards education as they had evolved in Tanganyika from the colonial period to post-colonial period. Education for self-reliance posed a critique of the inadequacies and inappropriateness of colonial education. It outlined the kind of society Tanzania was trying to build, a democratic socialist state and proposed changes that were designed to transform the education system in order to make it more relevant in serving the needs and aims of socialist society with a predominantly rural economy. The changes in the content of the curriculum itself was one of the targets of ESR. It called for selecting and organising content which was relevant the society and which could prepare learners for the life and revival of society. The curriculum should enable people to act upon their environment and change it for their benefit. ESR demanded a change in teaching, learning activities and interaction between teachers and learners. It called for learning by doing, and the integration of theory and practice through experimentation. It involves developing inquiring minds and self-confidence. It also called for change in the social interaction between teachers and learners and other members of the community. ESR demanded integration of schools with the community. Schools were to be both social and economic communities, and they had to contribute to their upkeep. Schools should develop positive attitudes of learners towards work. ESR called for the re-examination for the purpose of evaluation of student performance. It called for the reduction in the importance of examinations because they do not get across power to reason, character to or willingness to serve. They encouraged grassroot learning. The biggest initiative was the implementation of Universal Primary Education (UPE). Mbunda (1979, p. 93) shows that in the Second Five Year Development Plan (1969-1974) the government proposed a progressive increase in standard one enrolment with the percentage of enrolment rising from less that 50% in 1969 to universal entry by 1989. The 1974 TANU National Executive Meeting passed what came to be known as Musoma Resolution which reinforced the educational directives laid out in ESR. Schools were explicitly directed to integrate work into the curriculum. Primary school leaving examinations were decentralised so that they could be more relevant to the pupils' environment. Evaluations would re-emphasise the assessment of the pupils' day to day achievements. The Musoma Resolution decreed that within three years arrangements must be completed to make primary education accessible to all children of school age. Government policy also emphasised adult education. Starting 1969 adult education got a boost when it was transferred from the Ministry of Rural Development and Regional Administration to the Ministry of Education. Nyerere announced that 1970 would be the year of adult education. Financial and human resources were diverted to Adult Education. It was a means of making peasants understand socialism and self-reliance as well as rural development. Primary schools became centres for adult programmes as well. Despite the emphasis on education, and the great expansion of primary education the economic crisis that began in the 1970s took its toll on the sector. Resources for the education programmes declined. By the 1980s both UPE and Adult Education remained as goals, but lack of resources made schools reinstitute fees and school enrollment declined. Only after 2000, could the government move more resources into education and make the goal of UPE a realistic one for the country.

References

Collier, P. *Aid and Economic Performance in Tanzania*. 1987.

Maliyamkono T. L et al. *The Challenge for Tanzania's Economy*. Portsmouth, NH: Heinemann Educational Books, 1986.

Havnevik, Kjell. *Tanzania: The Limit to Development from Above*. Dar es Salaam: Mkuki na Nyota Publishers, 1993.

Mbunda, F. L. "Primary Education since 1961" in Hinzen, H and Hurdsforfer, V.H. (eds.), *The Tanzanian Experience*. Hamburg: Unesco Institute for Education, 1982.

Nyerere, Julius. "Arusha Declaration: Socialism and Self Reliance", in Nyerere, *Freedom and Socialism*. Dar es Salaam: Oxford University Press, 1968.

Rugumamu, M. *Lethal Aid: The Illusion of Socialism and Self-Reliance*. Trenton, NJ: Africa World Press, 1997.

Skarstein, Rune and Wangwe, Samuel. *Industrial Development in Tanzania: Some Critical Issues*. Uppsala: Scandinavian Institute for African Studies; Dar es Salaam, TPH, 1986.

Chapter Nineteen

Economic Liberalisation and Multiparty Politics

Introduction
The inherited colonial model failed to meet expectations of quick development in order to overcome problems inherited from the colonial regime. The adoption of *Ujamaa* in 1967 was a way of bringing in a new hope based on ideology. For most of the 1970s, this seemed to have offered solution, but towards in the end of the 1970s the hope disappeared. There was a deep crisis which started towards the end of the 1970s and became deeper and deeper in the early years of the 1980s. Economic liberalisation beginning mid-1980s was a response to the crisis which had touched many aspects of Tanzania society. By the end of the 1980s many inside and outside the country began to call for a return to plural politics. As the country was forced to adopt economic liberalization, it also faced demands for political liberalisation.

The Late 1970s Economic Crisis
According Mboya S. D. Bagachwa, the economic crisis in Tanzania a decline in economic growth in the real GDP from 5.1% between 1970-1976 to 1.2% between 1980-1985, mirrored by declining per capita income growth from 2.5% between 1965-1970 to 1.6% between 1980-1985, soaring inflation rates of less than 10% per annum between 1970-76 to 31% between 1980-1985 rising budget deficits to 19% of GDP in 1979 and deterioration of balance of payment from a surplus of US

Dollar 137 million in 1977 to deficit of US Dollar 395 million in 1985 (Bagachwa, 1991, p. 45-46). The economic crisis reflected a decline in both industry and agriculture. Furthermore, budgetary constraints increased as Tanzania was forced to spend a lot of its revenues to pay for increased costs of oil supplies after 1973 and the 1979 war with Iddi Amin's Uganda. The end result of the crisis the state's capacity to meet expectations of its people declined dramatically. Inefficient state economic management and the worsening terms of trade for Tanzania further drove the crisis. As the country struggled to pay for its imports, and shortages of essential goods spread, it had to turn to the multilateral institutions that oversaw the world economy for assistance. The World Bank and IMF and other donor agencies pushed the state to concede more leverage to private entrepreneurs, non-governmental organisations and other civil organisations at the expense of the welfare state. Economic liberalisation constituted one of the efforts of addressing the crisis.

Economic Liberalisation

One of the results of adoption of *Ujamaa* was state control of all economic activities. Under the economic crisis the state failed to meet requirements of the people. Hardships caused by lack of essential goods and rationing of food and other essential items caused long queues especially in urban areas. Economic liberalisation meant the reopening of retail trade and importation to the private sector. Such actions included import trade liberalisation, devaluation of the shilling, the introduction of school fees, the removal of subsidies on consumer goods and a reduction in the state workforce which led to the widespread retrenchment of workers. Some of these policies had the effect of undermining the earlier import substitution industry policy as domestic industries began to face competition from foreign products. While liberalisation of the economy was going hand in hand with efforts to restructure the economy under the influence of IMF and World Bank, the real effect was on individual citizens who began to assert themselves in the bid "to brace through the crisis in order to make a living" (Mmuya and Chaligha, 1992, p.16).

During the crisis (1980-1985), the government extended permits for access to state controlled food supplies inconsistently and often corruptly. Equality became only a slogan. A new basis of struggling for survival began to form. With the liberalisation of the economy from the mid-1980s there followed a liberalisation of ideas and institutional arrangements which supported them. Economic and business groups which included traders, industrial producers in towns and farmers. While economic in character, these groups also had political interests. Some big businesses began to sponsor political activities. Grassroots associations which range from local development agencies to non-governmental organisations spread throughout the country. Of the 168 non-governmental organisations (NGOs) registered by 1990, 80% were registered between 1984 and 1990. Some of the opposition political groups come from these organisations. Another phenomenon was the emergence of religious organisations. From the mid-1980s there was upsurge of both Islamic and Christian groups—some of them with forms of fanaticism. All of these indicated that in the face of the crisis, people began to look for alternative ways of understanding the world.

Political Liberalisation

Many people see the collapse of the Soviet Union and Eastern European regimes as the main source of introduction of multi-partyism in Tanzania and many other African states. The main reason for such intimation is the timing. Mikhail Gorbachev introduced *Perestroika* (or restructuring) and *Glasnost* (or openness) and started the political upheavals of 1989-90 that led to the collapse of the USSR and the Communist block. Monopolistic politics became a thing of the past. Shortly after the end of the Cold War, Tanzania initiated debate about abandoning the single party system. CCM was fast enough to learn from the development. Nyerere as Chairman of CCM initiated the debate in 1990. But in reality there was a long historical background to this growth of support for pluralism in politics. In the liberation period, the single party had become an important source of strength in unity but in time of crisis its inflexibility and lack of capacity to act quickly became frustrating. It became more bureaucratic and unable to act to solve problems of the people. The changing perception about the nature of society and politics appeared. The original idea of the leadership's image of simplicity and committed service was replaced by images of conflict, tension, greed and self-interest.

The intensity of the crisis appeared more visibly from the mid-1980s. It was indicated by three major features. The first was the policy shifts and turns resulting in pressures to give up its basic pillars of policy direction. In 1987, after almost two years of the first Economic Recovery Programme, CCM came up with 15 years Party Programme for Economic and Social Development. The two policies were wholly opposed. But while the government programme had budget that of CCM did not. The party itself had to finally give in to the new policies and their philosophical basis when it had to rework its Ujamaa formulation in February 1991 under the banner of the Zanzibar Proclamation. The second feature was the bureaucratic impact to which we have already referred. The third feature was budgetary constraints which reduced the capacity of the government to finance essential projects and services. The crisis of the state eventually drove the country towards multiparty politics. All these factors were internal; the collapse of Soviet Union and Eastern Europe was an external factor which brought about the timing. But there was another external factor which preceded it. This was Western pressures. The Western world had all along opposed single party system. Also for ideological and strategic grounds, they would prefer to see proliferation of the Western type of political regimes. So through pressures exerted from state to state relations and through the activities of IMF and World Bank, and influence of individual donor agencies, Tanzania faced pressure to allow opposition parties and free expression of ideas. Thus, in July 1992 Tanzania introduced legislation giving freedom of political association as a basic framework for development of multipartyism and hence democracy. It is interesting to note how fast this system was taken up. As of December 1992, 34 political organisations (or proto-political parties) had been formed. At their peak in 1993, the groups reached 51. By May 1, 1994 the number had declined and the political parties that received permanent registration became 13.

References

Iba Der Thiam and James Mulira. "Africa and the Socialist Countries", *General History of Africa*, Vol VIII. 1993.

Mmuya, Max and Amon Chaligha. *Towards Multiparty Politics*. Dar es Salaam: DUP, 1992.

Mmuya and Chaligha. *Political Parties and Democracy in Tanzania*. Dar es Salaam: DUP, 1994.

Chapter Twenty

From Neo-Colonialism to Globalisation

Introduction

The integration of Tanzanian communities into the international capitalist system developed by Western countries happened in four phases, each of which seemed to cause more hardship on the communities themselves while making the Western countries involved stronger and stronger economically. The reasons should be obvious if we realise that the capitalist system is exploitative; it always strives to maximise profits. During the competitive stage Tanzanian communities were drawn into the system through the caravan trade controlled from Zanzibar. This short period was succeeded by the monopoly phase of capitalism known as imperialism which ushered in the colonial period. After independence we have noted the period of frustration which continued to be more intense as time passed. Political independence did not mean economic independence. The phase has normally been known as neo-colonialism. Finally, the West came to see that capitalism was in complete control of global economic activities and advocated globalisation. The first two phases have been discussed. This final chapter covers the last two phases.

Neo-Colonialism

The concept of neo-colonialism describes the kind of relationship which remained after colonised territories received political independence from the metropolitan powers. Flag independence left most economic relations undisturbed. The economic characteristics of the colonial state were inherited by the independent state (See Chinweizu, 1993, p. 770-771). Neo-colonialism has another form which makes its exploitative apparatus more oppressive; this is multilateralism. It originated from the Bretton Woods agreement of 1945 which created under American leadership three primary economic institutions: International Monetary Fund (IMF), the World Bank (WB) and the General Agreement on Tariffs and Trade (GATT). Starting in 1947, the IMF sought to manage difficulties posed by balance of payments surpluses and deficits from international trade. The World Bank went into operation in 1946 with the task of encouraging "capital investment for the reconstruction and development of its member countries". The third institution, GATT which began its work in 1948 was intended to promote "multilateral trade through minimising trade barriers, reducing import tariffs and quotas, and discouraging preferential trade agreements between countries" (Chinweizu, 1993, p.772). As it can be seen the system came out of World War II intending to strengthen the international capitalist system. The United Nations (the UN) was the political forum for international affairs. Later the creation of the European Economic Community (EEC) and the Organisation for Economic Co-operation and Development (OECD) expanded multilateral trade beyond the colonial monopolistic system by the time Tanzania and other African states gained independence.

Neo-colonialism was a new form of colonialism in which a colonised African state found itself dependent not only on the former colonising power, but now was open to pressures from a number of multilateral organisations as well as multinational trading organisations. This was happening at the time independent African states remained dependent on the inherited colonial economic system with its emphasis on production of cash crops for export. In Tanzania, like many other African states, political independence came with an expectation of rising standards of living, increasing incomes, improving social services and provision of good infrastructure. In order to import what was required from the metropole to maintain satisfactory standards of living, more foreign exchange was required. The colonial system of emphasising cash crop for export had to be maintained and intensified.

As years passed, the rapid transformation in development failed to materialise. Foreign investment and foreign aid did not come as expected. The standard of living was not rising because incomes were falling and national debt was mounting. The need for foreign exchange was increasing. The independent state inherited the colonial structure which could not easily be transformed. The economy was still grossly dependent on the outside world despite political independence. The expanded metropole of the West was operating in a formula to continue to strengthen capitalist exploitation in its relationship with the periphery now considered the "Third World. Tanzania may have suffered more because of its radical liberal political position in the 1960s, but all African states faced the same kind of hardship. The Western recipe for development was intended to deepen the level of dependence. *Ujamaa* was introduced in 1967 as a way of breaking the cycle of dependence. Clearly socialism was not the road accepted by the West; African states which chose this method were treated harshly especially since this was the period of "cold war." The reaction of the West was also shaped by need to protect investments in the face of nationalisation. But since Tanzania maintained economic links with the West, the dependency syndrome continued. Between 1974 and 1984 the various efforts at economic decolonisation which did not work. The IMF and World Bank recipies in turn also did not help. By mid-1980s these efforts had completely failed to achieve what was intended. In the late 1980s the collapse of the "cold war" and triumph of the capitalist system created two tendencies: liberalisation of the economies and pluralism in politics. The liberalisation in economic activities was a triumph of the capitalist open market system which had come to be recognised as globalisation.

Globalisation

Samwel Wangwe (2000) defines globalisation as "more integration of different parts of the world into a global village. It is associated with rapid advances in technology, growth of world trade and competition and policy change toward economic liberalisation". Modern gobalisation resulted from the triumph of capitalism after the collapse of Soviet Union and the coming to an end of the Cold war which had divided the world into two competing camps. Tanzania's economic collapse occurred in part because "globalisation has transformed the way in which the dominant forces in the global economy have come to define their interest in the world outside their own home base. These are no longer focused, as they were in earlier phases, on ensuring access to cheap raw materials in the periphery plus whatever degree of access to foreign commodity markets could be obtained that was compatible with maintaining protected access to one's own home market. The current agenda of transnational capital now seeks much broader and far reaching breaking down of barriers to free movement of commodities and capital across national borders as well as the removal of impediments to the location of production processes in any part of the world. Globalisation has thus been accompanied by increasingly insistent demands for removal of regulatory and other barriers in national states impeding the free movement of commodities, finance and capital, but not labour across the globe." (Wangwe, 2000)

The colonial economic system with its emphasis on production of raw materials has gradually become marginalised. During the neo-colonial phase African countries struggled to maintain a small share in world trade through negotiations for preferential trading arrangements through Lome Conventions with the European Union. But the World Trade Organisation (WTO) had been created in the Atlantic system to push multilateral trading arrangements. During this time of globalisation, the Third World share of trade has continued to decline and, if preferential trade arrangements are pushed out altogether, prices of raw materials will continue to drop to make peasant production of them completely unattractive. By and large, globalisation is a return to the competitive economic system, but at this stage incorporating almost everybody. Most African states are unhappy because of being unprepared for this kind of competition. South-South cooperation has been emphasised as a way out. Multilateral negotiations can help to reduce some pains, but will not change the power of capitalism to destroy less developed modes of production. Chinweizu (1993, p. 789) tells us that we have to re-examine our own performance as well. It will not help to continue to blame our colonial background and inheritance forever.

References

Aina, Tade Akin, *Globalization and Social Policy in Africa: Issues and Research 4. Direction.* CODESRIA Working Paper Series 6/96.

Bagachwa, Mboya S. D. "Impact of Adjustment Policies on Small Scale Enterprise Sector in Tanzanian Economic Trends". *A Quarterly Review of the Economy*, Vol. 4, No. 2, July, 1991.

Chinweizu. "Africa and the Capitalist Countries" in Mazrui, Ali and Wondi C. eds., *Africa since 1935, General History of Africa*, Vol VIII, UNESCO, 1993.

Wangwe, Samwel M. "Globalisation and Marginalisation: Africa's Economic Challenge in the 21st Century" in Othman, H. (ed.), *Reflections on Leadership in Africa: Forty Year after Independence*, 2000.

Postscript

A Note on Sources and Methods

Salvatory S. Nyanto

The preceding chapters leave no doubt that Tanzania's history has not occurred in splendid isolation. It has, over time, undergone many processes with varying connections and disconnections that today characterise the country as a modern nation. This book has brought together ideas and processes stretching as far back as during the Stone Age. The volume has complemented the earlier book whose contributors recounted a history of Tanzania from the Stone Age to the Arusha declaration (Kimambo & Temu, 1969). While acknowledging the indelible contribution made by the earlier volume to the historiography of the nation, yet we found it imperative to reproduce a new volume that meets the needs of both students and instructors who have long wished to see a new all-inclusive book in print. Since the publication of the earlier volume, Tanzania has endured many processes that it would be unfair to leave them unattended. This volume, notwithstanding building on the earlier one, has inexorably diversified the subject matter in both its scope and temporal dimensions. This makes the title *A New History of Tanzania* plausible as it sets the tone for a history of Tanzania to appear in the flavour of its own.

History, like other disciplines in humanities, employs wide-ranging sources in reconstructing the past. We have expounded, in our first chapter, sources that historians use: archaeology, anthropology, historical linguistics, and oral traditions or oral histories. Archaeology has enabled both historians and archaeologists to go far deeper into the origins of culture and humanity over two million years ago where written records and oral traditions cannot reach. Furthermore, the advance in the use of DNA in archaeology has also provided an avenue for historians and archaeologists to either refute or prove faunal remains where contradictions about the nature of evidence of the material findings arise (Cf. Mapunda, 2010, Ehret 2001, p. 20). The development of historical archaeology, as a new discipline of archaeology, has provided an invaluable contribution to historical scholarship too. The Africanist Archaeologists have increasingly ventured into the field thereby supplementing to the existing body of knowledge about the Tanzanian past. Using historical archaeology—as both a method and an approach—Africanist archaeologists have used oral histories and archaeological excavations to provide new insights on the history of Tanzania. Among the areas that have received such a new light include histories of the caravan trade of the nineteenth century, iron smelting and symbolism, and human settlements to mention just a few both along the coast and in the interior of Tanzania (Schmidt 1978, 2006, Mapunda, 1995, Chami 2004, LaViolette, 2004, Lane 2009, Biginagwa 2012, 2014).

Other sources notably anthropology, historical linguistics, and oral traditions have provided groundbreaking interventions in the Tanzanian historical scholarship too. Although the works of early anthropologists—having been influenced by Social Darwinism and colonial projects—provided a negative portrayal of African socio-economic, and cultural systems of societies they studied, their works cannot be ignored wholeheartedly to have contributed nothing to the history of Tanzania (Cf. Moore, 1994, p. 8-10). It was their writings (reports and books) that provoked early Tanzanian and Africanist historians to criticise the dominant colonial historiography in favour of the 1960s nationalist historiography (Cf. Kimambo, 1967, Katoke 1974, Feireman, 1974). In contrast with other sources, historical linguistics remains the only source that primarily relies on language change as a key evidence of historical past (Campbell 2002, p. 1, Nurse & Spear 1985, p. 8). Using historical linguistics as a primary source, historians including Christopher Ehert and David Schoenbrun, have made an important contribution to the Tanzanian and African history by unearthing pertinent histories of societies of the distant past that have had hitherto been thoroughly unexplored (Cf Ehret, 1988, 1998, Schoenbrun, 1993). Oral histories and traditions have since the 1960s remained an important source in Tanzanian history. Indeed, its contributions have become inestimable in Africa due to lack of written sources that go back beyond the colonial period. It was oral sources—supplemented by available written sources—that enabled nationalist historians to write what Israel Katoke termed, "African history with an African flavour" (Katoke, 1973).

There is no doubt that environment shapes human societies and human societies shape the environment. It is largely in cognizance of this widely held view that this book started by navigating through key issues on the relations between environment and human activities. The physical features such as rivers, lakes, and the Indian Ocean, have, as suggested by archaeological evidence, enhanced throughout the period of consideration, networks of trade and communications between societies in the interior, those along the East African Coast, and across the Indian Ocean. The audacity of traders supported by climate led to constant migrations that in turn led to the formation of new societies on both the coast and in the interior (Sheriff, 2014, p. 6). Building on Sheriff's expositions, Mohamed Bakari has relied on linguistic evidence [of Swahili language] to establish linguistic and cultural similarities along the Eastern African coast calling it a zone of "linguistic and cultural continuum" (Bakari, 2014, p. 195). Zanzibar offers an example of a place along the coast that has for centuries been characterised by constant migrations and the formation of new societies, cultures, and identities. This view has been brought to light by Paola Ivanov who has probed into the formation of new ethnic categories in Zanzibar—exacerbated by migrations—that are not in good terms with the old social and cultural identities. Consequently, there has been a problem of defining the boundaries of citizenship in the island thereby affecting a number of immigrant communities including Comorians (Ivanov, 2014, pp. 209-237, Walker, 2014, pp. 239-266).

Constant migrations and formation of new societies along the coast are largely attributable to the place of the Indian Ocean. Neville Chittick, one of the earliest archaeologists of the 1960s and 1970s working along the East African coast, argued in favour of the Indian Ocean claiming that it was "arguably the largest cultural continuum in the world" (Chittick, 1980, p. 13-22, Sheriff, 2014, p. 1). Michel Mollat went further to describing the Indian Ocean as "a Mediterrannean…a zone of encounters and contacts [that] crisscrossed in all directions…" (Mollat, 1980, pp. 16-17, see also Sheriff, 2014, p. 1, 11-13) while Abdul Sheriff viewed the Indian Ocean as a zone of "cultural continuum" (Sheriff, 2010). Taking the Indian Ocean as an area of encounters of diverse communities, trade and goods, the zone corresponds to Fernand

Braudel's analysis of *la longue durée* in the Mediterranean Ocean. He views the Mediterranean world as a human unit composed of cities and communications, lines of force and nodal points that have imposed what he calls a "unified human construction on geographical space" (Braudel, 1995, p. 277). The legacy of the Indian Ocean, as a region of encounters and contacts, still continues to date. As Sheriff contends, in spite of the challenges imposed by European interventions in the Indian Ocean, and the incorporation of large parts of it into the capitalist world economy, the Ocean still retains a number of its *la longue durée* characteristics in cultural and social aspects (Sheriff, 2014, p. 1).

While the diversity of environments supports different human activities, the landscape can also be remade by human activities. This makes ecological particularism important in looking at the extent to which the environment can be remade by human activities (Cf. Anderson 2000, Schmidt, 1997, Giblin, 1992, 1996, Maddox, 1996, Kimambo 1996). Climate change itself spurs humans to adapt to and to modify their environments. Archaeological evidence from the coast of East Africa has demonstrated climate change and its impact on human settlement for the last 5000 years. As Chami has reported, for the first five centuries of the Christian era Early Iron Working communities experienced a wetter climate that forced them to relocate on hills and elevated landscape tilling the arable land. However, between 600 AD and 900 AD the climate became worse to the extent that communities that survived the disaster had to move to areas near lakes, rivers, and water tables. The Great Lakes region, and coral islands that had no stable water sources including the Mafia Island are said to have been abandoned. The area experienced several climatic fluctuations between 900 AD and 1300 AD. This period, as Chami assets, corresponded with the rise of the Swahili culture. It is indicated by coral and limestone being used for building water reservoirs or wells such as those discovered at Kilwa (Chami, 2003, p. 16-18).

Indeed, the making of human communities in Tanzania has brought together encounters of different communities. This book has provided an account of the processes of population movements that, at different times and places, gave rise to the creation of the communities and cultures of varied historical, ethnic, and linguistic backgrounds. We have delved the processes of population movements relying on two approaches: physical and linguistic classification. Although classification of human beings according to their physical features has now already fallen out of favour in scholarship, we found it imperative to remind our readers that racial constructs are complex and dynamic, always changing in response to changing social contexts. For this case, linguistic classification appears plausible in explaining the making of human communities in Tanzania. It has succeeded in demonstrating, with substantial pieces of evidence, the spread of Khoisan, Cushitic, Nilotic, and Bantu speakers into the today's Tanzania mainland. Using linguistic classification as a method of studying language families, post-colonial historians, archaeologists, and linguists managed to show how new settlers incorporated the economies and socio-political organisations of pre-existing communities. For instance, Cushitic speakers incorporated many Khoisan communities as they spread agriculture and animal husbandry in the area. However, while Khoisan speakers were assimilated into the new economy, other societies remained hunters and gatherers. Furthermore, linguistic classification has also revealed Cushitic influence on the Hadzabe, Qwaza, and Aramanik societies of the Tanzanian interior.

One of the issues that has raised contested debates among historians and archaeologists, as far as the making of human communities in Tanzania is concerned, is the question of Bantu migration. As noted in this book, Christopher Ehret, Roland Oliver, Jean Hiernaux, and Jan Vansina are among the scholars who have probed into the subject matter with different viewpoints and pieces of evidence on the origins and the spread of Bantu (Oliver, 1966; Hiernaux 1968, Vansina 1995, Ehret 2001). Today, the idea that there was a massive Bantu migration and such great migration was associated with the spread of iron technology can no longer be sustained in lieu of recent archaeological evidence in Africa in general and Tanzania in particular. As Chami has argued in his several works, the idea of Bantu movement contradicts with archaeological evidence of Early Iron Working pottery from both central and southern Africa that indicate similar cultural phases—Limbo/Urewe, Kwale, and Mwangia (Chami 2006, p. 126). Chami's argument challenges the received wisdom of "Bantu expansion" in Tanzania and Africa as a whole. Building on substantial pieces of archaeological evidence, Chami, first, shows that there were people in East and Sothern Africa before the Iron Working period—the time of the Bantu expansion—who had already adopted agriculture, domestication of animals, and pottery making. Secondly, he indicates that the influence—that include cultural and linguistic assimilation—on the Bantu from the coast to the interior of modern Tanzania was by way of trade and contact. The Graeco-Roman trade with East Africa, among other things, is related to the spread of the Early Iron Working tradition.

Hence, the spread of Bantu language need to be separated from the spread of iron technology and pottery ware (Chami, 1999, pp. 208-210, 2009a, p. 48, 2009b, p. 210).

Besides cultural and linguistic assimilation, the interaction of societies led to the formation of complex societies on both the coast and the interior. Community formation along the Tanzanian coast was an interplay of different forces. One of the forces was the integration of the Tanzanian coast to the outside world that gave rise to the formation of coastal societies that had a mixture of people of different cultural, linguistic, and ethnic backgrounds. Such intermingling of different societies with different cultures and languages gave rise to a distinctive civilisation—Swahili civilisation. Until now, the coast remains a place whose societies constantly interact with other societies from far and wide. The interaction of communities gave rise to the coastal city states that not only attracted traders but also goods from the interior and the Indian Ocean world. In due course, coastal city states became cosmopolitan and their inhabitants engaged in various activities including trade, fishing, seafaring, and agriculture. The dependence of coastal communities on the agricultural activities on the adjacent hinterland made regular movements of people in and out of cities leading to an urban-rural continuum (Sheriff 2010, 2014).

Archaeological works from Kilwa, Kunduchi, Mbuamaji, and Bagamoyo have shed light to the nature of the Tanzanian coast since the first millennium of the Christian era. All the works suggest that coastal city states among other things, developed a network of trade with distant communities and those of the outside world, and its inhabitants engaged in a range of activities including trade, farming, and sea-faring (Chittick 1960, Chami 1994; Chami & 1998, 2006, 2008, Ombori 2013, Masele 2007). Notwithstanding the enormous archaeological investigations, Rhapta--an ancient commercial city—remains unresolved problem. Various hypotheses have so far been offered on the exact location of the town. The Greek anonymous writer claimed that Msasani, which is north of Dar es Salaam, was the port of Rhapta. Freeman-Grenville on the other hand thought Rhapta was on the Pangani estuary, and Felix Chami thought it to be on the Rufiji delta. In supporting his argument, Chami relied on the latitudes provided by Ptolemy's *Geographia* that the region was between latitude 7^0 and 8^0. While this is the case, Amandus Kwekason, building on Lacroix's argument, thought that Rhapta would have been located further south towards Kilwa and the Ruvuma River (Freeman-Grenville, 1959, Chami 2006, p. 17, Kwekason, 2011, p. 26, Lacroix 1989, p. 80). However, until now, despite efforts from archaeologists, the location of Rhapta still presents a more formidable challenge as each claim suggests a different location along the Tanzanian coast. Given the many hypotheses, it is clear that locating Rhapta remains a challenging task in scholarship. What appears to be the most reasonable conclusion on this problem is that a lot more archaeological investigations, coupled with the discovery of new evidence, need to be undertaken before historians can provide conclusive statements on the exact location of ancient Raphta.

Like the coast, community formation and socio-economic developments of societies in the interior was an interplay of several factors. The Indian Ocean played an important role to the spread of foreign crops (bananas and eventually rice) to the interior—via the Kenyan and Somali coasts—in the seventh century of the Christian era. Both foreign and indigenous crops aided the development of food-production in the interior from the seventh century onwards. However, foreign crops did not spread to the interior via the Indian Ocean only. This book has also presented other directions (Southern route) from which banana as a staple crop spread in the Great Lakes Region (Ehret, 1988, p. 633). Moreover, the period between the sixth and eleventh centuries of the Christian era saw diversity in local economies that continued to be inclined to ethnic and geographical ranges. For instance, agriculture in particular grain cultivation, dominated Bantu speaking communities in the fertile regions while Nilotic and Cushitic speakers grew various crops and practiced animal husbandry in both the northern and central parts of the Tanzanian interior. Apart from economic specialisation, there was a considerable amalgamation of communities with different linguistic backgrounds. For instance, following the merging of Nilotes, Southern Cushites, and Bantu into the proto-Chagga in northeastern Tanzania, there emerged a new society that fused together ideas and practices of all the three groups (ibid, p. 641).

The development of complex agriculture among Bantu-speaking communities of the interior was due to the spread of iron-working that in turn replaced Stone Age tools. Prompted by iron tools, early Bantu farming communities spread in the Great Lakes region, the coastal hinterland, central, southern and northeastern Tanzania. Favourable climatic conditions which supported permanent settlement and agriculture enabled this expansion (Ehret, 1988 p. 624). Although farming communities spread in the interior, many areas of western and south western Tanzania, as demonstrated in this volume, had by the seventh century of the Christian era remained unoccupied by farming communities due to the presence of Khoisan hunter gatherers who remained independent living on collecting what nature could offer (ibid). Recent archaeological works by Kwekason and Chami have demonstrated an opposite view about foraging communities in northwestern Tanzania. Working in Muleba in the Great Lakes Region, Kwekason and Chami have demonstrated the existence of pre-iron working communities and settlements (Chami & Kwekason, 2003, p. 73). On the other hand, Schoenbrun has found that the Great Lakes Region was settled by people of Sahelian orgin domesticating animals, plants, and smelting iron before the advent of Bantu (Schoenbrun, 1993).

Further archaeological evidence about the pre-iron age farming communities have been discovered by Kwekason in southeastern Tanzania. The findings of pre-Iron Working (PIW) sites indicate an association with the tradition of early settled communities in southeastern Africa. Such a tradition corresponds to the late food-producing Pastoral Neolithic communities of the Rift Valley as the two have common designs and styles of artifacts (Kwekason, 2011, p. 141). Kwekason further reiterates that the PIW tradition predates the Early Iron Working tradition of the central and southern coasts of Tanzania. What he calls the "tillers of the soil" as mentioned in the ancient Graeco-Roman documents were responsible for the pre-iron working tradition (ibid). Kwekason's findings provide an important contribution to our understanding of Neolithic communities. For a number of decades, Neolithic sites have yielded numerous animal remains that indicate domestication of animals before the advent of Iron Age. Conversely, evidence of plants domesticates for decades received a relatively little attention from archaeologists in Tanzania. What accounts for such a neglect is because of the tropical climate whose high rainfall leads to the poor preservation of faunal and floral remains.

The Swahili civilisation has been tangled into the web of scholarly inquiries with diferent viewpoints. For decades, scholarship tended to portray the Swahili civilisation as the sum of the activities of the outsiders. However, such a viewpoint no longer holds water in scholarship. The dominant position of which this book relies is that even at the height of the Swahili civilisation, coastal societies had already undergone diverse transformations. More importantly, archaeological pieces of evidence have also posed a rebuttal on the architecture of the Swahili civilisation. Archaeologists have found that despite foreign and Islamic influences, the stone buildings were of local origin and the coral building materials were mined locally (Masao & Muturo 1988: p. 608, Matieviev, 1984, p. 198). Local initiatives, however, do not deny foreign influences as no society that develops in isolation of other influences. It is therefore pulpable to argue that Coastal Swahili communities might have in one way or another been influenced by foreign influences in the course of meeting their local needs.

The primacy of local influence in shaping the Swahili civilisation is also evident in Chami's works that is corroborated by archaeological evidence. Like other scholars, Chami's analysis of the architecture of Swahili towns has indicated that "the architecture was conditioned by available resources for building..." (Chami 2008, p. 552). Besides architecture, the other area that substantiates local initiative is the general culture of the Swahili. As Chami asserts "the culture of the Swahili towns is African with an infusion of Islamic traits. It is these infused traits such as religion, law, language writing and costume which have made many students of the Swahili culture identify the people as Arabs" (Chami, 2008, p. 551). Chami's analysis of pottery suggests that the people of the Triangular Incised Ware (TIW) tradition were the descendants of the Early Iron Working (EIW)–Mwangia tradition—people who exploited the same environment that was in the past used by their ancestors. Such TIW cultural materials recovered in numerous sites along the coast further suggest that the early phase of TIW tradition occurred before Islam was introduced along the East African coast in the eighth century (Chami 1998, p. 210).

Amandus Kwekason's pottery findings on the southeastern coast of Tanzania have indicated a new pottery tradition labeled "proto-Swahili ware" whose dating lies between the plain and Swahili pottery traditions. His findings have added a new understanding of Swahili pottery to Chami's contextual pottery seriation for the Swahili coast. For Chami, the contextual pottery seriation includes that of Early Iron Working (EIW) or Early Iron Age (EIA, 1st to 6th centuries A.D that includes three sequential ceramic phases namely Limbo, 2nd century BC to 3rd A.D, Kwale 3rd to 5th century A.D, and Mwangia, 6th century. Other sequential pottery seriations are Triangular Incised Ware (TIW) 6th to 10th centuries, Plain Ware (PW) 10th to 13th centuries, A.D), and Swahili Ware or Neck Punctating (SW/NP) (13th to 15th centuries A.D). These pottery traditions have been identified along the coast and on Mafia Island (Chami 1998, p. 202, 1999, p. 1, 2000, p. 1). The proto-Swahili tradition, as Kwekason argues, seems to have succeeded the Plain pottery ware tradition in the southern coast of Tanzania that dates earlier than the known dates from the central coast of Tanzania and Mafia Island. He further contends that though the proto-Swahili ware succeeded the Plain ware cultural tradition yet it was already a well-established tradition along the Southern coast before the known Swahili pottery tradition that is identified with vestigial rims, carnated form and neck or shoulder dating from the thirteenth to the fifteenth centuries of the Christian era. Despite the variations in the occurrence of the pottery ware, the range of economic activities that characterised Swahili people as people who commuted from the urban areas to the countryside for agricultural purposes parallels with the idea raised in the book that Swahili towns developed "urban-rural continuum" as the dominant characteristic of the dwellers of coastal Swahili towns (Cf. Chami, 2008, p. 552).

The traditional view of the Swahili language, like other aspects of the Swahili civilisation, has for decades been linked to the rise of Islam along the East African coast (Spear & Nurse, 1985, p. 6). However, such a viewpoint is no longer credited in scholarship. It is now beyond doubt that the beginning of Swahili language goes many centuries back before the rise and spread of Islam along the coast. Derek Nurse and Thomas Spear challenge the idea of external invention on Kiswahili language arguing that it fails to distinguish between what was inherited in Kiswahili and what was absorbed later. They further argue that Kiswahili is an African language in its sound system and grammar closely related to the Bantu languages of East Africa and the Comoro islands. The language is proven to have shared a common development long before the spread and adoption of Arabic vocabulary. In their view, "the Arabic material is a recent graft onto an old Bantu tree" (ibid). Recent scholarship has shown that the beginning of Swahili language can be traced many centuries before the rise and spread of Islam along the coast. Its emergence and spread, as Massamba reiterates, was never from a single point. Rather, its emergence was simultaneous at different points along the East African coast and at different rates of development. Such a simultaneous development was exacerbated by a process of linguistic contact. Towns such as Rhapta created a convergence of ethnic groups of the Stone Age period making it a trading language (Massamba 2007, p. 72, Chami 2009, p. 210). It was after 1300 of the Christian era that Islam became a ruling ideology and subsequently adopted the language to make it a *lingua franca* (Chami 1998, p. 214).

Agricultural communities gradually experienced more noticeable socio-economic and political changes from the eleventh century onwards in response to two motives. The first motive was the increasing contact with different linguistic and cultural groups while the second was the possession of iron technology by Bantu, Nilotes, and other communities. Consequently, there was an increase in population, production, and more complex communities with greater social and economic differentiation leading to the formation of centralised political instituitions. This book has demonstrated the importance of environment and climatic conditions to the economy and to the formation of centralised institutions. Northwestern and northeastern Tanzania, which are part of the Great Lakes Region, developed large centralised kingdoms because they had favourable climate (fertile soil and abundant rainfall) that could support high population density and specialisations among communities. In western and central Tanzania on the other hand there emerged ntemiship system of organisation due to abundance of land that encouraged people of one *ntemi* state to move and form other smaller ntemi states. The region had also less fertile soil and less rainfall that made rulers unable to extract surplus with great regularity. Though environment tends to select what kinds of political institutions can be established on a particular area this was not always the case. Other areas such as the southern highlands—with exception of the Fipa plateau—never developed centralised political institutions notwithstanding the favourable environment with fertile soil and abundant rainfall.

The increase in greater social and economic differentiation corresponded with the development of commodity production and exchange in the Tanzania's interior due to the distribution of resources and regional specialisation. As we have demonstrated, unequal distribution of resources and regional specialisation stimulated the development of networks of trade and regional exchange from about 1000 A.D to 1800 A.D. The integration of the interior into the global network was largely influenced by the Zanzibar Commercial Empire by the 1840s. The establishment of the Zanzibar commercial empire led to the subordination of subsistence economies of the interior into the global economy that affected societies in political, economic, and social aspects. On the whole, the position of the commercial empire created a setting upon which economic and political processes had resultant transformative impacts on the economies and social formations of the East African interior. This affirms Lawrence Hollingsworth's claim that "when one pipes in Zanzibar, they dance on the lakes..." (Hollingsworth 1953:6). Such a view was supported by Abdul Sheriff and Nicholls who held that the position of the Zanzibar commercial empire and its integration into the capitalist economic system was the main stimulant to the changes of the interior (Sheriff 1980: 36). However, John Iliffe argued that changes were not uniformly transformative of the old systems. What he calls "enlargement of scale" was unevenly experienced by the people in the interior (Iliffe, 1979, p. 40).

Building on Iliffe's concept of enlargement of scale, Stephen Rockel's study on the caravan porters of the nineteenth century-East Africa has showed how the porters, in their course of meeting the demands of the Zanzibar commercial empire, developed friendships and joking relations (*utani*) with communities along the caravan routes (Rockel 2000, & 2006). He argues that long distance caravan porters shared a lot in common with the sea men in the dhow trade of the western Indian Ocean. East African caravan porters were actors in the same international economy of production, consumption, and desire that paralleled with those of sailors of the western Indian Ocean and beyond (Rockel, 2014, p. 95-96). The joking relations and networks of friendships—as an African institution—was one of the forms of cultural networks that moved from the domestic arena to the caravan ports and towns of the Swahili coast (ibid, p.98). Nyamwezi caravan porters emerged as one of the groups that carried the coastal ethos inland through the institution of *utani*. As Rockel has argued, the Nyamwezi developed complex relationships during the nineteenth century that deepened in residential areas of coastal traders in the trading centres of the interior. Such complex relationships were manifested by regular visits, marriage ties, blood brotherhood relationships, the spread of Kiswahili language, and Islam in the interior (ibid, p. 107, Rockel, 2006, 1995, 2000).

The Ngoni invasion is one of the nineteenth-century movements whose legacy remains in the history of Tanzania (Omer-Cooper, 1987, p. 59). The spread of Nguni speakers affected Tanzanian societies in various ways. It led to the formation of Ngoni ethnic groups due to the amalgamation of indigenous communities and Nguni speakers. Today, the Ngoni of Ruvuma region and the Tuta of Kahama-Shinyanga remain as a legacy of the Ngoni invasion in Tanzania. In the military field, the Ngoni introduced fighting techniques that were copied by Mkwawa, Nyungu ya Mawe, and Mirambo. Thus, the Ngoni necessitated the formation and efficiency of fighting warriors as *ruga ruga* in Ukimbu, Unyanyembe, Sangu and Hehe States who could fight against local enemies and against the imposition of colonial rule. Although the Nguni's influence on the making of modern Tanzania cannot be downplayed, its invasion can also be looked as one of the movements that created tensions and havoc in many societies of the Tanzanian interior. They disrupted caravan routes, staged constant raids on societies of Western Tanzania and weakened the pre-existing political institutions. For the Nyamwezi, Kimbu, Konongo, Bende, Tongwe, Ha, Vinza, and the Sumbwa, the Ngoni invasion was more of a curse than a blessing (Cf. Roberts, 1969, p. 69-78)

Besides the Zanzibar commercial empire and the Ngoni invasion, the expansion of European activities in the second half of the nineteenth century affected Tanzanian societies in numerous ways. Driven by imperialism, European traders, explorers, and missionaries frequented both the coast and the interior of modern Tanzania beginning in the 19th century. Traders, with the help of chartered companies, ventured into the interior to open up new markets for their goods—trade in legitimate goods. Explorers investigated strategic areas such as the high mountains, rivers and lakes to be used for imperialistic interests. Missionaries, Catholic and Protestant, ventured into the interior with more than one agenda of spreading the gospel. They were instrumental in opening both the coast and the interior to what Dr. Livingstone called "Christianity, Commerce, and Civilisation" (Hastings 1994, p. 251-252). It is worth emphasising that the link between Christianity, commerce, and civilisation gained momentum in the nineteenth century during the heyday of territorial expansion. Nonetheless, such a notion cannot be sustained wholeheartedly in scholarship to demonstrate relations between Christianity and Empire. Incidentally, not all missionaries supported the relations between Christianity and commerce. Drawing examples from India, Porter argued that the Evangelical missionaries, whose influence was felt among Indians, did nothing to improve India during the reign of the East India Company (Porter, 1985, pp. 597-604, Stanley, 2003, pp. 58-84). All in all, the development of European capitalism enabled Europeans to extend their influences in Tanzania. The activities of explorers, traders, and missionaries meant extension of European interests in Tanzania and Africa in general.

Driven by the reports of traders, explorers, and missionaries, Germany rushed into German East Africa under the auspices of Karl Peters' *Deutsch-Ostafrikanische Gesellschaft* (Germany East Africa Company). Karl Peters' treaties with local chiefs made it possible for the Germans to claim—during the Berlin Conference—German East Africa as their own sphere of influence. Effective colonisation of German East Africa began in 1890 after the failure of Karl Peters' company to govern the colony (Koponen 1994:77-83). The partition of Africa in general and German East Africa (Today's Tanzania mainland) created the colonial boundaries during the Berlin Conference (paper partition). On the whole, colonial boundaries never considered the ethnic and linguistic composition of societies. It is no wonder today to see Luo and Maasai in both Kenya and Tanzania, Makua and Makonde in both Tanzania and Mozambique to mention just a few (Mbwiliza, 1991, p. 19, Aminzade 2014). This situation partly poses a problem on defining the limits of citizenship in regions bordering neigbhouring countries where linguistic and ethnic composition transcend colonial boundaries that used today as national boundaries. The other idea that deserves a note is the idea of "sphere of influence." Missionaries also recognised spheres as they rushed into different corners of Tanzania in their attempt to extend "religious spheres of influence". For instance, the White Fathers regarded Western, Northwestern, Southwestern Tanzania, and the heart of Africa as their own "specialised ministry". The Benedictines had a considerable influence in Southern Tanzania, and the Holy Ghost Fathers along the Coast. The Moravians had a desire of creating a strongest mission field from Lake Nyasa to Lake Victoria, the Anglican LMS and CMS ventured into the interior in response to Dr. Livingstone's plea while the UMCA made Southern Tanzania a considerable project. The German Lutheran missionaries spread and made north-eastern Tanzania a successful ministry (Lema 1999; Hastings 1996, p. 255, Nolan 1978, J.T. Hamilton & K.G. Hamilton, 1983, p. 574).

The imposition of German colonialism was not welcomed wholeheartedly throughout the Tanzanian mainland. As demonstrated in this book, kings and chiefs along with their subjects waged numerous wars of resistances against the Germans to protect their political and economic interests. African resistance varied and employed different justifications and strategies. The Maji Maji resistance is an example of African resistance that covered large area and involved many ethnic groups, employed different tactics, and notwithstanding its fighters' diversities, were inspired by Prophet Kinjekitile Ngwale's *maji* ideology (cf. Iliffe 1969 &1979, Gwasa & Iliffe 1967, Giblin and Monson 2010). What strikes historians is how such a movement spread the entire southern Tanzania, and how diverse ethnic groups were mobilised and organised for war. Scholars have long regarded communication as the main factor for widespread movement and organisation. However, as Giblin and Monson contend, communication puts [historians] at a disadvantage for there is little evidence to support the substance of the messages and instructions that accompanied the administering of *maji* medicines (Giblin & Monson, 2010, p. 17-19). Building on John Iliffe, Giblin and Monson argue for the complexity of circuits of communication, including communication between Africans and Germans. In their view, "communication became a cause of action, but a cause which could not be regulated or directed" (ibid, p.20).

These days, archaeology has provided us with new insights on the Maji Maji resistance. Betram Mapunda's work on the archaeology of Maji Maji in Ungoni has employed archaeology to verify, clarify, and supplement written and oral information about the resistance (Mapunda 2010, p. 220-238). His works have also shed light on issues of interest to historians. For many decades, it was accepted that the Matumbi ethnic group initiated the war against German forced cotton scheme. With the aid of archaeological evidence, Mapunda argues that the stimulus for the Matumbi to initiate the war was their earlier experience with the Arabs in Kilwa who for years forced Matumbi to work in the plantations. Driven by the conduct of the Arabs, Matumbi migrated west of Kilwa (in Ungoni) by the second half of the nineteenth century. Mapunda contends that because of such experience, Matumbi were "injured buffaloes who, when the Germans introduced similar policies, found it easy to mobilise themselves against the invaders". His argument on the Matumbi's migration has been supported by beads recovered from numerous trenches in Ungoni [Mapunda, forthcoming]. Although all resistance movements were violently suppressed, they first remain in the history of Tanzania as early attempts to defend economic and political interests, and neither were they "blood thirsty" and "primitive" as argued by colonialists and subsequent scholars. Secondly, from the nationalist viewpoint, African resistance movements represented an early form of nationalism because they involved movements and the mobilization of mass support that enabled nationalists of the 1950s and 1960s to draw on memories of heroic past (Temu 1969:189).

The failure of African resistance movements at the turn of the twentieth century paved the way for the effective establishment of both the colonial economy and administration in German East Africa. The colonial economy based on peasant, plantation, and settler agriculture emphasised production of cash crops for export. Consequently, Africans were made to produce what they did not consume and consumed what they did not produce. What D. A Low, John Lonsdale, and John Iliffe call "the second colonial occupation" after the Second World War saw the British emphasising the production of more cash crops to revamp the economy affected by the war (Low and Lonsdale, 1976, Iliffe, 1979). Thirdly, colonial economies in particular plantation agriculture created uneven development of the country between productive regions and labour *reservoir*. It also laid the foundation for the development of migrant labour system (*manamba*). Young men from labour reserve zones (Kigoma, Rukwa, Njombe, Songea & Tabora) left for *manamba* to make their cash necessary to pay taxes and purchase newly available consumer goods (Tambila *et.al* 1983, Sago, 1974, p. 174, Giblin, 2005, pp. 107-133). Migrant labour system has remained a legacy of the colonial economies. Today, rural-urban migration remains a characteristic of many young men and women. Apart from *manamba*, Indirect Rule, as a form of the British administration, affected societies too. The "tribalisation" and institutionalisation of "chiefship" hampered national unity, slowed down independence struggles in Tanganyika, and created conflicts even within local communities (Beidelman 2012: 228-278). Such sentiments continued for decades after independence as certain peoples considered themselves more superior and advanced than others.

Struggles for independence took different forms in both Tanganyika and Zanzibar. Julius K. Nyerere and TANU nationalists employed non-violent methods for Tanganyika's independence while Zanzibar's independence was obtained—after the failure of democratic means—by way of revolution. The effects of Indirect Rule lingered during the struggle for Tanganyika's independence. Despite the growing influence of tribalism and racial sentiments the use of Kiswahili as a *lingua franca*, the struggle for independence transcended linguistic and tribalistic divisions. This unity found expression first in TAA and then in TANU. In other East African countries, the petty bourgeois class tended to organise in groups as civil servants, wealthy farmers and traders that made it more difficult to unite into one strong nationalist movement. After the independence of the two countries, on 26th April 1964, Tanganyika and Zanzibar united to form the United Republic of Tanzania, a union that exists to date. Various reasons have been put forward to explain the rationale for the union. Some argue that the union was aimed to strengthen historical unity and cooperation that the mainlanders and those from the islands have made for centuries. Conversely, Ronald Aminzade argues that the union of Tanganyika and Zanzibar was in response to global cold war among Russia and USA and their allies and there was no pressure from below (Aminzade 2012:99).

Although Tanganyika gained its independence and subsequently united with Zanzibar, the dependent economy created during the colonial period remained unchanged. This prompted the launching of the national building project that went hand in hand with the process of Africanisation in the administration, political system, civil service, commerce, industry, and agriculture. However, despite good intentions, nation-building projects, race, and citizenship raised contentious debates and animosities among nationalist leaders. As

Aminzade contends, such conflicts involved issues on who deserved membership in the newly established independent nation, and which political, economic, and cultural rights to be offered to qualified citizens (Aminzade 2013:8). Even in rural areas such as Ukaguru, many locals opposed what Nyerere and TANU had done (Beidelman 2012:278). The process of Africanisation also raised debates over the legalisation of selected cultural forms as "national", and campaigns to ban miniskirts, wigs, male tight trousers, and other forms of clothes that were considered "indecent dress". Supporters of the campaigns argued that miniskirts, wigs, and male tight trousers undermined Tanzania's culture while opponents criticised the movement as unfair to condemn the new styles as imitation of foreign culture (Ivaska 2011: 15, 63-64). It was therefore the increasing conflicts during the early years of independence that prompted the independent government to launch the Arusha Declaration in 1967 (Aminzade 2013: 30).

On the whole, the Arusha declaration changed the direction of development that made the TANU leadership, the bureaucrats and the social base of the nationalist movement match together. The declaration empahasised equality and self-reliance, and offered ethical codes that controlled the exercise of political powers by both the party and government leaders, sought to increase production in the villages, encourage population growth in rural areas, and its policies appealed to many people including religious institutions. For instance, *Ujamaa* (brotherhood) influenced Catholics, Anglicans, and Lutherans to establish Small Christian Communities with corresponding goals to that of *Ujamaa* villages (Healey, 1981, p. 62-63.). That said, it does not mean that the policies of socialism had no drawbacks. For instance, the villagisation programme, despite its achievements, was criticised for its consequent impact on the environment, over utilisation of resources, deterioration of farming systems, increasing burden on women and disturbed people's relationship with nature and associated spirits to mention just a few (Chriansson & Tobison 1989:62, McCall 1985, Kjekshus 1996: xxxvii, Swantz 1996: 165, Giblin, 1991, p. 182-183, Lawi 2007: 82).

No sooner had the policies of *Ujamaa* earned international recognition in Africa and beyond than the economic crisis brought the system to a grinding halt. By the mid-1980s it was clear that the policies of socialism could no longer be maintained. In 1989, twenty two years after the Arusha declaration, Tanzania was neither socialist nor self-reliant (Maliyamkono & Bagachwa 1989:1). In the late 1970s and early 1980s, hardship increased due to lack of food and other essentials. Under this context, the adoption of economic liberalisation and multiparty politics became imperative in addressing the critical situation. President Julius Nyerere stepped down in 1985 and Ali Hassan Mwinyi became the President. Unlike his predecessor, President Mwinyi was more liberal and opened the country into multi-party politics in 1992. President Benjamin Mkapa moved forward the privatisation programme of state-owned industries to foreign investors who could provide capital, equipment, and technology. However, the privatisation programme was criticised on two grounds. First, the late Rev. Christopher Mtikila advocated indigenisation policies (*sera za uzawa*). He wanted the economy to be in the hands of the indigenous citizens. He also called for the expulsion of Indians, Arabs, and Somalis who he claimed profited off the work of Tanzanians (Aminzade 2013: 329). Secondly, the privatisation programme was strongly opposed in the Parliament during President Jakaya Kikwete's first term leading to the rejection of the government's plan to sell the National Insurance Company. The Parliament too opposed, with no success, the government's plan of privatising Commercial Rural Development Bank (CRDB) and National Bank of Commerce (NBC). Similar agitations against foreign multinational companies were reported in gold mining areas (ibid, p. 279-288). These instances provide an indication that the road towards economic liberalisation was not smooth. It was characterised by endless conflicts between indigenous citizens and investors on one hand, and between the Parliament and the government on the other.

Besides economic liberalisation and multiparty democracy, ideas of race, citizenship, and politics have continued to attract considerable scholarly attention in Tanzania. The works of Ronald Aminzade, James Brennan, J. M. Lusugga Kironde, Andrew Burton, and Jonathon Glassman have delved into these isssues covering the pre-colonial, colonial and post-colonial periods (Burton, 2005, 2007; Kironde, 2007; Glassman, 2011; Brennan, 2007, 2012; Aminzade, 2013). Glassman's work challenges an assumption that racial thinking in the colonial period reflected only western ideas nudging aside local initiatives on race and racial constructs in pre-colonial, colonial and post-colonial Zanzibar. His work shows how Africans in the islands also crafted competing ways of categorising race and politics during the Arab Sultanate, the British period and post-independence period. Racial politics also dominated the multiparty elections of 1995, 2000, 2005, and 2010 in Zanzibar. As Glassman contends, Zanzibar's multiparty politics is being polarised on two axes. The first is ethnic whereas the majority Zanzibaris of Arab origin vote in support of CUF and Zanzibaris of Tanzania mainland vote for CCM. The second is regional whereas Shirazi Pemba vote in favour of CUF while the Shirazi of Unguja vote in support of CCM (Glassman, 2011, p. 285). Drawing examples from Dar es Salaam's urbanisation, Andrew Burton has demonstrated how the German and British colonial states set up laws to restrict "natives" from entering and living in the city. The rationale was to reserve Dar es Salaam for White and Indian populations. Africans who had no wage work were marked *kupe* (parasites), *wazurulaji* (loiterers), *wavivu* (lazy people), and *maadui wa Siasa ya Ujamaa na Kujitegemea* (enemies of the policy of Socialism and Self-Relience) (Burton, 2005, p. 4, 2007, pp. 136-146). Likewise, the works of James Brennan and Andrew Burton, and J. M. Lusugga Kironde have traced the racial constructs between the custodians of the city (*wenyeji, wenyemji*) and foreigners (*watu wa kuja, wahuni*), colonial constructions of zones of settlements for Europeans, Asians, and Africans, and post-independent ideas of race and nationalism (*kujenga taifa*/building the nations versus *unyonyaji* (see Brennan, 2012, pp. 21-165, 2007, pp. 118-130, Brennan and Burton, 2007, pp. 31-42, Lusugga Kironde, 2007, pp. 97-115).

Today, Tanzania, like other African countries is still tied to neo-colonial relations. Though the nation became independent from the former colonial master (Britain) it was open to pressures from a number of multinational orgnanisations and multinational trading organisations. This was so because Tanzania remained dependent on the inherited colonial economy that put emphasis on the production of cash crops for export. Besides the extension of neo-colonial relations, the influences of globalisation cannot be left unattended. Despite the fact that Tanzania was integrated into the global trading networks since the era of the Greeks and Romans, such integration was limited to economic spheres only. Today, Tanzania is tied to the web of new global integration that emphasises the removal of regulatory and other barriers, finance, and capital. It is no wonder therefore that what happens today in the developed world reaches Tanzania and other developing countries in a few days or even few hours. On the other hand, the influence globalisation has negatively affected indigenous cultures. Foreign culture is increasingly affecting the younger generation. Campaigns of the 1960s that were targeted towards promoting "African" culture are no more.

References

Aminzade, Ronald. *Race, Nation, and Citizenship in Post-Colonial Africa: The Case of Tanzania*. Cambridge: Cambridge University Press, 2013.

Anderson, David. *Eroding the Commons: The Politics of Ecology in Baringo, Kenya 1890-1963*. Oxford: James Currey; Nairobi: E.A.E.P; and Athens: Ohio University Press, 2002.

Bakari, Mohamed. "The State of Swahili Civilisation: Swahili Language and Society, Indian Ocean Antecedents and Anthropological Research" in Abdul Sheriff & Engseng Ho.eds., *The Indian Ocean: Oceanic Connections and the Creation of New Societies*. London: Hurst & Company, 2014.

Beidelman, Thomas. *The Culture of Kaguru: The Cultural Subjection of Ukaguru*. Bloomington and Indianapolis: Indiana University Press, 2012.

Biginagwa, Thomas, J. "Historical Archaeology of the Nineteenth-Century Caravan Trade in North-Eastern Tanzania: A Zooarchaeological Perspective", University of York: PhD Thesis, 2012.

_____."East Africa: Historical Archaeology", *Encyclopedia of Global Archaeology*. New York: Springer Science and Business Media, 2014.

Braudel, Fernand. *The Mediterrannean and the Mediterrannean World in the Age of Philip II*, Volume 1. Los Angeles: University of California Press, 1995.

Brennan, James R. and Andrew Burton, "The Emerging Metropolis: A History of Dar es Salaam, circa 1862-2000" in James R. Brennan, Andrew Burton, and Yusufu Lawi, eds., *Dar es Salaam: Histories from an Emerging African Metropolis*. Dar es Salaam: Mkuki na Nyota Publishers, Nairobi: BIEA, 2007a.

Brennan, James R. "Between Segregation and Gentrification: Africans, Indians, and the struggle for housing in Dar es Salaam, 1920-1950" in in James R. Brennan, Andrew Burton, and Yusufu Lawi, eds., *Dar es Salaam: Histories from an Emerging African Metropolis*. Dar es Salaam: Mkuki na Nyota Publishers, Nairobi: BIEA, 2007b.

_____. *Taifa: Making Nation and Race in Urban Tanzania*. Athens: Ohio University Press, 2012.

Burton, Andrew. *African Underclass: Urbanisation, Crime and Colonial Order in Dar es Salaam*. Nairobi: BIEA; Oxford: James Currey; Dar es Salaam: Mkuki na Nyota and Athens: Ohio University Press, 2005.

_____. 'Brothers by Day': Policing the urban public in colonial Dar es Salaam, 1919-1961 in James R. Brennan, Andrew Burton, and

Yusufu Lawi, eds., *Dar es Salaam: Histories from an Emerging African Metropolis*. Dar es Salaam: Mkuki na Nyota Publishers, Nairobi: BIEA, 2007.

Campbell, Lyle. *Historical Linguistics: An Introduction*. Cambridge, Massachusetts: The MIT Press, 2004.

Chami, Felix, A. "Limbo: Early Iron-working in south-eastern Tanzania", *Azania*, Volume XXVII, 1992.

_____. *The Tanzanian Coast in the First Millennium AD: An Archaeology of the Iron Working, Farming Communities*. Uppsala: Societas Archaeological Uppsaliensis, 1994.

_____. "A Review of Swahili Archaeology", *African Anthropological Review*, Vol. 15, No.3, 1998.

_____. "The Early Iron Age on Mafia Island and its relationship with the mainland", *Azania*, Volume XXXIV, 1999a.

_____. "Graeco-Roman Trande Link and the Bantu Migration Theory", *Anthropos*, 94. 1999.

_____. "A Response. To Christopher Ehret's "Bantu Expansions", *International Journal of African Historical Studies*, Vol 34, No.3, 2001.

_____. "The Swahili World" in Felix Chami and Gilbert Pwiti, eds., *Studies in the African Past 2*, Dar es Salaam. Dar es Salaam University Press, 2002.

_____. "Climate Change on the Coast of East Africa Since 3000 BC: Archaeological Indicators" in Felix Chami, Gilbert Pwiti & Chantal Radimilahy, eds., *Studies in the African Past 3*. Dar es Salaam University Press, 2003.

_____. *The Unity of African Ancient History 3000 BC to AD 500*. Dar es Salaam: E &D Limited.

_____."Cities and Towns in East Africa" in Helaine Selin, ed. *Encyclopaedia of the History of Science, Technology, and Medicine in Non-Western Cultures, Volume 1*. Berlin, Heidelberg, New York: Spring, 2008.

_____. "The Longue Duree of Zanzibar and the Western Indian Seaboard" in Felix Chami, ed., *Zanzibar and the Swahili Coast from c 30,000 Years Ago*. Dar es Salaam: E & D Vision Publishing, 2009a.

_____. "The Atomic Model View of Society: Application in Studies of the African Past" in Peter R. Schmidt, ed., *Postcolonial Archaeologies in Africa*. Santa Fe, New Mexico: School for Advanced Research Press, 2009b.

Chittick, Neville. "East Africa and the Orient: Ports and Trade before the arrival of the Portuguese" in Menaud, ed., *Historical Relations Across the Indian Ocean*. Paris: UNESCO, 1980

Christiansson, C. and Tobisson, E. "Environmental Degradation as a consequence of Socio-Political Conflicts in Eastern Mara" in Hjort of Ornas and Salih, M. *Ecology and Politics, Environmental Stress and Security* in Africa. Uppsala, The Scandinavian Institute of African Studies, 1989.

Ehret, Christopher. "The East African Interior" in M. Elfasi & I. Hrbek, eds., *General History of Africa Volume III: Africa from the Seventh to the Eleventh Century*. Heinemann, California: UNESCO, 1988.

_____.*An African Classical Age: Eastern and Southern Africa in World History 1000 BC to AD. 400*. Charlottesville: University Press of Virginia; Oxford: James Currey, 1998.

_____.*The Civilizations of Africa: A History to 1800*. Charlottesville: University Press of Virginia, 2002.

_____. "Bantu Expansions: Re-Envisioning a Central Problem of Early African History", *The International Journal of African Historical Studies*, Vo. 34, No. 1. 2001.

_____. "Writing African History from Linguistic Evidence" in John Edward Philips, ed., *Writing African History*. Rochester, NY: University of Rochester Press, 2005.

Feierman, Steven. *The Shambaa Kingdom: A History*. Madison: The University of Wisconsin Press, 1974.

_____. *Peasant Intellectuals: Anthropology and History in Tanzania*. Madison: The University of Wisconsin Press, 1990.

Glassman, Jonathon. *War of Words, War of Stones: Racial Thought and Violence in Colonial Zanzibar*. Bloomington and Indianapolis: Indiana University Press, 2011.

Giblin, James and Jamie Monsoon, "Introduction", in James Giblin & Jamies Monsoon, eds., *Maji Maji: Lifting the Fog of War*. Leiden & Boston: Brill.

Giblin, James L. *The Politics of Environmental Control in Northeastern Tanzania, 1840-1940*. Philadelphia: University of Pennsylvania Press, 1993.

_____. "The Precolonial Politics of Disease Control in the lowlands of Northeastern Tanzania" in Gregory Maddox, James Giblin & Isaria Kimambo, eds., *Custodians of the Land: Ecology and Cultures in the History of Tanzania*. London: James Currey; Dar es Salaam: Mkuki na Nyota, Nairobi: E.A.E.P; Athens: Ohio University Press, 1996.

Hamilton, J.T and K.G. Hamilton. *History of the Moravian Church, the Renewed Unitas Fratrum 1722-1957*. Winston-Salem, Inter Provincial Board of Christian Education, Moravian Church of America, 1983.

Hastings, Adrian. *The Church in Africa 1450-1950*. Oxford: Clarendon Press, 1996.

Healey, Joseph G. *A Fith Gospel: In Search of Black Christian Values*. Maryknoll, Orbis Books, 1981.

Hiernaux, Jean. "Bantu Expansion: The Evidence from Physical Anthropology Confronted with Linguistic and Archaeological Evidence", *The Journal of African History*, Vol.9, No. 4, 1968.

Hollingsworth, Lawrence W. *Zanzibar under the Foreign Office*. London: Macmillan and Company Ltd, 1953.

Iliffe, John. *A Modern History of Tanganyika*. Cambridge: Cambridge University Press, 1979.

Ivaska, Andrew. *Cultured States: Youth, Gender, and Modern Style in 1960s Dar es Salaam*. Durham and London: Duke University Press, 2011.

Ivanov, Paola. "Cosmopolitanism or Exclusion? Negotiating Identity in the Expressive Culture of Contemporary Zanzibar" in Abdul Sheriff & Engseng Ho.eds., *The Indian Ocean: Oceanic Connections and the Creation of New Societies*. London: Hurst & Company, 2014.

Katoke, Israel. *The Making of the Karagwe Kingdom: Tanzanian History from Oral Traditions*. Nairobi: East African Publishing House, Historical Association of Tanzania, Paper No.8, 1973.

Kjekshus, Helge. *Ecology Control and Economic Development in East African History, The Case of Tanganyika 1850*. Dar es Salaam, Mkuki na Nyota Publishers, 1996.

Keita, S.O.Y. "Physical Anthropology and African History" in John Edward Philips, ed., *Writing African History*. Rochester, NY: University of Rochester Press, 2005.

Koponen, Juhani. *Development for Exploitation, German Colonial Policies in Mainland Tanzania 1884-1914*. Helsinki, Finish Historical Society, 1994.

Kimambo, Isaria N. *A Political History of the Pare of Tanzania c. 1500-1900*. Nairobi: East African Publishing House, 1969.

_____. Environmental Control and Hunger in the Mountains and Plains of Northeastern Tanzania" in Gregory Maddox, James Giblin & Isaria Kimambo, eds., *Custodians of the Land: Ecology and Cultures in the History of Tanzania*. London: James Currey; Dar es Salaam:

Mkuki na Nyota, Nairobi: E.A.E.P; Athens: Ohio University Press, 1996.

Kironde, Lusugga J. M. "Race, Class and Housing in Dar es Salaam: The colonial impact on landuse structure, 1891-1961" in in James R. Brennan, Andrew Burton, and Yusufu Lawi, eds., *Dar es Salaam: Histories from an Emerging African Metropolis*. Dar es Salaam: Mkuki na Nyota Publishers, Nairobi: BIEA, 2007.

Kwekason, Amandus. *Holocene Archaeology of the Southern Coast of Tanzania*. Dar es Salaam: E & D Vision Publishing, 2011.

Kwekason, Amandus and Felix Chami. "The Archaeology of Muleba, South West of Lake Nyanza: A Pleriminary Report" in Felix Chami, Gilbert Pwiti & Chantal Radimilahy, eds., *Studies in the African Past 3*. Dar es Salaam University Press, 2003.

Lawi, Yusufu Q. Tanzania's Operation Vijiji and Local Ecological Consciousness: The Case of Eastern Iraqwland, 1974-1976 in *Journal of African History*, 48, 2007.

Low, D. A. and John Lonsdale, "Introduction: Towards the New Order 1945-1963" in D. A. Low and Alison Smith, eds., *Oxford History of East Africa, Volume Three*. Oxford: Clarendon Press, 1976.

LaViolette, Adria. "Swahili Archaeology and History of Pemba, Tanzania: A Critique and Case Study of the Use of Written and Oral Sources in Archaeology" in Andrew Reid & Paul Lane, eds., *African Historical Archaeologies*. New York, Boston, London: Kluwer Academic/Plenum Publishers, 2004.

Lema, Anza, A. "Chaga Religion and Missionary Christianity in Kilimanjaro: The Initial Phase, 1893-1916" in Thomas Spear and Isaria N. Kimambo, eds., *East African Expressions of Christianity*. Oxford: James Currey; Dar es Salaam: Mkuki na Nyota; Athens: Ohio University Press, 1999.

Maddox, Gregory. "Environment and Population Growth in Ugogo Central Tanzania" in Gregory Maddox, James Giblin & Isaria Kimambo, eds., *Custodians of the Land: Ecology and Cultures in the History of Tanzania*. London: James Currey; Dar es Salaam: Mkuki na Nyota, Nairobi: E.A.E.P; Athens: Ohio University Press, 1996.

Maliyamkono, T.L & M.S.D. Bagachwa, *The Second Economy in Tanzania*. London: James Currey; Athens: Ohio University Press; Nairobi: Heinemann Kenya; Dar es Salaam: ESAURP, 1990.

Mapunda, Betram. "An Archaeological View of the History and Variation of Iron Working in Southwestern Tanzania", Ph.D. Thesis, University of Florida, 1995.

_____. *Contemplanting the Fipa Ironworking*. Kampala: Fountain Publishers, 2010a.

Mapunda, Betram. "Reexamining the Maji Maji War in Ungoni With a Blend of Archaeology and Oral History" in Giblin James and Jamie Monson, eds., *Maji Maji: Lifting the Fog of War*. Leiden, and Boston: Brill, 2010b.

Massamba, David, P.B. *Kiswahili Origins and the Bantu Divergence-Convergence Theory*, University of Dar es Salaam: Institute of Kiswahili Research, 2007.

Matveiev, V. V. "The Development of Swahili Civilization" in D.T. Niane, *General History of Africa Volume IV: Africa from the Twelfth to the Sixteenth Century*. Heinemann, California: UNESCO, 1984.

Masao, F. T and H.W. Mutoro. "The East African coast and the Comoro Islands" in M. Elfasi & I. Hrbek, eds., *General History of Africa Volume III: Africa from the Seventh to the Eleventh Century*. Heinemann, California: UNESCO, 1988.

Mollat, Michel. "The importance of maritime traffic to cultural contacts in the Indian Ocean", *Diogenes*, 111, 1-18, 1980.

Mbwiliza, Joseph F. *A History of Commodity Production in Makuani 1600-1900: Materialist Accumulation to Imperialist Domination*. Dar es Salaam: DUP, 1991.

McCall, M. "Environmental and Agricultural Impacts of Tanzania's Villagisation Programme" in J.I. Clarke *et. al.* eds., *Population and Development Projects in Africa*. Cambridge University Press, 1985.

McIntosh, Susan K. "Archaeology and the Reconstruction of the African Past" in in John Edward Philips, ed., *Writing African History*. Rochester, NY: University of Rochester Press, 2005.

Nicholls, Christine S. *The Swahili Coast, Politics, Diplomacy and Trade on the Eastern African Littoral 1798-1856*. London: Geroge Allen & Unwin Ltd, 1971.

Nolan, Francis P. *Mission to the Great Lakes: The White Fathers in Western Tanzania, 1878-1978*. Kipalapala: TMP Book Department, 1978.

Nurse, Derek and Thomas Spear. *The Swahili: Reconstructing the History and Language of an African Society, 800-1500*. Philadelphia: University of Pennsylvania Press, 1985.

Oliver, Roland. "The Problem of Bantu Expansion", *The Journal of African History*, Vol.7, No. 3, 1966.

Ombori, Titus L. "Archaeological and Historical Investigations of Mbuamaji Site, Kigamboni, Dar es Salaam-Tanzania", University of Dar es Salaam: MA Dissertation, 2012.

Omer-Cooper, J.D. *History of Southern Africa*. London: James Currey, Postsmouth NH:Heinemann, 1987.

Porter, Andrew. "Commerce and Christianity": The Rise and Fall of a Nineteenth-Century Mission Slogan" *The Historical Journal*, Vol. 28, 3, 1985.

Roberts, Andrew. "Political Change in the Nineteenth Century" in I.N. Kimambo & A.J. Temu, eds., *A History of Tanzania*. Nairobi: East African Publishing House, 1969.

Rockel, Stephen J. "A Nation of Porters: The Nyamwezi and the Labour Market in Nineteenth-Century Tanzania", *Journal of African History*, 41, 2, 2000.

_____.*Carriers of Culture: Labor on the Road in Nineteenth-Century East Africa*. Portsmouth,NH: Heinemann, 2006.

_____. "Slavery and freedom in 19th east Africa: the case of Waungwana caravan porters", *African Studies*, Vol 68, 1, 2009.

_____. "Between Pori, Pwani and Kisiwani: Overlapping Labour Culture in the Caravan, Ports and Dhows of the Western Indian Ocean", in Abdul Sheriff & Engseng Ho.eds.,*The Indian Ocean: Oceanic Connections and the Creation of New Societies*. London: Hurst & Company, 2014.

Sally, Moore, F. *Athropology and Africa: Changing Perspectives on a Changing Scene*. Charlottesville & London: The University Press of Virginia, 1994.

Sago, Laurenti. "A History of Labour Migration in Kasulu District, 1928-1960," University of Dar es Salaam: MA Dissertation, 1974.

Schmidt, Peter. *Historical Archaeology: A Structural Approach in an African Culture*. Westport, CT: Greenwood Press, 1978.

_____. "Archaeological Views on a History of Landscape Change in East Africa", *Journal of African History*, Vol. 38, No.3, 1997.

_____. *Historical Archaeology in Africa: Representation, Social Memory, and Oral Traditions*. Lanham, New York, Toronto, Oxford: Atamira Press, 2006.

Sheriff, Abdul. "Tanzanian Societies at the Time of Partition" in Martin H.Y. Kaniki, ed., *Tanzania under Colonial Rule*. London: Longman Group Limited, 1980.

_____.*Dhow Cultures of the Indian Ocean: Cosmopolitanism, Commerce, and Islam*. London: Hurst & Company; New York: Columbia University Press, 2010.

_____. "Introduction" in Abdul Sheriff & Engseng Ho.eds., *The Indian Ocean: Oceanic Connections and the Creation of New Societies*. London: Hurst & Company, 2014.

_____. "Globalisation With a Difference: An Overview", in Abdul Sheriff & Engseng Ho.eds., *The Indian Ocean: Oceanic Connections and the Creation of New Societies*. London: Hurst & Company, 2014.

Stanley, Brian. "Church, State, and Hierarchy of "Civilization": The Making of the "Missions and Governments" Report at the World Missionary Conference, Edinburgh 1910" in Andrew Porter, ed. *The Imperial Horizons of British Protestant Missions, 1880-1914*. Grand Rapids; Michigan; Cambridge, UK: William B. Erdman Publishing Company, 2003.

Swantz, Marja-Liisa, "Village Development: On Whose Conditions" in Marja-Liisa Swantz and Aili Mari Tripp, eds., *What Went Right in Tanzania: People's Response to Directed Development*. Dar es Salaam: DUP, 1996.

Tambila, Kapepwa, et.al. *Migrant Labour in Tanzania during the Colonial Period: Case Studies of Recruitment and Conditions of Labour in Sisal Industry*. Hamburg: Institut fur Afrika Kunde, 1981.

Temu, Anold J. "The Rise and Triumph of Nationalism" in I.N. Kimambo and A.J. Temu, eds., *A History of Tanzania*. Nairobi: East African Publishing House, 1969.

Vansina, Jan. "New Linguistic Evidence and 'the Bantu Expansion', *Journal of African History*, Vol. 36, No.2, 1995.

Walker, Iain. "Identity and Citizenship among the Comorians of Zanzibar, 1886-1963" in the Expressive Culture of Contemporary Zanzibar" in Abdul Sheriff & Engseng Ho.eds., *The Indian Ocean: Oceanic Connections and the Creation of New Societies*. London: Hurst & Company, 2014.

www.ingramcontent.com/pod-product-compliance
Lightning Source LLC
Chambersburg PA
CBHW071408300426
44114CB00016B/2222